Getting Started with OpenVMS™

Getting Started with OpenVMS™
A Guide for New Users

Digital Press is an imprint of Elsevier Science.

Library of Congress Cataloging-in-Publication Data

ISBN: 1-55558-279-6

British Library Cataloguing-in-Publication Data

A catalogue record for this book is available from the British Library.

The publisher offers special discounts on bulk orders of this book.
For information, please contact:

Manager of Special Sales
Elsevier Science
200 Wheeler Road
Burlington, MA 01803
Tel: 781-313-4700
Fax: 781-313-4882

For information on all Digital Press publications available, contact our World Wide Web home page at: http://www.digitalpress.com or http://www.bh.com/digitalpress

Transferred to digital printing 2009

For Carol, who patiently tolerated many months of evenings and weekends practically alone.

Table of Contents

Preface

Intended Audience

This book is intended to introduce the reader to Hewlett-Packard's OpenVMS operating system. It assumes some familiarity with modern computer operating systems, such as UNIX or Microsoft Windows. It will also be helpful to the reader to have access to an OpenVMS system upon which to try the examples given in this book.

Those readers accustomed to UNIX will probably notice that OpenVMS has features that will seem somewhat familiar; UNIX and OpenVMS have similar (but far from identical) approaches to memory management, multi-user access, command line interfaces, devices, and processes. OpenVMS also uses the Common Desktop Environment (CDE) GUI, identical to that in use on several different UNIX systems.

The Windows user may find OpenVMS to be somewhat less intuitive than the UNIX user, but those readers familiar with the MS-DOS command prompt interface will notice some similarities to the Digital Command Language command structure. The Windows user may also find the mechanics, if not the design and layout, of the CDE GUI environment to be fairly intuitive.

Users of either Windows or UNIX will already be familiar with the concepts of a multi-level directory structure, multiple disk drives, and perhaps printer queues and e-mail.

How to Use This Book

This book is divided into three major parts:

- Introduction

A brief history of OpenVMS, an outline of its current status, and what to expect in the near future.

- Practical Guide

Introduces some of the concepts behind multi-user, multitasking operating systems and the OpenVMS terminology describing them. Afterward, it shows the reader how to log into the system for the first time and begin using OpenVMS.

- Technical Introduction

The technical introduction describes details which a user does not need to know in order to successfully use the system, but which the curious reader may find interesting. Such topics as process structure, scheduling, memory management, and the file system are discussed.

Conventions Used in This Book

Differences Among Hardware Architectures

Most material presented in this book applies equally well to the VAX, Alpha, and Itanium versions of OpenVMS. Where there are differences, the VAX model is often chosen. The VAX model is usually adequate to illustrate the concept being described, but is often simpler than the Alpha and Itanium equivalents. In several instances, differences among the three architectures are specifically mentioned.

Format of DCL (Digital Command Language) Commands

Many notations used in this book follow the traditional OpenVMS conventions as found in the online help files and OpenVMS documentation set.

When showing examples of DCL commands, it is customary to precede them by a dollar sign ($), as in this example of the SHOW TIME command:

```
$ SHOW TIME
```

The dollar sign is the default command prompt, and so is usually shown in DCL examples. Dollar signs are required only within command procedures. When entering commands from your terminal, it is customary to omit the dollar sign.

It is customary to show DCL commands in upper case, although you may enter them in lower case if you wish. DCL converts most items to uppercase internally, except for items included in quotation marks (" "). Commands typed at the command line are shown in uppercase in this book. Commands in command procedures are usually shown in lowercase, following the author's usual practice. You may use any mixture of upper- and lower case you wish.

Examples in this book spell out each DCL command line element fully, although any command may be abbreviated to any length at which it remains unambiguous.

Optional Elements of DCL Commands

When part of a DCL command is not always required, it may be shown in square brackets ([ ]). Consider this example:

```
$ SHOW QUOTA [/DISK=diskname]
```

In this example of the SHOW QUOTA command, the /DISK qualifier is necessary only if the disk about which you are requesting information is different from your current default disk. Examples of this command include:

```
$ SHOW QUOTA
$ SHOW QUOTA /DISK=DKA400:
```

Negatable DCL Command Qualifiers

Certain qualifiers may be negated by placing "NO" before them. These negatable qualifiers are sometimes shown with "[NO]" before the qualifier name. Consider this example:

```
$ SET TERMINAL/[NO]BROADCAST
```

This means that "SET TERMINAL/BROADCAST" and "SET TERMINAL /NOBROADCAST" are both valid commands. The former directs that the BROADCAST characteristic should be enabled, and the latter directs that it should be disabled.

Notations for Keyboard Keys

Your keyboard may have either a RETURN or an ENTER key on the main keyboard. Unless otherwise noted, they are considered equivalent in this book. Note that this does not refer to the ENTER key at the lower right of the numeric keypad, which sometimes has a separate function.

Sometimes you must press one key and then press a second key before releasing the first. If you must use the CTRL and Z keys in this fashion, it is denoted as "CTRL/Z".

Use of Bold Face in Examples

In examples that show user input along with system responses, user input is usually shown in **bold face**. Exceptions are made when the reader's attention must be called to some other aspect of the example.

"System Manager" Versus "System Administrator"

The person who oversees the general operation of an OpenVMS computer system is known as the "system manager." The term "system administrator" is usually used to describe the corresponding role in a UNIX environment. Just as UNIX has a long history of culture and tradition, so too does OpenVMS. This tradition calls for using the term "system manager," and is observed in this book.

Acknowledgments

The author would like to thank several individuals whose efforts were crucial to the publishing process and whose work is very much appreciated. In order of their involvement, they are: Pam Chester and Theron R. Shreve, who got the project off the ground and supported it throughout, Jim Hibbits, who provided a thorough technical review, and Tim Donar, who painstakingly incorporated the numerous edits and changes inherent in such a project. There were other individuals who declined to be mentioned. They know who they are.

Chapter 1 — Introduction

The computing world is a fast-moving one. Leading-edge technology may become obsolete in three to five years, and sometimes even sooner. Technology workers scramble to earn certifications in technologies that sometimes evaporate before the certificates expire.

But occasionally a technology proves to be so well designed and executed that it thrives long after competing technologies fade away, even outlasting some newer products that were predicted to replace it.

In 1977, Digital Equipment Corporation introduced the world to two such products: the VAX computer and an operating system designed to run upon it—VAX/VMS. Even though the VAX could run other operating systems and VAX/VMS would later be ported to other types of computers, they were designed largely with one another in mind.

The VAX and VAX/VMS had several ambitious design goals. Among them were to allow the same software to run unmodified on hardware with a wide range of capabilities and sizes, to be easy to use, and to remain viable for 15 to 20 years.

The VAX exceeded these goals, and lasted for longer than the upper design goal of 20 years, with new VAX systems being sold until the year 2000. As this book is written, a few vendors even have some remaining stock of new VAX systems.

Hewlett-Packard has promised hardware support to existing VAX and Alpha installations for many years into the future, and even now, is porting the VMS operating system, now called OpenVMS, to the Intel Itanium architecture. Actively being developed and improved today, almost 25 years after its introduction, OpenVMS promises many more years of viability to come.

History

Throughout the 1960s, Digital developed and sold a very successful line of computers known as the PDP series. In the early 1970s, Digital began to recognize that the larger programs and data sets being developed were beginning to outgrow the limitations of the 16-bit PDP architecture. Increasingly, programmers had to split large programs into smaller units that would run on their computers. One PDP model, the PDP-11/70, was designed as an attempt to increase the useful data capacity of the PDP hardware, but it was still restricted by having to use portions of the same 16-bit software architecture.

Digital began to envision a line of computers that would be compatible with the PDP series and, yet, lift the restrictions on program and data size resulting from the PDP design. In March 1975, a team was assembled whose purpose was to propose a "32-bit PDP" product. The result was a new line of computers, the VAX, and a new operating system designed specifically for it, VAX/VMS.

The first VAX systems were ready in late 1977, a remarkably short time for the development of a hardware architecture and a new operating system. After the introduction of the VAX, the PDP line was developed for many more years. The PDP-11 continued to serve markets where a 32-bit system was not needed, or where its excellent real-time data-collection capabilities were required. Of course, the VAX became Digital's flagship product.

The VAX and VAX/VMS were enormously successful, both in business and in academia. So many universities had VAX computers in their labs that computer science graduates of that time were sometimes referred to as "the VAX generation." The VAX was smaller than a mainframe, but larger than a microcomputer. It was about the size of what was then known as a "minicomputer," but had better performance. The VAX came to be classified as a "supermini."

Over its first 15 years, the VAX architecture underwent numerous upgrades in hardware technology. Its CPU performance, memory capacity, disk capacity, and I/O performance all increased by several orders of magnitude. The later examples of the VAX architecture featured literally hundreds of times more performance than the original. All this was achieved with very little change to the original VAX architecture design.

In the 1980s came the MicroVAX; a VAX small enough to sit beside a desk, running a subset of VAX/VMS called MicroVMS. Within a few years, the MicroVAX had advanced to the point that MicroVMS was no longer required; all subsequent machines would run the full VAX/VMS system. The MicroVAX II, which came in five major variants, proved so successful and so flooded the marketplace that during the late 1980s, the average VAX system manager had less than three years of experience.

The VAX and MicroVAX lines were developed in parallel, and the MicroVAX spawned a line of graphics workstations called VAXstations. These machines were the first VAX/VMS machines to have a graphics display and mouse (although previous VAX machines did have some limited graphics capabilities via graphics terminals such as the VT240).

In 1991, Digital announced that the VAX/VMS operating system would be renamed "OpenVMS."

The late 1980s and early 1990s had seen popularity gains in "open" systems. One rather simplistic definition of "open" is a system for which the source code is readily available to anyone. Sometimes, users may develop enhancements that eventually become part of the official version.

Critics wondered aloud, "How can you call a proprietary system like VMS 'open'?" But OpenVMS proponents point out that OpenVMS passes many tests for an open system and, in fact, earned several open-systems certifications *before* some versions of UNIX, the system around which much open systems development is based. The change of name was liked by some OpenVMS users and disliked by others.

At about the same time as the name change, Digital's new hardware platform supporting OpenVMS became available, the Alpha AXP architecture.

Enter the Alpha AXP

The VAX architecture was developed to go beyond the 16-bit capabilities of the PDP-11. The 32-bit VAX environment provided a luxury to programmers who no longer needed clever tricks to fit applications and data into a 16-bit machine. However, applications continued to grow, and today some high-end applications require even more addressing space than 32 bits can provide.

Today, a 32-bit architecture is more than adequate for most computing tasks; virtually all new personal computers are still 32-bit machines. But some applications, including weather forecasting, fluid dynamics modeling, and very large databases need still more addressing capability.

Digital recognized the impending need for such a machine and developed the Alpha AXP architecture. The Alpha is a full 64-bit architecture with an addressing space as impressive in 1992 as 32 bits was in 1977. To illustrate, a 32-bit machine has approximately four thousand million bytes of addressing space. A 64-bit machine has four thousand million bytes for every byte that a 32-bit machine has.

The Alpha was designed to run multiple operating systems, which included OpenVMS, Digital UNIX, and Microsoft Windows NT. After about a decade of development, the first Alpha AXP computer and OpenVMS AXP V1.0 were shipped in 1992. By the late 1990s, revenues from Alpha systems far exceeded those of the VAX, which itself had been very successful. The VAX and Alpha versions of OpenVMS were developed roughly in parallel until the late 1990s, when the discontinuation of the VAX architecture was announced.

In 2001, Compaq Computer Corporation (which had acquired Digital a few years before) began porting OpenVMS to a third hardware architecture, the Intel Itanium. The Alpha processor line will undergo upgrades through 2004, and the last major variant, the EV79, will be the basis for what is now being called "the next generation server family," to be released in late 2004 or early 2005. Afterward, the Itanium architecture, described next, will be the primary 64-bit platform for OpenVMS.

Enter the Itanium

In 2001, Compaq Computer Corporation announced plans to port OpenVMS to the Intel Itanium processor, also known as the IA-64. At the time of this writing, the Itanium version is not available for testing, but Intel has made detailed technical documents available for review. The description of Itanium contained here is based on those documents.

The Itanium is a 64-bit architecture, featuring the same amount of addressing space as the Alpha. Those features of the Alpha that allow it to emulate complex VAX characteristics and to support multiple operating systems, collectively known as "PALcode," will have Itanium counterparts. Specifically, certain Alpha-style PALcode functionality will be included in the Itanium version of OpenVMS itself, while other portions may be contained in a computer's firmware. In the Alpha design, PAL stands for "privileged architecture library," and under Itanium, "processor abstraction layer," but the functionality is quite similar. Some combination of hardware, firmware, and software PALcode support will provide an environment for the successful porting of OpenVMS to Itanium.

Based on comparisons of the VAX, Alpha, and Itanium architectures, the porting of OpenVMS from Alpha to Itanium should prove to be less difficult than the porting from VAX to Alpha was a decade ago. The first OpenVMS Itanium machines are scheduled to be available for third-party testing in 2003 with the production release scheduled for early 2004.

Continued Support for VAX and Alpha Systems

Itanium will eventually become the primary platform for OpenVMS, but for the next several years, OpenVMS will be available on three separate hardware architectures: VAX, Alpha, and Itanium. Existing VAX and Alpha systems will eventually be replaced by Itanium systems, but there will be a large amount of overlap during the next several years.

Over 500,000 VAX systems were sold during more than two decades of development, and many are still in service. As of 2002, some VAX systems are still available through certain channels, and new generations of the Alpha architecture are under development at the time of this writing.

In May 2002, Compaq merged with Hewlett-Packard. Compaq had previously made commitments to support existing VAX machines until at least 2010, and existing Alpha systems for significantly longer. Hewlett-Packard has since affirmed its intention to honor these commitments.

The Roles of OpenVMS

When Digital designed VAX/VMS in the 1970s, its goal was to create a 32-bit operating system for the new hardware line, the VAX. From the start, it was designed so that many people could use a single VAX/VMS computer at once. The techniques used to accomplish this goal naturally led to a system that could perform a variety of tasks: The system must keep track of many separate, but overlapping, computations and manage access to finite resources in a way transparent to the users. The system had to delay computations momentarily when certain resources were unavailable, such as while waiting for certain memory contents or access to a disk drive. The system had to delay and resume computations in such a way that a programmer did not have to worry about the details of shared access or scheduling while writing a program.

These inherent abilities make OpenVMS suitable for a wide variety of tasks. It can be used as a personal system, a multiuser timesharing system, a batch engine, a network server, or a network client, and it can serve several of these uses at the same time.

Out of this development effort came an operating system with outstanding reliability, despite the complexities involved. It is not unusual for OpenVMS systems to run continuously for months or years, shutting down only because of prolonged power failures or scheduled upgrades. Combined with Open VMS's flexibility, this reliability naturally translates into a system well suited to environments that cannot tolerate system failures. OpenVMS is used extensively by hospitals and other medical facilities, by major stock exchanges and banks around the world, by one of the very largest Internet search engines, and by many Fortune 500 companies for which downtime would mean the loss of hundreds of thousands, or perhaps millions, of dollars per hour. In short, OpenVMS is used extensively where system reliability is crucial.

Users of the OpenVMS operating system enjoy a feature many other systems claim, but few deliver: scalability. The high end of the OpenVMS performance line currently includes systems with multiple CPUs, several gigabytes of physical memory, and terabytes of disk capacity. On the other end of the spectrum are systems the size of two telephone directories stacked atop one another. OpenVMS can effectively manage the resources of a wide variety of machines, which in the next couple of years will certainly include even more impressive hardware models, both large and small.

The following sections highlight some of the various roles OpenVMS currently performs around the world.

As a Desktop System

OpenVMS first appeared on physically large computers, at least by today's standards. In 1977, a computer system 5 feet tall and almost 15 feet long qualified as a "minicomputer." The largest OpenVMS systems today are of roughly comparable physical size, but, of course, they vastly outperform the early VAX machines, while consuming far less electricity and generating far less heat. However, most modern OpenVMS systems are much smaller, many being desktop systems suitable for personal use.

OpenVMS will run successfully (but without much elbow room) on a modest system with 8MB of memory and less than 500MB of disk space.[1] Most popular "personal computer" operating systems can no longer come close to this accomplishment.

Today, there are a variety of desktop OpenVMS systems, some with impressive graphics capabilities, disk capacity, and CPU performance.

Later versions of OpenVMS use the Common Desktop Environment (CDE) graphical interface, the same interface found on several other operating systems, including many versions of UNIX. This means that many users who have never used OpenVMS before will nevertheless find a familiar interface, easing their learning experience.

Desktop systems can use all the features of OpenVMS; there is no "client" or "server" version. A desktop system can act as an interactive system, a network client, a network file server, a Web server, a mail server, and a batch engine, all at the same time. The only practical differences between the desktop OpenVMS system and large corporate systems are speed and storage capacity.

A desktop system might also be used as a personal system by one user, while simultaneously serving as a multiuser interactive system for other users.

New OpenVMS systems have traditionally been either too large or too expensive for home users, but for about the past decade, systems small enough to be used in a private home or office have been available on the used market.

A decade ago, this meant a MicroVAX II or VAXstation 2000 system. Today, perhaps it's an AlphaStation or MicroVAX 3000 series system. There is also at least one software-based VAX emulator that runs on Windows PCs. A few years from now, used (or even new) Intel Itanium–based machines should be available at prices affordable for home users.

---

1. The early versions of VAX/VMS ran just fine on systems with 0.25MB of memory and 1 MIPS of CPU performance, often serving dozens of users, multiple disk and tape drives, and several printers simultaneously.

For the past few years the OpenVMS hobbyist program has been available. Individuals may acquire free software licenses for OpenVMS and several third-party programs. The hobbyist kit contains several programming languages, including C and Java, DECnet and TCP/IP networking, and DCOM, to name only some of its contents. The hobbyist program is available to members of Encompass, a large users group counting many OpenVMS users among its members. Encompass also provides its membership with access to a library of software contributed over the years by other members. (See Appendix B, "Additional Resources.")

As a result, more and more private individuals are able to afford their own OpenVMS systems with which to experiment at will.

As a Multiuser System

Acting as a multiuser interactive system was one of the original purposes of the VAX and OpenVMS. Originally, text terminals connected each user to the system. Today, the concept of a text terminal has expanded to include network terminals, such as Telnet sessions. The ability to act as an X Window System server was added later, allowing other users on the network to run GUI applications on a remote OpenVMS system, while displaying their output on local client systems.

Several users may log into and use an OpenVMS system at the same time. This introduces a number of complicated issues related to the sharing of computer resources. OpenVMS has features that arbitrate access to the CPU(s), disks, files, shared memory, private memory, and other system resources.

As a multiuser system, OpenVMS provides comprehensive support for file and object ownership, protection, and access. Access methods may range from exclusive access by one user to shared write access by many users, with accesses coordinated across the entire cluster, if applicable. (See "As a Clustered System," which follows.)

OpenVMS includes a 32-bit (VAX) or 64-bit (Alpha and Itanium) virtual memory management system that supports both paging and swapping. This means that the system can divide its memory into small units called pages and allocate them to users depending on their needs. When there is insufficient physical memory to meet demands, some memory contents can be automatically moved to disk, freeing memory. The process of moving things in and out of memory occurs automatically, with no need for users or even programmers to be concerned with the details.

In addition to pageable virtual memory, OpenVMS includes both paged and nonpaged dynamic memory pools. Uses of the pools range from transient storage for I/O requests to semi permanent data structures describing disks and other devices.

OpenVMS uses the process as its basic unit of scheduling, and threads are supported. You may think of each simultaneous user as a separate process. Each process has its own memory, which cannot be directly accessed from another process. In addition, some memory is shared among all processes—the area in which OpenVMS and system-wide data reside on the running system. This means that each user process has separate memory, but things that are shared (e.g., OpenVMS itself) need not be duplicated for each user.

> **Note:** explanations for the terms used in the preceding paragraphs may be found in Part 2, "A Technical Introduction."

As a Clustered System

Joining computer systems together to form clusters became a popular trend in the computer industry several years ago. Several operating systems now have some type of clustering capability, but OpenVMS started the trend with Digital introducing VAXcluster systems in the mid-1980s.[1] Most other clustering strategies have directly resulted from study and imitation of the OpenVMS clustering technology.

Clustering is a technology for coupling separate computers together to form, in some ways, a single computing entity. This is a technique for increasing total computing capacity, while avoiding some of the problems with using totally separate computers.

A cluster is more tightly integrated than a traditional network, but not as tightly as a single computer with multiple CPUs. For example, OpenVMS clusters can allow users to share disks and files among all nodes (cluster systems) with record-level granularity, but they cannot yet migrate a process from one node to another. All systems in a cluster can use a shared copy of the User Authorization database, so that any authorized user can log into any node in the cluster.

Clustered systems can share disks, whether the disk is connected directly to one computer or to a dedicated storage controller. For most purposes, a user may log into any node in the cluster and never see any differences compared with any other node. If so configured by the system manager, the user environment looks exactly the same: All of the user's programs and data are there, and all of the same printers are available no matter which node is used. On the other hand, the system manager may decide to assign different responsibilities to different nodes and elect to have certain programs or devices available only on selected nodes.

Since clustered systems can share devices, such as disks and printers, different nodes in a cluster can help one another execute work more quickly. For example, a user may

---

1. One hardware vendor had previously marketed a "clustered" system, but the technology does not satisfy the modern definition of a "cluster."

submit a batch job (or a print job) to a generic, clusterwide queue. Whichever node in the cluster has the necessary resources available can assume responsibility for that job. The user may not know or care which node actually performs the work.

As a Network Server

Network servers can take many forms: a file server offering file, disk, and printer services; a company wide mail hub; an Internet Web server; an FTP site; or a system offering other network services. OpenVMS includes two kinds of networking: DECnet, a proprietary networking product originally developed by Digital, and TCP/IP, the networking scheme of the Internet. Third-party implementations of TCP/IP networking are also available for OpenVMS. Using one or both of these network types, OpenVMS systems can offer all of the network services mentioned above and more (many TCP/IP functions have roughly equivalent DECnet counterparts.) These services include file services; disk services; NFS and FTP for file access and transfer; DNS for Internet name resolution; SMTP, POP3, and IMAP for remote e-mail delivery; Telnet for remote access; SSH, SCP, and other related components for secure access; LPD for network printer access; and many more.

As an added benefit, OpenVMS has some fundamental differences from other systems that make it much less vulnerable to popular "buffer overflow" network attacks. Even if the OpenVMS system is using the very same network software as the other systems, the OpenVMS design catches the underlying problem and prevents many common attacks from working as intended.

As a Back-End System

Back-end systems have much in common with some types of network servers. They sit alone in a closet or computer room, often with no interactive users logged in, their only task to answer requests from other computers. Perhaps a company sets up a large database system residing on an OpenVMS system in a central computer room. Each user of the database has a personal computer on his or her desk running a *front-end* application. This application serves as the user interface, through which the user examines and modifies the database. User requests for database access are passed from the front-end personal computers to the back-end OpenVMS system, which manages the database.

There are many possible advantages of such a two-tiered approach. The personal computers do not have to hold large portions of the database. This allows smaller disk and memory requirements for the front-end machines, lowering cost. In addition, the OpenVMS server can concentrate all its resources on managing the database, relieved of the need to manage a graphical interface for each user. Each user can enjoy the quick response of a local, dedicated machine that also runs other office applications along side the database software.

OpenVMS runs both TCP/IP and DECnet, comes with a file system designed for access by multiple parties, can be clustered, and comes with a distributed resource lock manager. These aspects make it suitable for use with the multitiered approach just described.

Summary

The outstanding design of OpenVMS includes features suitable to any or all of the roles described above. In many ways, OpenVMS was a more advanced system 20 years ago than many cutting-edge operating systems are today. Rather than remaining static, OpenVMS has continued to improve for the past two decades, incorporating features that make it an excellent choice for the most sophisticated modern applications.

Part 1 — A Practical Guide

Chapter 2 — Hardware Platforms Supporting OpenVMS

As described previously, the OpenVMS operating system was originally designed for the VAX computer. Later, the system was ported to the Alpha series of processors, and, as this book is being written, it is being ported to the Intel Itanium line of processors. Let's have a brief comparison of these three architectures, highlighting the most important characteristics of each.

The VAX

As mentioned earlier, the VAX architecture was designed hand-in-hand with the VAX/VMS operating system. This is believed to have been the first time this approach had ever been used for an interactive computer system. Several hardware features were designed specifically to assist with the VMS operating system functions, such as selecting which task to run next ("context switching") and manipulating linked lists of data structures.

The VAX is a 32-bit CISC architecture. The term "32-bit" means that the natural size of a datum used by the CPU is 32 bits (4 bytes) in size. CISC stands for "complex instruction set computing." In short, this means that the VAX has numerous instructions of different in-memory sizes, and they vary in their execution times.

True to its scalability goals, the VAX processor lies at the heart of computers varying enormously in size, speed, and capabilities. The fastest VAX machine is several hundred times quicker than the slowest, while storage capacity and physical size vary by corresponding amounts. The biggest, fastest VAX systems achieve performance comparable to mid-range IBM 3090 mainframe systems.

The VAX is truly a well-engineered architecture, one that is well thought out, well planned, complete, and well executed. Its adherence to its design and reliability are legendary. But even the best-engineered products eventually become obsolete, and the VAX is no longer manufactured. Let's take a look at why this is and why it means little to the future of OpenVMS.

The VAX is a 32-bit machine. In practical terms, this boils down to one fact that is perhaps more important than any other: a 32-bit machine can effectively use a maximum of 4 gigabytes of memory space.[1]

---

1. There are techniques that allow a computer to use a memory address space greater than its natural data size would imply. In fact, some of these techniques were successfully applied to the VAX's predecessor, the PDP-11.

Generous when it was designed in the mid-1970s, its 32-bit nature is now becoming a liability for a small, but increasing, number of applications.

Early in the lifespan of the VAX, engineers at Digital examined the rate at which computer memory requirements were growing and predicted that 32-bit architectures would begin to run out of steam in the mid-1990s. This turned out to be a very accurate estimate.

The VAX also has characteristics that do not naturally lend themselves to executing several instructions simultaneously, an increasingly popular technique.

These factors, coupled with a relatively high cost, are the primary reasons the VAX is no longer being carried forward. Digital foresaw these events well in advance and began work on a successor to the VAX, the Alpha AXP architecture, which overcomes many limitations of the VAX.

"CISC" versus "RISC" architectures

"CISC" stands for "complex instruction set computer" and "RISC" for "reduced instruction set computer." Although there is some overlap between the two categories, some generalizations apply. CISC machines have a large number of built-in instructions, whereas RISC machines have a smaller number of simpler instructions. RISC machines usually execute a larger number of instructions in a given time, but each one performs less work, negating some or all of the implied performance benefit. However, the simpler instruction set of a RISC architecture has characteristics that make it easier to have many instructions in progress at one time. With proper programming techniques, a serious performance advantage can be had over a CISC design by virtue of executing several instructions simultaneously.

The Alpha

Also designed by Digital, the Alpha, otherwise known as the AXP, is a 64-bit RISC design, the world's first 64-bit architecture. (Source: "VAX & OpenVMS at 20," Digital Equipment Corp., 1997.)

Since its debut in 1992, the Alpha architecture has set many performance records, and except for a few brief periods when competing products have temporarily leapfrogged it, the Alpha has outperformed all of its competitors.

As a RISC architecture, the Alpha faced a challenge in supplying the kinds of services that the OpenVMS operating system relied on in the VAX. Long, complex instructions were out of the question, exactly the kind that OpenVMS depended on heavily. To solve this challenge, the designers put together a system called "PALcode," short for "privileged architecture library." This system breaks down the complex instructions into sequences of small RISC instructions and allows the operating system to execute them almost as if they were single instructions. This system is adaptable to allow several different operating systems to run on the Alpha, including UNIX and Windows NT. Windows 2000 was also partially developed on Alpha machines, although there was never a production version of Windows 2000 for Alpha.

Throughout the early and mid-1990s, OpenVMS was developed in parallel on VAX and Alpha machines, with new features appearing first on VAX, then being added later to the Alpha version. As time went on, however, this relationship was reversed, with new features appearing first on Alpha. As of today, some features of OpenVMS are available only on Alpha, particularly those having to do with 64-bit addressing and support for a new file system structure.

The Intel Itanium

Like the Alpha, the Itanium is a 64-bit design. Its strategy for supporting complex instructions like those found on the VAX is quite similar to the Alpha approach.

The Intel Itanium is an Explicitly Parallel Instruction Computing (EPIC) design rather than a RISC design. However, some features of the Itanium are similar to a RISC architecture, as the term is used in this book. Namely, having relatively few instructions easily executed in parallel.

Just as with the Alpha architecture, some features required by OpenVMS are not supported by Itanium as native features. However, Itanium supports the copying of PALcode procedures from firmware to memory, providing a solution. It has also been written that some of these functions will be written into the Itanium version of OpenVMS itself, rather than in firmware. Although not all of the details are available as of this writing, one or both of these techniques will likely be employed.

In many ways, the porting of OpenVMS to the Itanium architecture will be less challenging than the previous port from VAX to Alpha because of similarities between the Alpha and Itanium hardware designs.

Like Alpha, Itanium will support multiple operating systems and provide support for both big- and little-endian data types, even though some aspects of instruction coding are little-endian only. The Itanium also supports 32- and 64-bit instruction sets, although this feature will likely be of more use to other operating systems than to OpenVMS.

Those features of OpenVMS that now support 64-bit addressing can be ported directly to Itanium. The Itanium architecture also provides four access modes (called

"Privilege Levels" in Itanium nomenclature). OpenVMS requires four access modes, a feature found on relatively few CPU architectures, many of which supply only two modes.

Chapter 3 — Multiuser Concepts

Multiuser systems like OpenVMS have several features not typically found on single-user operating systems. The following sections describe some of the OpenVMS features that provide for a multiuser environment.

Many operating systems are designed primarily for the use of only one person at a time, even though they may include most of the features required to support multiple users. The evolution of Microsoft Windows and the Apple Macintosh operating systems are examples of these. These systems have been retrofitted to some extent to allow access by more than one user simultaneously.

OpenVMS, like UNIX, evolved from the opposite direction. It was designed first as an interactive system to be used by many people at once, each using a command line interface (CLI). Single-user graphical user interfaces (GUIs) were added later. An OpenVMS system can support the simultaneous use of multiple terminal-based users and X Window System clients.

Both types of OpenVMS interfaces, CLI and GUI, are described later in this book.

Concurrent Access by Many Users

As mentioned earlier, OpenVMS can support many simultaneous users while also running other tasks. This can be accomplished on computers that may have only a single processor.

How does a computer system with only one processor perform many tasks at once? The answer is that it presents a clever illusion. In reality, a processor can be working on only one task at a given instant. The operating system switches rapidly between tasks, giving each a very brief amount of attention, just milliseconds, before moving on to the next. This gives a very convincing sense that many tasks are proceeding at once, even though the CPU is really working on one at a time.

Suppose you are typing an e-mail message on your OpenVMS system. The system spends a very brief amount of time processing the key you pressed and displaying your keystroke on the screen. Between your keystrokes, the system switches to other tasks while waiting for your next keystroke. Only when you press another key does OpenVMS need to turn its attention back to you, just for long enough to process and display the next character.

In this manner, OpenVMS can manage thousands of users, multiple disk drives, multiple printers, network communications, and more. But, in order to pull off this grand illusion of everything happening at once, some very complicated software has to keep track of everything in progress.

Before OpenVMS can take its attention away from you and your e-mail message, it must first ensure that it can pick up where it left off. Every minute detail of your activities, your open files, your terminal, and the current state of the processor must be *exactly* preserved, so that the system can switch its attention back to you when required.

Some mechanism must exist to store all of this information for every task, some *unit of scheduling* has to be saved and another loaded each time the system switches its attention from one task to the next. This unit is called the *process*.

Processes, Jobs, and Threads

The Process

These independent tasks, each able to be scheduled separately from the others, are called *processes*. When you log into the system, a new process is created for your use. Your login session becomes one of the tasks the system can switch among.

But the process is not just an entity that can be scheduled for CPU attention; it provides the environment in which you work. The process keeps track of which program you are running, what files you have open, your current directory, your identity, your priority, your access rights, and your privileges, to name just a few.

Many parts of OpenVMS itself are also implemented as processes, but these processes are automated and proceed without a human user to direct their actions. Other automated processes can run under the identity of a certain user and enjoy the same access rights to files and other objects as that user would.

Different types of processes are grouped into *modes*, according to their characteristics. The modes are described in the following subsections.

The Interactive Process

An *interactive process* is one directly associated with a user. An interactive process is created for you when you log into the system. This process executes your commands to the system, and when you log out, the process is destroyed.

This type of process is referred to as *interactive*, because you, the user, interact with the system through it. An interactive process is associated with your terminal, whether it is an actual physical terminal or a terminal emulator program used from a different computer.

None of the other types of process described below is normally associated with a user's terminal (except a subprocess, via the ATTACH command).

The Detached Process

A *detached process* is one that exists totally independently of other processes. It can continue to exist after the process that created it has terminated. OpenVMS itself uses a number of permanent detached processes to perform various system functions.

Some detached processes are used to perform tasks that need to be performed often, but at unpredictable times. They usually hibernate when there is no work to be performed, but awaken in response to certain events, as needed. Other detached processes awaken at regular intervals to check whether there is any work to do.

A user holding the proper privileges may create detached processes, but depending on the type of work to be performed, it may be more appropriate (and easier) to use a batch process for repetitive tasks.

The Batch Process

A *batch process* is a process that executes a command procedure that you submit to be executed on your behalf. A *command procedure* is a file containing CLI commands that are executed sequentially, like a program. You request the execution of a batch job by submitting the command file to a batch queue, discussed later. Batch jobs are often used to perform time-consuming or recurring tasks.

Technically, a batch process is quite similar to a detached process, except that batch processes are associated with an entry in a batch queue, and they terminate when the command procedure ends. Batch jobs that need to run at intervals can include a command to resubmit themselves for a later time.

The Subprocess

A *subprocess* is a child process of an existing process and depends upon its parent process for its existence and resources. It usually performs some service for the parent process—for example, using CLI commands from within a compiled program or executing a command that may take a long time. Using a subprocess to execute a time-consuming command allows you to continue entering and processing commands while the subprocess works on the time-consuming one.

Normally, a subprocess finishes its work and terminates before its parent process does. A subprocess that still exists when the parent process ends is automatically destroyed, whether its work is finished or not.

When you create a subprocess from an interactive process, the subprocess will also be an interactive process. Likewise, a batch process will create a batch-mode subprocess.

The Network Process

A *network process* is essentially a detached process that performs network functions. For example, if you request access to a file on a remote OpenVMS system, the remote system will create a network process to carry out the request for you. It works with your process to pass data back and forth or to manipulate the remote file as needed.

Please note that some processes may be dedicated entirely to network-related functions but not be in network mode.

The Other Process

There is one final process mode, *other*, which really only means that the process is not marked as being in any of the previously described modes. These processes are relatively infrequent and can usually be considered equivalent to detached processes.

Examining System Processes

To see a list of processes currently present on your system, use the Digital Command Language (DCL) command SHOW SYSTEM, as shown in Figure 3-1:

```
$ SHOW SYSTEM
OpenVMS V7.3  on node PHOEBE  27-OCT-2002 13:15:17.22  Uptime  5 01:52:10
  Pid    Process Name     State  Pri     I/O        CPU       Page flts  Pages
00000081 SWAPPER          HIB    16        0    0 00:00:26.08         0        0   (2)
00000084 LANACP           HIBO   13       --    swapped  out  --             482   (2)
00000086 IPCACP           HIB    10        7    0 00:00:00.23       159       92   (2)
00000087 ERRFMT           HIB     8     4278    0 00:00:19.68      2443      112   (2)
00000089 OPCOM            HIB     8    15579    0 00:01:19.92     54144      117   (2)
0000008A AUDIT_SERVER     HIB    10     5711    0 00:01:11.87     68318      175   (2)
0000008B JOB_CONTROL      HIB    10     9227    0 00:00:32.84     57855      139   (2)
0000008C QUEUE_MANAGER    HIB    10    13013    0 00:03:29.95    100718      365   (2)
0000008D SECURITY_SERVER  HIB    10      590    0 00:00:53.93    180636      144   (2)
0000008E TP_SERVER        HIB    10    30010    0 00:05:18.78     64589      159   (2)
0000008F NETACP           HIB    10    18555    0 00:01:07.38     11114       87   (2)
00000090 EVL              HIB     6       59    0 00:00:00.62     13001       73  N (2)
00000091 REMACP           HIB     8       67    0 00:00:00.27       244       62   (2)
00000092 MIKE             LEF     5     3774    0 00:00:34.81     25784      311   (1)
00000093 MULTINET_SERVER  LEF     5    93461    0 00:02:45.87      1069     1095   (3)
00000094 NAMED_SERVER     HIB     6    67687    0 00:02:43.62     69791      964   (3)
00000095 SMTP_SYMBIONT    HIB     5     8159    0 00:01:08.35     48831       82   (3)
00000097 WWW server 80    HIB     6   105114    0 00:08:03.21     20325     1153  N (3)
00000098 WEBSERVER_1      LEF     6       39    0 00:00:00.49      8620       55  S (5)
00001EB8 MIKE_RTA1:       CUR     4     4003    0 00:00:19.79     14998      600   (1)
00001F2D BATCH_223        COM     2    52914    0 00:13:04.27    202133      388  B (4)
```
Figure 3-1 System Processes

Each line in the display describes one process. This display includes most of the process types described previously.

There are two interactive processes for user MIKE (1): the normal system detached processes (2); some detached processes performing TCP/IP network functions (3); a batch process (4); and a subprocess (5). An "S" at the right edge of the display denotes a subprocess, an "N" denotes a network mode process, and a "B" denotes a batch process.

The Job

In OpenVMS terminology, the term job refers to a collection of processes consisting of a parent process, all of its subprocesses, all of their subprocesses, and so on.

In the previous example, the process WEBSERVER_1 is a subprocess of WWW server 80. Taken together, they are called a job. The letter "S" at the right of the display indicates a subprocess.

To prevent a single job from consuming an excessive number of system resources, certain resources are shared among all processes in a job. The total amount of a particular resource used by all processes in the job cannot exceed a certain limit. Resource quotas and limits are discussed in Chapter 4, "User Accounts". This concept bears repeating: Some system resources are shared among processes in a job, a concept that can guide the development of complex applications, portions of which may have high demand for system resources. This implies that the root cause of a resource-limit problem can sometimes lie outside the process experiencing the problem.

The Thread

A *thread* refers to a schedulable entity within a process that is able to execute independently. Just as a process is a separate schedulable task under the operating system, a thread is a separate schedulable task within a process.

Multiple threads allow different parts of the same program to execute simultaneously on different processors, potentially improving the performance of an application. Threads may also be used to divide a complex program into simpler conceptual units.

Threads are generally of interest only to programmers writing complex applications and are not covered in detail in this book.

Summary

This section has introduced the various types of processes you will encounter on an OpenVMS system. Creating batch processes and subprocesses is discussed in Chapter 7, "The User Environment."

Queues: Print, Batch, and Server

Queues are clusterwide lists of jobs scheduled for execution. The OpenVMS queuing system is used for three main purposes: (1) sending output to printers (print queues), (2) scheduling the execution of command procedures (batch queues), and (3) submitting files to be processed by a given program, which usually runs as a detached process (server queues).

The DCL commands PRINT, SUBMIT, SHOW QUEUE, SET QUEUE, SHOW ENTRY, SET ENTRY, and DELETE/ENTRY are the principal commands used to interact with queues. Their use is described in Chapter 7, "The User Environment:", "Working with Queues."

Some queues are generic and route jobs to the next available execution queue to perform the work. For example, a generic print queue routes print jobs to the next available printer queue.

Printer execution queues can execute one job at a time. Batch execution queues can execute multiple jobs simultaneously, but this number is limited by the system manager and can be adjusted while the system is running. Server queues may be able to process more than one job at a time, depending on the application processing the work.

A generic queue may be assigned to execution queues on different systems in the cluster. For example, a print job might be routed to a printer attached to another system.

Requests are assigned a queue entry number based on the order in which they arrive. If all execution queues are busy, as when several users request printing at approximately the same time, the remaining jobs wait in the generic queue until an execution queue is available.

Queue entries are assigned priorities, with the highest-priority jobs executing first. Within a priority level, the oldest job is executed first. Printer queues may optionally be set to print the smallest waiting job first.

Print Queues

Print queues keep track of print jobs submitted by system users. For example, several users may wish to print files at approximately the same time. Let's imagine an OpenVMS system with three printers. Let's say that printers LASER1 and LASER2 are ordinary small-office printers, but that BIGPRINTER is a very-high-speed, heavy-duty printer suited to printing very large print jobs.

In this case, the system manager might set the queues for LASER1 and LASER2 to accept jobs of 200KB or less, but that BIGPRINTER to accept jobs of 150KB or more.

The default generic printer queue SYS$PRINT can accept print jobs of any size and route them to a printer with the right capabilities. When a user issues a PRINT command without specifying a particular queue, the job will be entered into the generic printer queue SYS$PRINT. The OpenVMS queuing mechanism will route the job to the next available execution queue whose capabilities match the print job. A job of 50KB will be routed to either LASER1 or LASER2, whichever becomes available first. A job of 175KB can be routed to any of the three, but a job of 500KB will be routed only to BIGPRINTER.

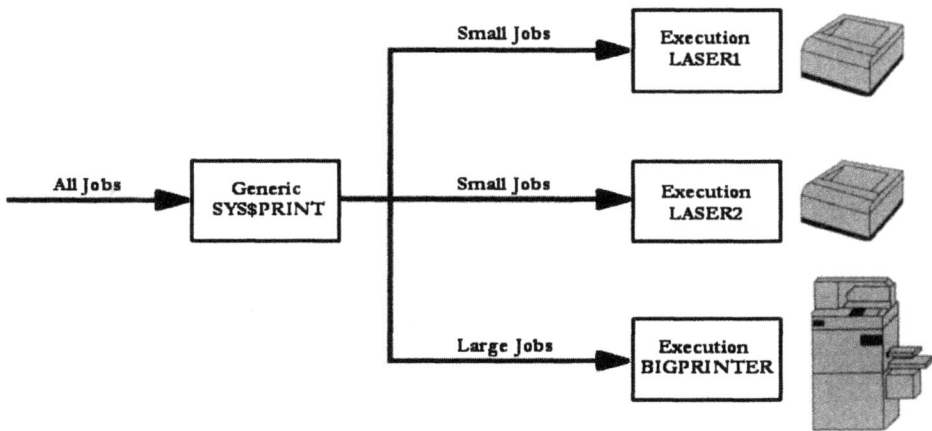

Figure 3-2 Generic and Execution Queues

Similarly, system managers can define a number of site-specific forms (paper stock) that users may specify for their jobs (e.g., letterhead, plain paper, 132-column continuous-form paper) as well as site-defined characteristics that can represent any printer attributes the system manager chooses.

A user may decide to place a job into a particular execution queue. However, this will not result in faster service; any jobs in the generic queue that would have been printed before it will still be executed first.

See Chapter 7, "The User Environment," for information about printing files.

Batch Queues

Collections of commands called *command procedures* can be submitted to a *batch queue* to be executed on a user's behalf. When a batch job starts, a batch process is created to execute the command procedure. Optionally, a logfile is produced, recording the progress of the batch job and any system messages generated during the execution of the procedure.

Batch jobs can be scheduled to run at a certain time and can be programmed to resubmit themselves at intervals.

A batch execution queue may execute several jobs simultaneously. Even so, the system manager can place a limit on the number of batch jobs that can execute at a given time, so a batch job is not guaranteed to start at the time specified by the user.

Server Queues

Virtually any type of file may be processed with *server queues*. Because this is a rather ambiguous description, this book will provide an example based on a popular real-world application.

An OpenVMS system may be directly connected to the Internet to act as an e-mail server for many users. When an e-mail message arrives, it is in the form of a text file received over the network from some other computer. It may be from a remote server, bound for some local user, it may be from a local user's personal computer, bound for someone on another continent.

The e-mail program must process each incoming and outgoing message to determine its destination and forward it to the next server or place it in a local user's mailbox.

The e-mail program may choose to use an OpenVMS server queue to hold a list of messages waiting to be processed. The program can take the first job in the queue and process it without worrying about any other pending messages. If there is a network problem, such as an unreachable remote server, the e-mail program can simply place the job back in the queue, scheduling it to be reprocessed at a later time, and move on to the next job in the queue.

The details of list maintenance and scheduling waiting messages need not be done by the e-mail program, but can be handled by the OpenVMS built-in queuing mechanism.

Summary

This section has introduced some of the concepts relevant to a multiuser operating system. Additional issues, such as file-ownership user profiles (accounts), are described in later sections.

Chapter 4 — User Accounts

Because OpenVMS is designed for many users, it must have some way of telling those users apart. For each authorized user, OpenVMS maintains a *user account*. Each account has a unique name, known as the *username*, and an associated password.[1]

When you log in to an OpenVMS system, you supply your username, identifying yourself to the system, and your password as proof of your identity. Your system manager will supply you with a username and an initial password. If you are installing OpenVMS on a new system, you will be asked to choose the initial passwords for several built-in accounts during installation.

The first time you use your account, you may be required to change your password. Afterward, you may be required to change your password at regular intervals as defined by your system manager. Your user account does far more than simply identify you to the system. It also specifies the location of your home directory; when and where you are allowed to log in; and the rights, resource quotas and limits, and privileges you are allowed on the system. Figure 4-1 contains a listing of a user account record.

```
Username: MIKE                          Owner:  Mike Duffy
Account:  SYSTEM                         UIC:    [1,100] ([MIKE])
CLI:      DCL                            Tables: DCLTABLES
Default:  DKA100:[MIKE]
LGICMD:   LOGIN
Flags:
Primary days:   Mon Tue Wed Thu Fri
Secondary days:                  Sat Sun
No access restrictions
Expiration:            (none)   Pwdminimum:  8   Login Fails:     0
Pwdlifetime:        30 00:00    Pwdchange:  12-OCT-2002 10:04
Last Login: 30-OCT-2002 16:41 (interactive), 30-OCT-2002 17:31 (non-interactive)
Maxjobs:         0  Fillm:       300  Bytlm:        32768
Maxacctjobs:     0  Shrfillm:      0  Pbytlm:           0
Maxdetach:       0  BIOlm:       160  JTquota:       4096
Prclm:          10  DIOlm:       160  WSdef:          256
Prio:            4  ASTlm:       190  WSquo:          512
Queprio:         0  TQElm:        30  WSextent:      2048
CPU:       (none)  Enqlm:       4000  Pgflquo:      40960
Authorized Privileges:
  ACNT        ALLSPOOL    ALTPRI      AUDIT      BUGCHK     BYPASS    CMEXEC    CMKRNL
  IMPERSONATDIAGNOSE  DOWNGRADE EXQUOTA    GROUP      GRPNAM    GRPPRV    IMPORT
  LOG_IO      MOUNT       NETMBX      OPER       PFNMAP     PHY_IO    PRMCEB    PRMGBL
  PRMMBX      PSWAPM      READALL     SECURITY   SETPRV     SHARE     SHMEM     SYSGBL
  SYSLCK      SYSNAM      SYSPRV      TMPMBX     UPGRADE    VOLPRO    WORLD
Default Privileges:
  ALTPRI      AUDIT       MOUNT       NETMBX     OPER       SECURITY  SETPRV    SYSNAM
  TMPMBX
```

Figure 4-1 A User Account Record

---

1. Your system manager may create user accounts that require zero, one, or two passwords, but accounts with one password are the norm.

User account records are stored in the system User Authorization File and, so, are known as UAF records.

Resource Quotas and Limits

Each user account has limits as to how much of the system's resources its processes are allowed to consume. Some of these limits apply to a single process, and some are shared among all processes in a job. These limits are known as *limits* and *quotas*. These terms have subtly different technical meanings, but the new user needs only to recognize that they are limits placed on system-resource usage.

The general user also has little need to understand the exact meaning of each item; they are introduced here only to illustrate that OpenVMS includes such a concept.

For example, the number of processes you may create at once, the number of I/O operations that may be outstanding at one time, the number of open files allowed, and the amount of memory a process can use are limited by your user account.

As an example, a UAF record includes an item called WSextent. In the example, it has a value of 2048, meaning that a process owned by this user may consume a maximum of 2048 pages of physical memory (known as its working set extent) at one time. Working sets are described in Part 2, "A Technical Introduction."

Note: A value of zero indicates there is no limit for that item. The exceptions are "Prio" and "Queprio," which refer to relative priority levels, not resource limitations.

Your system manager is responsible for setting appropriate values for these items. The goal is to provide the best overall system performance within the limits of the computer's resources.

Disk Quotas

Your system manager may elect to enable disk quotas. Disk quotas place limits on the consumption of disk storage space on a per-disk, per-user basis.

Use SHOW QUOTA [/DISK=disk] to examine your disk-space restrictions on a given disk. A message indicating that quotas are not enabled means that there are no limits other than the free space available on the disk.

Privileges

Privileges grant a user the ability to do things a typical user cannot. Privileges are required, for example, to set the system time, to examine the system security logs, or to read any file regardless of its protection.

The most basic user accounts have only the TMPMBX and NETMBX privileges, which are adequate for most ordinary purposes. Your system manager will grant additional privileges on an as-needed basis.

For reference, the full list of privileges (taken from OpenVMS VAX version V7.3) is as follows:

ACNT	may suppress accounting messages
ALLSPOOL	may allocate spooled device
ALTPRI	may set any priority value
AUDIT	may direct audit to system security audit log
BUGCHK	may make bug check log entries
BYPASS	may bypass all object access controls
CMEXEC	may change mode to exec
CMKRNL	may change mode to kernel
DIAGNOSE	may diagnose devices
DOWNGRADE	may downgrade object secrecy
EXQUOTA	may exceed disk quota
GROUP	may affect other processes in same group
GRPNAM	may insert in group logical name table
GRPPRV	may access group objects via system protection
IMPERSONATE	may impersonate another user
IMPORT	may set classification for unlabeled object
LOG_IO	may do logical i/o
MOUNT	may execute mount acp function
NETMBX	may create network device
OPER	may perform operator functions
PFNMAP	may map to specific physical pages
PHY_IO	may do physical i/o
PRMCEB	may create permanent common event clusters
PRMGBL	may create permanent global sections
PRMMBX	may create permanent mailbox
PSWAPM	may change process swap mode
READALL	may read anything as the owner
SECURITY	may perform security administration functions

SETPRV	may set any privilege bit
SHARE	may assign channels to non-shared devices
SHMEM	may create/delete objects in shared memory
SYSGBL	may create system wide global sections
SYSLCK	may lock system wide resources
SYSNAM	may insert in system logical name table
SYSPRV	may access objects via system protection
TMPMBX	may create temporary mailbox
UPGRADE	may upgrade object integrity
VOLPRO	may override volume protection
WORLD	may affect other processes in the world

Note: On older versions of OpenVMS, the IMPERSONATE privilege was called DETACH. Historically, it was used to create detached processes under the User Identification Code (introduced in the next section) of another user. Over time, the power granted by DETACH grew until a name change to IMPERSONATE was warranted.

User Identification Codes

A User Identification Code (UIC) is associated with each user account. A UIC is the combination of a *group* number and a *member* number.

A UIC takes the format "[group,member]." If you are member 100 of group 35, your UIC is [35,100]. These numbers are displayed in octal format, so they may contain only the digits 0 through 7. UICs may be displayed as alphanumeric names rather than numbers (see "Identifiers," below).

A system manager usually defines UIC groups to associate users who are related in some way, such as the faculty as opposed to the students at a university or all the employees in a given department of a corporation—say, the accounting department.

Your UIC is used to grant or deny access to system objects, such as files. When a file is created, the UIC of the owner is associated with the file. Later, when some user requests access to the file, his or her UIC is used to determine whether access will be allowed. File protection is divided into four categories, based on the requesting user's classification:

- *SYSTEM user*. The requestor is either OpenVMS itself, the system manager, or another user with a SYSTEM UIC, as defined by the system manager. The system manager may assign an arbitrary number of users to this category, usually system operators or those who perform system backups.

- *File OWNER*. The requestor's UIC exactly matches the UIC attached to the file.

- *GROUP member*. The requestor is in the same UIC group as the file owner.

- *WORLD user*. This category includes every other user not mentioned above.

Each of these four categories may be granted or denied the ability to read (examine), write (modify), execute (if the file is a program or procedure), or delete the file.

The ability to change the protection of the file (CONTROL access) is granted automatically to the OWNER and SYSTEM categories. As a practical matter, this means you cannot accidentally deny yourself access to your files (as you can always grant yourself access again), nor can you prevent SYSTEM users from gaining access. You can also grant other users CONTROL access via Access Control Lists (ACLs).

File protections and ACLs are described further in Chapter 7, "The User Environment."

UICs Are Not Necessarily Unique

It is important to note that a UIC does not necessarily identify one particular user. It is possible for the system manager to assign the same UIC to two or more user accounts. It is also possible to reuse a UIC previously assigned to a user account that has been deleted.

Because UICs are closely related to file protection, most system managers ensure that no two current users share the same UIC, and many avoid reusing an old UIC. Sharing of UICs can also cause confusion with identifiers (described later) and allow one user to view the private files of another with whom he or she shares a UIC. Further, if a malicious user were to damage the system, but shared a UIC with other users, it might be difficult, or impossible, to determine which user was responsible.

Of course, a system manager may find valid reasons for violating either of these guidelines on a case-by-case basis.

Identifiers

An *identifier* is a credential held by one or more users. Identifiers are usually used to indicate that their holders have certain types of access to certain objects.

All users in a company's accounting department might belong to the same UIC group, but not all of them may be authorized to view payroll files. The system manager might create an identifier called PAYROLL and grant it only to the specific users authorized to view payroll data.

> **Note:** Identifiers are used in conjunction with ACLs to grant this type of special access to files. ACLs are described in Chapter 7, "The User Environment."

Thus, UIC-based protection adequately handles most situations, but the PAYROLL identifier provides special access to specific individuals.

In addition, OpenVMS usually creates a separate identifier for every UIC. Some system managers choose to prevent this, and doing so does not interfere with users' ability to access files. The only real difference most users will notice is whether or not file ownership is shown by UIC or by identifier.

For example say user MIKE has a UIC of [1,100], but the system manager has prevented the identifier MIKE from being created. Ownership for MIKE's files will be listed as follows:

```
$ DIRECTORY /OWNER LOGIN.COM

Directory DKA100:[MIKE]

LOGIN.COM;51          [1,100]

Total of 1 file.
```

If, however, the identifier MIKE was created to go along with his UIC, file ownership for his files will be displayed in the following format:

```
$ DIRECTORY /OWNER LOGIN.COM

Directory DKA100:[MIKE]

LOGIN.COM;51          [MIKE]

Total of 1 file.
```

Summary

Your user account defines nearly every aspect of your identity on the system: your username, the location for your files, your rights and privileges, your limits on resource consumption, and more. You need not understand all aspects of it in great detail, as your system manager will assign the appropriate settings. However, your interactions with the system will be more intuitive if you have a general understanding of your user account.

Chapter 5 — Logging In and Out of the System

Logging in for the First Time

This section takes the reader through the steps necessary to establish a connection and log into an OpenVMS system. Once you are logged in, you are ready to try the examples in Chapter 6, "The Digital Command Language." If you have access to an OpenVMS system, you may log in now; however, you may find it helpful to read Chapter 6, "The Digital Command Language" first.

For the purposes of this section, it is assumed that you will be using a terminal or terminal window to access the system. If you are using an OpenVMS workstation equipped with a GUI interface, please see Chapter 15, "The OpenVMS GUI."

Obtaining a User Account

First, you must acquire a user account. If you are using an existing OpenVMS system, the system manager will supply you with a username and initial password. If you have just installed OpenVMS on a computer, use the SYSTEM account and the password that was determined at installation time.

Note: the SYSTEM account is, by default, a fully privileged account. Please exercise caution when using it, as it is possible to cause any number of unpleasant results, including the accidental deletion of very important files. On a newly installed system, the best course of action is to use the SYSTEM account to create a normally privileged account, and then use the new account for experimentation. For complete information on maintaining accounts, see the *OpenVMS System Management Utilities Reference Manual* in the OpenVMS documentation set. Within it, locate the chapter on the Authorize Utility.

Connecting and Initiating a Login

This section shows you how to connect to the system and log in. Each of the following subsections is specific to a different kind of access. If you do not know what type of access you have, consult your system manager.

You should read the entire sequence of events before trying it for the first time because the login sequence must be completed within a certain amount of time. Otherwise, you will have to begin again.

Please locate the subsection appropriate for yourself, perform the steps shown there, and then skip ahead to "The Login Sequence."

If You Have a Directly Connected Terminal

A terminal directly connected to an OpenVMS system (without a terminal server or other intervening hardware) has the simplest method for beginning a login: just press RETURN or ENTER.

If pressing ENTER does not result in a Username: prompt, one of several things might be the cause. Is your terminal powered on? Is it actually connected to the system? Check the cabling. Is your terminal set to the proper communication rate? The combination of 9,600 baud, 8 data bits, no parity, and one stop bit is a good first assumption on most OpenVMS systems. Your system may or may not be set to automatically detect the terminal baud rate; press ENTER a few times, waiting a couple seconds between presses. If you cannot get a response after checking these items, please consult your system manager or technical support staff.

Please see Chapter 11, "Using Your Terminal" for more information about terminals.

If You Have Telnet Access

Telnet is a TCP/IP program allowing a user on one computer to connect with another system and establish a terminal session. The originating computer must have a Telnet client program installed. GUI Telnet interfaces typically present a window allowing you to specify the remote system name and network port. CLI Telnet programs allow you to specify these items on the command line. Consult the documentation for your particular Telnet client.

You will need to know the following things about the OpenVMS system. Is your OpenVMS system running TCP/IP? It is required for Telnet access. Is Telnet access enabled on the OpenVMS system? What is the network name (or IP address) of the OpenVMS system? What network port is used for Telnet access? The default is port 21. Is your user account permitted to log in from a remote location? Your system manager can answer these questions.

Supply your Telnet client with the name (or IP address) and port number (if different from 21) for your OpenVMS system. Then, instruct your Telnet client to connect. A connection will be established, and a login sequence will be started. It is usually not necessary to press ENTER to begin a login session; a Username: prompt should appear when the connection is made.

If You Have Modem Access

If your terminal or computer is equipped with a modem, you may use dial-up access if your OpenVMS system is also equipped with a modem.

Your modem must be instructed to dial the OpenVMS system. Many terminal emulation programs and Telnet clients have the ability to control the modem; consult your modem and software documentation for instructions.

After your modem indicates that a connection has been made, you may or may not need to press ENTER to start a login sequence. If a "Username:" prompt does not appear within a few seconds of a connection, try pressing ENTER.

If You Have Terminal Server Access

Terminal servers are network devices designed to allow more flexible network access for terminals. Each terminal server allows several terminals or other devices to be connected to it. The terminal server communicates over the network using protocols such as LAT and TCP/IP to allow access to multiple network hosts instead of being directly connected to one host.

It is possible to have modem access to a terminal server. In that case, use your modem to connect to the terminal server first, and then use the terminal server to reach the OpenVMS system.

Consult your terminal server documentation or system manager for instructions on how to connect to the terminal server and establish an outgoing connection. Usually, Digital-style terminal servers behave as follows: To establish a connection with the terminal server, press ENTER. The terminal server will present the LOCAL> prompt. At that prompt, specify the OpenVMS host you'd like to reach with the CONNECT command, followed by the name of the OpenVMS system—for example, CONNECT ALPHA4, followed by ENTER.

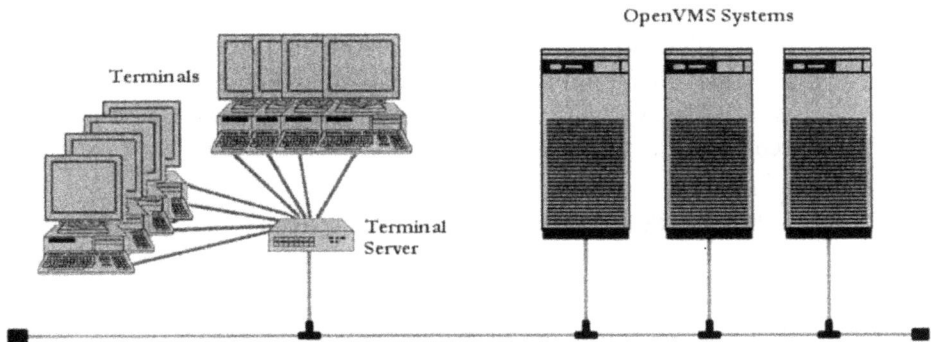

Figure 5-1 Terminal Server Access

Later, when you log out from node ALPHA4, you will be returned to the terminal server LOCAL> prompt. You may log out of the terminal server with the LOGOUT command.

If You Have a GUI-Based Workstation

The OpenVMS GUI handles logins in a different fashion. This interface uses an attached monitor, keyboard, and mouse, just as if the system were a personal computer.

When the system is booted, the GUI starts automatically as one of the final steps in the startup sequence. A large dialog box appears at the center of the screen, asking for a username. When a username is entered, the dialog box changes to one asking for a password. Chapter 15 includes an illustration showing the GUI login screen.

When a valid username and password are entered, a customizable user environment appears and you are logged in.

Once logged in, you may establish a DCL terminal session by starting the DECterm application from the Application Manager. DECterm does not ask for a username or password; the terminal session runs under the same username that you entered at the beginning of the GUI session. Using the GUI interface is covered in more detail in Chapter 15, "The OpenVMS GUI ."

The Login Sequence

Most of the connection methods discussed above except that for the directly connected terminal will automatically begin the login process when the connection is made. If nothing happens, press ENTER or RETURN to begin the login.

> **Note:** Some OpenVMS systems have a system password enabled. This is a rarely used, extra security feature. Such systems require you to type a password, which will not be displayed, even before presenting you with a Username: prompt. You will have no indication that anything at all is happening until the system password is accepted. Consult your system manager to determine whether this feature is enabled.

At this point the system may or may not display a message indicating the identity of the system, its name, the version of OpenVMS it is running, or any other message the system manager has defined. Many system managers use this feature to alert the user community of important events, such as a scheduled system downtime. Others choose to display a stern warning against unauthorized attempts to access the system.

The system will then ask you for your username and password. The username and password are not case-sensitive; you may type them in any combination of upper and lower-case letters you wish. Older versions of OpenVMS will display your username in upper case, regardless of how you type it, whereas newer ones will display it exactly as you enter it. While you type your password, it will not be displayed.[1]

> **Note:** Your system manager can configure your account to require two passwords. This is done infrequently, and this book assumes each account has one password. Your system manager will notify you if your account is to have two passwords.

Login Failures

If you enter your username or password incorrectly, or if your account has been disabled for some reason, the message "User authorization failure" will be displayed. This message is intentionally ambiguous to prevent giving any hints to someone who may be trying to break into the system.

After some number of failures, usually three to five, your account will be temporarily disabled. While your account is disabled, even entering the proper password will not work. This is a security feature intended to prevent break-ins from malicious users trying many possible passwords.

Once your username and password have been accepted, the system may or may not display a welcome message, as defined by the system manager. If present, this message will typically display a banner welcoming you to the OpenVMS system. OpenVMS then shows the date and time of your last interactive and noninteractive logins. If you have any new mail messages waiting, you will be notified.[2] If the system has recorded any login failures from your account since last time you logged in, you will be notified. This is a security feature intended to alert you to someone trying to guess your password or use your account to break into the system. Figure 5-2 shows a typical login sequence.

```
    This system is for the use of authorized personnel only. (1)
    All other access strictly prohibited.

Username: MIKE (2)
Password:      (3)
```

1. If your terminal has the LOCAL ECHO characteristic turned on, the terminal itself will display your password, and OpenVMS will not be able to prevent it from happening. The vast majority of OpenVMS sites do not use LOCAL ECHO, and you may assume that your site is the same unless you are told otherwise.
2. The system manager can disable new mail notifications. This is helpful in cases where the user might retrieve his or her mail some other way, such as through a POP3 client.

```
Welcome to OpenVMS (TM) VAX Operating System, Version V7.3 on node ABBY (4)
    Last interactive login on Friday,  1-NOV-2002 16:51      (5)
    Last non-interactive login on Friday,  1-NOV-2002 17:19  (6)
        1 failure since last successful login    (7)

            You have 1 new Mail message.  (8)

$  (9)
```

Figure 5-2 A Login Sequence

The points of interest in the Figure 5-2 are as follows:

1. *The system announcement message.* This is shown before you log into the system
   and can be any message the system manager wishes.

2. *The username prompt.* Enter your username here—in this case, MIKE. Older
   versions of OpenVMS may display the username in all upper case letters, but
   newer versions display in the same manner that you type it. The username itself is
   not case-sensitive; enter it in any case you wish.

3. *The password prompt.* Enter your password here. For security reasons, the
   password will not be displayed as you type it. Should you make a typing error,
   BACKSPACE will work, even though you cannot see it, or you may use CTRL/U
   to delete the entire password and begin again. The password is not case-sensitive;
   enter it in any mixture of upper and lower case letters.

4. *The system welcome message.* In this example, the default message is shown, but the
   system manager may change it at will.

5. *Last interactive login notification.* This displays the time of your last interactive
   login. This is a security feature that can alert you to the fact that someone else has
   used your account, perhaps by stealing your password. Few users examine this
   message carefully, but it can help alert you to potential security problems. If you
   see a login reported for which you know you are not responsible, notify your
   system manager.

6. *Last noninteractive login notification.* This is similar to (5), but it notifies you of
   logins other than interactive ones—for example, batch jobs submitted from your
   account.

7. *Previous login failure notification.* This is a security feature that alerts you to
   unsuccessful attempts to log in to your account. Each incorrect password causes
   this number to increase. At the next successful login, the number of previous
   failures is shown here. If login failures are reported for which you know you are
   not responsible, notify your system manager. This message will be shown only at
   the next successful login and will then be reset.

8. *New mail notification.* If you have any waiting mail messages, you will be notified here. This message can be suppressed by the system manager; typically, it would be disabled for users who use POP3 or something similar to access their mail (see Chapter 12, "E-mail").

9. *The system prompt.* The dollar sign ($) is the normal OpenVMS DCL prompt that indicates that the DCL CLI is waiting for a command. This prompt may be changed via the SET PROMPT command, if you wish.

Once your username and password are accepted, OpenVMS creates an interactive process for you. This process automatically executes SYS$MANAGER:SYLOGIN.COM and SYS$LOGIN:LOGIN.COM before presenting you with the DCL prompt.

SYLOGIN.COM is a systemwide command procedure automatically executed for every user on the system. Its contents are determined by the system manager, and it includes commands relevant to all system users.

LOGIN.COM is your personal login command procedure, located in your home directory. You may use it to customize your OpenVMS environment. LOGIN.COM is described in Chapter 7, "The User Environment."

The CLI

When you log in via a terminal or terminal emulator, you will enter the DCL command line environment. You interact with the system by typing commands at the DCL prompt and noting any messages the system issues while executing your command.

DCL stands for Digital Command Language, which dates back to OpenVMS having been a product of Digital Equipment Corporation.

Entering Commands

Once you have successfully logged in to your OpenVMS system, you may begin entering commands. The DCL Command Line Interpreter (CLI) is the program that accepts the commands you type; it ensures that they are valid commands and carries them out.

OpenVMS provides a type-ahead buffer. This allows you to continue entering commands while a previous command is still processing. While a previous command is executing, your keystrokes will not be shown, but will be carried out when the current command completes.

If you continue typing ahead until the system cannot accept any more keystrokes, the terminal will beep each time you press a key. If this happens, stop typing until the system catches up.

Please see Chapter 6, "The Digital Command Language," for information on entering commands.

Logging out

When you have finished using the system, you should log out. Leaving your terminal session unattended poses a security risk, as someone else could approach your terminal while you are away. Leaving an idle session logged in also consumes a small, but real, portion of system resources.

Log out using either the LOGOUT or the LOGOUT/FULL command:

```
$ LOGOUT
  MIKE            logged out at 12-DEC-2002 19:07:39.58
```

or

```
$ LOGOUT/FULL
  MIKE            logged out at 12-DEC-2002 19:08:52.31

  Accounting information:
  Buffered I/O count:          127     Peak working set size:    1771
  Direct I/O count:             50     Peak page file size:      5955
  Page faults:               10417     Mounted volumes:             0
  Charged CPU time:     0 00:00:04.80  Elapsed time:     0 00:00:48.02
```

Chapter 6 — The Digital Command Language

This chapter introduces the Digital Command Language (DCL) command line interpreter (CLI). For users who access OpenVMS through a terminal or terminal emulation program, DCL will be the primary interface to the system. Those users who have access to a GUI interface should also read this chapter; DCL commands and command procedures are an integral part of OpenVMS, even for GUI users.

Those readers with access to an OpenVMS system may find it helpful to try the examples presented throughout this book.

What is a CLI?

A CLI is a piece of software that accepts commands typed by a user at a terminal keyboard and causes them to be carried out. A program may have its own internal CLI, but the default CLI for commands typed at the OpenVMS system prompt is DCL.

When a command is entered, DCL determines whether it is a valid command. If it is not valid, DCL displays an appropriate error message and awaits further commands. On receiving a valid command, DCL determines which program, if any, should be executed to carry out the command. Most commands require the attention of a program, but some commands are carried out internally by DCL.

If a separate program must execute to carry out the command, DCL causes the program to run and supplies it with information from the command line. After the program has finished, DCL again takes over and awaits the next user command.

While waiting for you to enter a command, DCL presents a prompt, a signal that it is waiting for your input. By default, that prompt is a single dollar sign ($).[1]

Format of DCL Commands

DCL commands follow a uniform format, separating DCL from most other CLIs. On many other systems, the command line is simply passed in its entirety to the program. Each program performs its own command line processing, resulting in some inconsistencies between the command line formats for different programs.

DCL, on the other hand, performs full command line processing and rejects many invalid commands without the need to invoke the corresponding program. Most

---

1. DCL, unlike a UNIX system's CLI, does not present a different prompt when the user has root access. The concept of root access has no exact equivalent in OpenVMS.

OpenVMS programs retrieve command line elements from DCL during execution and never examine the full command line as typed by the user.

Once you understand the general DCL command format, you will be able to apply that experience to OpenVMS programs you have never used before.

For those programs that process their own command lines, DCL does provide a mechanism for passing the command line directly to them (see "Foreign Commands" in Chapter 7, "The User Environment").

Parts of a DCL Command

DCL commands consist of four main elements: *verbs, qualifiers, parameters*, and sometimes *keywords*.

The functions of these elements can be remembered using the following guidelines: verbs describe what to do, qualifiers describe how to do it, and parameters describe what objects to act on.

Keywords sometimes behave like parameters and other times serve as qualifier values. They are discussed later.

Consider this example:

```
$ PRINT SCHEDULE.LIS/COPIES=4
```

In the example above, PRINT is the verb. Verbs appear first and tell DCL the action you wish to perform—in this case, to print a file.

SCHEDULE.LIS is a parameter. In this case, it is the file you wish to print. Parameters appear after verbs and are preceded by a space. Some commands accept more than one parameter, as will be shown in upcoming examples.

/COPIES=4 is a qualifier specifying that you wish to print four copies. If /COPIES is not specified, a *default* value of one copy will be assumed. Qualifiers are preceded by a slash (/) and can appear in more than one place on a command line. When they appear in different places, they sometimes have different meanings, as is shown in the following example.

This command

```
$ PRINT SCHEDULE.LIS/COPIES=4
```

is equivalent to the following command:

```
$ PRINT/COPIES=4 SCHEDULE.LIS
```

Now, let's consider the same basic command, but with some variations that demonstrate how the position of qualifiers can change the meaning of a command.

```
$ PRINT/COPIES=2 SCHEDULE.LIS,PAYROLL.DAT
```

The above example places the qualifier /COPIES=2 just after the verb. When it appears after the verb, it is applied to each parameter. Two copies of each file, SCHEDULE.LIS and PAYROLL.DAT, will be printed.

Compare that with the next example:

```
$ PRINT SCHEDULE.LIS,PAYROLL.DAT/COPIES=2
```

This example places the qualifier /COPIES=2 after a parameter. When appearing after a parameter, it affects only that parameter. In this example, one copy of SCHEDULE.LIS and two copies of PAYROLL.DAT will be printed.

A qualifier whose behavior is dependent upon where it appears is known as a *positional qualifier*. A qualifier that behaves the same way regardless of its position is called a *command qualifier* or *global qualifier*.

An example of a command qualifier for the PRINT command is the /QUEUE qualifier. It carries the same meaning in each of the following two commands:

```
$ PRINT SCHEDULE.LIS,PAYROLL.DAT/QUEUE=PRINTER2
$ PRINT/QUEUE=PRINTER2 SCHEDULE.LIS,PAYROLL.DAT
```

Both files will be printed on PRINTER2.

Entering Commands

You may enter DCL commands in either upper-case or lower-case letters or in any mixture of the two. DCL will convert any items not enclosed within quotation marks (" ") to upper case before processing the command. In keeping with the history of the OpenVMS documentation set, examples in this book are shown in upper case. When entering commands at the DCL prompt, you do not enter the leading dollar sign ($) shown in these examples. Dollar signs are required only within command procedures (see Chapter 9, "Command Procedures").

To enter a DCL command, type the verb first. Next, place any positional qualifiers you wish to apply to all parameters. Next come parameters (or keywords), the first of which must be preceded by a space. After each parameter, you may place any positional qualifier you wish to affect only that parameter. This positional qualifier is allowed to override the same qualifier appearing after the verb, as shown in examples that follow. A global qualifier may appear anywhere on the command line.

Some verbs, such as COPY and RENAME, accept multiple parameters. Others, such as PRINT and DELETE, accept lists of parameter values separated by commas (,) or plus signs (+) (see the following table).

You will encounter all of the following formats (and more) depending on the requirements of each command verb:

```
General format                          Example
$ VERB                                  $ DIRECTORY
                                        $ LOGOUT

$ VERB/QUALIFIER                        $ DIRECTORY/FULL
                                        $ LOGOUT/BRIEF

$ VERB PARAMETER (or KEYWORD)           $ DELETE file
                                        $ SHOW TIME

$ VERB PARAM1 PARAM2                    $ COPY existing-file new-file
                                        $ RENAME old-name new-name

$ VERB PARAM1+PARAM2                    $ PRINT file1+file2
                                        $ DELETE file1,file2

$ VERB/QUALIFIER PARAM,PARAM/QUALIFIER  $ PRINT/COPIES=2 file1,file2/COPIES=3
```

When the command is complete, press ENTER.

Before pressing ENTER, you may edit the command to correct any mistakes by using the backspace or delete key; in addition, you may use the arrow keys to move the cursor. Use CTRL/A to toggle between insert and overstrike modes. It is not necessary for the cursor to be at the end of the line when you press ENTER.

You may sometimes omit required elements and have DCL prompt you for them (see the section on "Entering Incomplete Commands" below).

Keywords

Some DCL commands may include an additional element known as a keyword. Keywords can appear in two different places. Sometimes, a keyword supplies a value to a qualifier. Other times, it appears after a verb, just as a parameter would.

Keywords are predefined words, not arbitrary text. When one appears on a command line, it must appear in the right place and be one of the values allowed by the command verb or qualifier with which it appears. For example:

```
$ DIRECTORY LOGIN.COM /DATE=MODIFIED

Directory DKA100:[MIKE]
```

```
LOGIN.COM;45        30-AUG-2001 16:18:45.96

Total of 1 file.
```

This command instructs the DIRECTORY program to show the modification date of the file LOGIN.COM. In this example, MODIFIED is a keyword for the /DATE qualifier. Other possible keywords for DIRECTORY/DATE include BACKUP (the date the file was last backed up), CREATED (the date the file was created), and EXPIRATION (the date the file will expire or has expired).

Note: File expiration dates are used fairly infrequently, but may be used to help identify certain files that may no longer be needed. The system itself takes no action when a file expires.

Some qualifiers allow their keywords to appear in a list. Place them within parentheses, separated by commas. Colons (:) and equals signs (=) can be used interchangeably to supply a value to a keyword. The following two commands are equivalent:

```
$ SET FILE DATA.TXT /PROTECTION=(SYSTEM=RWED,OWNER=RWED,GROUP=RW,WORLD=R)
$ SET FILE DATA.TXT /PROTECTION=(SYSTEM:RWED,OWNER:RWED,GROUP:RW,WORLD:R)
```

When using only one keyword, the parentheses may be omitted. The following two commands are equivalent:

```
$ SET FILE DATA.TXT /PROTECTION=(SYSTEM=RWED)
$ SET FILE DATA.TXT /PROTECTION=SYSTEM=RWED
```

When appearing after a verb, keywords can behave like parameters. Let's consider a previous example:

```
$ PRINT SCHEDULE.LIS
```

As we have seen, the verb (what to do) is PRINT. The parameter (what to PRINT) is SCHEDULE.LIS. Now let's introduce a command verb that uses keywords:

```
$ SHOW TIME
   6-NOV-2002 17:33:34
```

In this example, the verb (what to do) is SHOW, and the keyword (what to show) is TIME. When used this way, a keyword and a parameter are similar, but there are some important differences.

Parameters may appear as lists of items to be processed together, such as with a PRINT command specifying multiple files. The following commands

```
$ PRINT SCHEDULE.LIS
```

```
$ PRINT PAYROLL.DAT
```

may be combined as follows:

```
$ PRINT SCHEDULE.LIS,PAYROLL.DAT
```

Keywords, however, are usually not permitted in that kind of combination:

```
$ SHOW DEFAULT
  DKA0:[MIKE]
$ SHOW TIME
   6-NOV-2002 17:22:47
```

Each of these commands is fine alone, but they cannot be combined. An attempt to do so results in an error message (more on those later):

```
$ SHOW DEFAULT,TIME
%DCL-W-NOLIST, list of parameter values not allowed - check use of comma (,)
 \DEFAULT,TIME\
```

DCL Keywords

Why is there a distinction between parameters and keywords used where parameters usually appear? The answer lies in the OpenVMS command definition utility (CDU). CDU is the tool that allows programmers to define the command line elements that their programs will use. Keywords allow the same command verb to execute one of several programs, depending on the keyword. For example, the program that performs the SET PASSWORD command can be separate from the program that performs the SET TIME command. This allows for smaller, more modular programs when a single verb, like SHOW or SET, makes sense for a variety of different functions.

Abbreviation of Command Line Elements

You need not always enter the full text of DCL verbs, qualifiers, or keywords. You may abbreviate them to the shortest length that is unambiguous with other valid entries. For example, you may abbreviate the DIRECTORY command verb to DIRECT or DIR. Yet you may not abbreviate it to DI, because that abbreviation also matches the DIAGNOSE, DIFFERENCES, DISABLE, DISCONNECT, and DISMOUNT verbs.

Should you abbreviate a command element to the point at which it becomes ambiguous, DCL will produce a message to that effect:

```
$ DI
%DCL-W-ABVERB, ambiguous command verb - supply more characters
 \DI\
```

Entering Commands Longer Than One Line

DCL can accept commands longer than one line. When your command nears the edge of the screen, you may simply continue typing and allow the line to wrap to the next line automatically. This method works for command lines shorter than 255 characters, or a little more than three lines on most terminals. If you exceed this limit, DCL will terminate your command entry and display an error message.

To manually continue a long command on the next line, end the current line with a hyphen (-) and press ENTER. DCL will not process the line you just entered, but will wait for you to continue your command on the next line. DCL indicates it is waiting for continuation by preceding the prompt by an underscore (_). A single command can be continued over several lines, as shown here:

```
$ PRINT CONTENTS.TXT,CHAPTER1.TXT,CHAPTER2.TXT -
_$ /QUEUE=PRINTER3/FORM=SINGLE_LETTER/AFTER="11:00" -
_$ /JOB_COUNT=4/NOTIFY [enter]
```

When you continue a line with a hyphen, DCL will check for a valid command verb as soon as you move on to the first continuation line.

Once you have moved on to a continuation line, you may no longer correct any mistakes you may have made on a previous line. If you have made a mistake, you may press CTRL/Y to cancel the entire command.

Entering Incomplete Commands (DCL Prompts)

If you enter a DCL command, but do not include all required parameters, DCL will prompt you for the input it needs to process your command. If you wish to RENAME a file, but do not tell DCL what file to rename or what the new name should be, DCL will prompt you for these items:

```
$ RENAME [enter]
_From: DRAFT4.TXT [enter]
_To: FINAL.TXT [enter]
```

If you simply press ENTER in response to a prompt, the prompt will be repeated until you enter a value or cancel the command. To cancel the command, press CTRL/Z.

```
$ RENAME [enter]
_From: [enter]
_From: [enter]
_From: [ctrl/z] *Exit*
```

Note that DCL will prompt only for required elements; it is up to you to enter any optional elements, such as qualifiers. If a valid verb and all required parameters are present when you press ENTER or CTRL/Z, the command will be issued.

Comments

The DCL comment delimiter is an exclamation mark (!). When you place an exclamation mark on a DCL command line (except within quotation marks), everything to the right of it will be ignored by DCL.

This feature is used mainly in DCL command procedures (files containing commands to be executed sequentially) to provide internal documentation. A comment delimiter may also be used in an interactive command, as follows:

```
$ SHOW TIME ! This is a comment and will be ignored.
  21-NOV-2002 17:27:09
```

An exclamation mark appearing within quotation marks will not be treated as a comment character, but will be processed as part of the string in which it appears. For example, you may define a symbol whose value contains an exclamation mark as follows (symbols are introduced later in this chapter):

```
$ PHRASE :== "Hey! That's my car!"
$ SHOW SYMBOL PHRASE
  PHRASE == "Hey! That's my car!"
```

Informational, Warning, and Error Messages

In many cases, DCL simply executes your command without displaying a message. In general, if you see no message, you may assume that the command completed successfully.

If the command was unsuccessful or DCL has other information it must provide you, DCL will display an appropriate message. DCL messages, like DCL commands, follow a specific format. This section will show you how to interpret a DCL message.

Let's say you wish to obtain the current time:

```
$ SHOW TIME
  22-NOV-2002 18:28:49
```

But, you make a typographical error:

```
$ SHOW TOME
%DCL-W-IVKEYW, unrecognized keyword - check validity and spelling
 \TOME\
```

In the above example, TIME is misspelled as TOME, causing DCL to respond with a message indicating that it could not process the command.

Let's take a closer look at the message, breaking it down into its various parts to illustrate the uniform way that DCL reports errors. Consider the message

```
%DCL-W-IVKEYW, unrecognized keyword - check validity and spelling
   \TOME\
```

Messages begin with a percent sign (%) unless several related messages are displayed together (discussed below).

Next come three fields that identify the program issuing the message (here, DCL), the severity of the error (in this case W, meaning warning), and the error mnemonic (IVKEYW).

After this, the error is explained in plain English: "unrecognized keyword."

Finally, the message may include advice on how you may correct the error: "check validity and spelling."

Note: Any or all of these fields may be disabled via the SET MESSAGE command. See the OpenVMS online help facility for information.

Severity Levels

Every OpenVMS error message has an associated severity level, as follows. The numeric equivalents are shown in parentheses. Note that the numeric values follow the OpenVMS convention that odd values indicate success (or TRUE) conditions, while zero and even values indicate failure (or FALSE) conditions.

```
-S-   (1) Success
-I-   (3) Informational
-W-   (0) Warning
-E-   (2) Error
-F-   (4) Severe (fatal) error
```

Multiple Messages from the Same Command

Sometimes a command may generate more than one error message in response to a single command. There are two principal reasons for this. One is that the command must perform several operations, more than one of which generates a separate message. The other main reason is to clarify the preceding message further. Both types are shown in the following example:

```
$ PRINT/QUEUE=PRINTER4 NOFILE1.TXT,LOGIN.COM
%PRINT-E-OPENIN, error opening DKA0:[MIKE]NOFILE1.TXT; as input (1)
-RMS-E-FNF, file not found (2)
```

```
%PRINT-F-CREJOB, error creating job (3)
-JBC-E-NOSUCHQUE, no such queue (4)
```

This command attempts to print two files, LOGIN.COM, which exists, and NOFILE1.TXT, which does not. It attempts to print them on print queue PRINTER4, which also does not exist. The messages are interpreted below:

1. This message indicates that the PRINT facility cannot open the file NOFILE1.TXT. This is an error message, indicated by the severity field "-E-."

2. This message begins with a hyphen (-), indicating that it clarifies the previous message. It states the reason the file could not be opened: The file could not be found. This message is from the OpenVMS Record Management Services (RMS).

At this point, DCL continues to process the command, as it may still be possible to complete it partially. Had there been a Failure or Fatal error, processing would stop, but since the worst previous problem was an Error, processing continues.

3. The PRINT facility reports that it cannot create the print job (now consisting of just LOGIN.COM). This is a Fatal or Failure condition, as indicated by the severity code "-F-." Command processing stops upon encountering a Failure condition.

4. This message clarifies message (3), indicating the print job cannot be created because the specified printer queue, PRINTER4, does not exist. This message is from the Job Controller (JBC).

DCL Symbols

A DCL *symbol* is a symbolic name for a character string or integer. A symbol may be used in place of a literal value. For example, symbols may be used as a shorthand substitute for long command lines, or they may be used much like variables, as found in compiled programming languages.

Before we demonstrate the use of symbols, it is important to understand the two types of symbols: *local* and *global*.

Symbol Scope

The term *scope* refers to the context in which a symbol is recognized. A symbol with local scope has meaning only within a limited environment, but a symbol with global scope is recognized throughout the process.

A local symbol is one that is valid only for the current command level, whereas a global symbol is valid at any command level. When you log in, your process is at command level 0. If you execute a command procedure, the procedure is at command level 1. If that procedure executes another procedure, the second one will execute at command level 2. DCL supports up to command level 31; level 0 is the highest command level, and level 31 is the lowest. Command procedures are described in Chapter 9 "Command Procedures."

DCL maintains a separate table of local symbols for each command level. When a command level is ended, all of its local symbols are destroyed.

On the other hand, global symbols are active at all command levels in the process. A global symbol created or modified at any level is accessible by all levels. If a global symbol is created at any command level, the symbol endures even after the command level ends.

If a local symbol and a global symbol of the same name exist at a particular command level, the local symbol takes precedence. Each of these commands is described in the upcoming paragraphs:

```
$ TOTAL = 15        ! Create a local symbol
$ TOTAL == 10       ! Create a global symbol of the same name
$ SHOW SYMBOL TOTAL ! The local symbol takes precedence
  TOTAL = 15   Hex = 0000000F  Octal = 00000000017
```

The next few paragraphs demonstrate the creation and use of some symbols.

Creating a Symbol

Use one of the following operators to create a symbol:

- = creates a local character string or integer symbol.

- : = creates a local character string symbol.

- = = creates a global character string or integer symbol.

- : = = creates a global character string symbol.

The general format for creating a symbol is as follows:

```
$ symbol_name [:=]= value_to_assign
```

Specific examples of symbol creation are contained in the following sections.

Examining the Value of a Symbol

You may examine the value of an existing symbol using the SHOW SYMBOL command, such as in the following example:

```
$ TOTAL = 10
$ SHOW SYMBOL TOTAL
  TOTAL = 10   Hex = 0000000A  Octal = 00000000012
$ TEXT := "This is a character symbol"
$ SHOW SYMBOL TEXT
  TEXT = "This is a character symbol"
```

Integer symbols are displayed in decimal, hexadecimal, and octal representations.

Deleting a Symbol

Symbols may be deleted via the DELETE/SYMBOL command. Local symbols are assumed; the /GLOBAL qualifier is required to delete a global symbol:

```
$ TOTAL == 10
$ SHOW SYMBOL TOTAL
  TOTAL == 10   Hex = 0000000A  Octal = 00000000012
$ DELETE/SYMBOL/GLOBAL TOTAL
$ SHOW SYMBOL TOTAL
%DCL-W-UNDSYM, undefined symbol - check validity and spelling
```

Using a Symbol in Place of a DCL Command

Certain DCL commands can be quite lengthy. To save keystrokes, symbols are often used in place of long or frequently used commands.

You may wish to use your LOGIN.COM file to create such symbols automatically when you log in. LOGIN.COM is described in Chapter 7, "The User Environment."

Let's say that your preferred EDIT command is as follows:

```
$ EDIT/EDT/COMMAND=SYS$LOGIN:EDTINI.EDT
```

Rather than typing such a long command over and over, you may define a short symbol to represent the entire command:

```
$ EDT :== EDIT/EDT/COMMAND=SYS$LOGIN:EDTINI.EDT
```

Once the symbol is assigned, you may use EDT in place of the complete command, treating it as if it were a command verb:

```
$ EDT filespec
```

Some users choose to redefine existing DCL verbs to apply the qualifiers they use most often automatically:

```
$ PRINT :== PRINT/NOBURST/NOFLAG/NOTRAILER/NOTIFY
```

After the above symbol assignment is made, the command PRINT automatically includes the qualifiers shown. If you would like to override any of the qualifiers, you may apply conflicting qualifiers to your command symbol. This example keeps all of the qualifiers associated with the symbol, but cancels the /NOTIFY qualifier:

```
$ PRINT/NONOTIFY SCHEDULE.LIS
```

The command above results in the following command being executed:

```
$ PRINT/NOBURST/NOFLAG/NOTRAILER/NOTIFY/NONOTIFY SCHEDULE.LIS
```

The resulting command effectively contains both /NOTIFY and /NONOTIFY, but DCL acts only on the latter (/NONOTIFY).

Be warned that Hewlett-Packard, like Compaq and Digital, recommends against defining symbols with names exactly matching existing command verbs. Many users do so anyway, accepting the undesirable effects, which consist mostly of confusion.

As an example of an undesirable effect of this practice, consider a command symbol from the author's LOGIN.COM:

```
$ DEL*ETE :== DELETE/CONFIRM
```

The author uses this symbol because he occasionally issues a DELETE command that deletes more files then he actually intended. To prevent such occurrences, he uses the symbol DEL*ETE (The asterisk denotes the length to which the symbol may be abbreviated) so that DELETE commands automatically include the /CONFIRM qualifier, which prompts for confirmation before deleting each file.

Usually, this causes no trouble at all. The problem arises when the author issues the DELETE/SYMBOL command. Since DCL does not consider DELETE/CONFIRM to be consistent with DELETE/SYMBOL, it issues a message that may confuse a user who does not know what is going on:

```
$ DELETE/SYMBOL/GLOBAL PRINT
%DCL-I-IGNQUAL, qualifiers appearing before this item were ignored
 \SYMBOL\
```

The command completes successfully, but DCL issues an informational message warning that the implicit /CONFIRM qualifier was ignored.

Also, if the author executes a command procedure containing DELETE commands and those commands do not explicitly include /NOCONFIRM, the command procedure pauses to ask for confirmation of each file deletion.

Many users believe that side effects such as these are a minor inconvenience compared with accidentally deleting important files.

Symbols as Character or Text Variables

Another common use for symbols is to store integer or text values.

Symbols are indispensable in command procedures, where they take the place of variables as found in a compiled programming language. Using symbols in this way is also supported directly at the DCL prompt.

Creating an Integer Symbol

To create an integer symbol, assign a value to it using "=" for a local symbol or "==" for a global symbol. This example creates a symbol called APPLES and assigns it a value of 10:

```
$ APPLES = 10
$ SHOW SYMBOL APPLES
  APPLES = 10   Hex = 0000000A  Octal = 00000000012
```

Symbols may be used in mathematical calculations, as shown here:

```
$ APPLES = 2 * (4+5)
$ SHOW SYMBOL APPLES
  APPLES = 18   Hex = 00000012  Octal = 00000000022
$ !
$ ORANGES = 15
$ SHOW SYMBOL ORANGES
  ORANGES = 15   Hex = 0000000F  Octal = 00000000017
$ !
$ TOTAL_FRUIT = APPLES + ORANGES
$ SHOW SYMBOL TOTAL_FRUIT
  TOTAL_FRUIT = 33   Hex = 00000021  Octal = 00000000041
```

The assignment of TOTAL_FRUIT was the result of adding the values of APPLES and ORANGES. DCL supports several integer arithmetic operators, which include the following:

- + for addition or to denote a positive number

- – for subtraction or to denote a negative number

- * for multiplication

- / for division

- ( ) to specify the order of mathematical operations

Creating Character String Symbols

As seen earlier, symbols can also represent text data. In our earlier example, a symbol was used to represent a DCL command. In addition, symbols may represent arbitrary text:

```
$ COLOR = "blue"
$ SHOW SYMBOL COLOR
  COLOR = "blue"
$ !
$ ! Character-string symbols may be manipulated or combined:
$ !
$ COLOR = "greenish-" + color
$ SHOW SYMBOL COLOR
  COLOR = "greenish-blue"
```

The example above first sets COLOR to "blue," and then changes it to "greenish-blue." Note that the symbol COLOR appears on both sides of the equals sign. The right-hand side of an expression is calculated first, and then the result is assigned to the symbol COLOR. This allows the new value of COLOR to depend on the old value. This is a common feature of many programming and scripting languages.

How Symbols Are Evaluated by DCL

Symbols are substituted (replaced by their values) automatically in the following circumstances:

- On the right side of the =, ==, :=, and :== operators

- In a lexical function (discussed later)

- Within brackets on the left side of an assignment (for performing character or bit overlays, not covered in this book).

- As the first element on a command line (in place of a DCL verb).

Should you need to force a symbol substitution in another circumstance, enclose it in single quotes:

```
$ FILENAME = "login.com"
```

```
$ TYPE 'filename' ! the file LOGIN.COM will be typed
```

If you need to force symbol substitution within a set of double quotes, use two leading single quotes and one trailing single quote:

```
$ FILENAME = "login.com"
$ TYPEIT = "TYPE ''filename'"
```

A word of caution for the inexperienced user: Pay particular attention to the use of = or = = versus : = or : = = to assign a value to a symbol. When assigning a symbol with the = or = = operator, the value must be enclosed in quotes. Using : = or : = = allows you to omit the quotes and automatically converts the value to upper-case letters and compresses multiple spaces or tabs into one space. It also has some potentially frustrating effects, which are shown in the following example.

```
$ !
$ ! The := or :== operator works with this syntax:
$ !
$ color = "blue"
$ color := "greenish-''color'"
$ show symbol color
  COLOR = "greenish-blue"
$ !
$ ! But := or :== does not work as you might intend
$ ! with this syntax:
$ !
$ color = "blue"
$ color := "greenish-" + color
$ show symbol color
  COLOR = "greenish-+ COLOR"
$ !
$ ! On the other hand...
$ !
$ ! The = or == operator behaves identically with either syntax:
$ !
$ color = "blue"
$ color = "greenish-" + color
$ show symbol color
  COLOR = "greenish-blue"
$ !
$ color = "blue"
$ color = "greenish-''color'"
$ show symbol color
  COLOR = "greenish-blue"
```

WRITE and WRITE SYS$OUTPUT

The examples in this book make extensive use of the DCL command *WRITE SYS$OUTPUT value*, where *value* is some datum we'd like to examine.

The WRITE command instructs DCL to perform an output operation, and SYS$OUTPUT represents the location to which the output should be sent. SYS$OUTPUT is an OpenVMS-supplied logical name that usually equates to the user's terminal. So, WRITE SYS$OUTPUT value means "put this value on my screen."

For more information on the WRITE command, see "Reading And Writing Files" in Chapter 9, "Command Procedures."

Lexical Functions

DCL provides a set of *lexical functions* that perform a wide variety of tasks, such as returning information about processes, files, devices, and queues and manipulating character strings along with other useful tasks.

Lexical functions can be used on the command line in much the same way as symbols. Lexical functions are easily recognized: Their names begin with "f$" and end with a pair of parentheses containing various elements of information (arguments) the functions may require.

Why Are They Called Lexical Functions?

Lexical functions are so named because they are performed during the lexical phase of command processing. This occurs early enough in command processing that the results of lexical functions may be used in many of the same ways a symbol can.

To use a lexical function, you must supply the name of the function you wish to use and any *arguments* the function requires. Once executed, the *return value* of the function (the result of the operation) is substituted into the command as if you had typed the return value directly.

To illustrate this concept, a lexical function will be used here to determine the length of a string of text. The *f$length()* function performs this task. Its *argument* is the string of text to examine, and its *return value* is the length of the piece of text (in this case, 20):

```
$ WRITE SYS$OUTPUT F$LENGTH("This is the argument")
20
```

During the processing of the command above, the lexical function is evaluated at an early stage, and its return value is substituted into the command. In effect, DCL changes the command line to the following before continuing:

```
$ WRITE SYS$OUTPUT 20
```

To illustrate the usefulness of lexical functions, consider the following example. It demonstrates how to use the convert time lexical function f$cvtime() to determine on which day of the week a given date will fall:

```
$ WRITE SYS$OUTPUT F$CVTIME("17-MAR-2003,","WEEKDAY")
Monday
```

The next example uses get job and process information function f$getjpi() to determine which account you are logged into:

```
$ WRITE SYS$OUTPUT "My username is ''F$GETJPI(0,"USERNAME")'"
My username is BENNY
```

Lexical functions may, of course, be used in command procedures. This line, when executed in a procedure, will cause the command procedure to terminate if the process is not a BATCH process (this type of comparison is described later):

```
$ IF F$MODE() .NES. "BATCH" THEN $ EXIT
```

This example shows how to create a symbol containing the username you are logged in under:

```
$ MY_USERNAME = F$GETJPI(0,"USERNAME")
$ SHOW SYMBOL MY_USERNAME
  MY_USERNAME = "MIKE          "
```

Notice that the username MIKE has some extra spaces at the end, as returned by f$getjpi() (the extra spaces take into account the maximum length of an OpenVMS username). The next example shows how to get rid of the extra spaces by using the f$edit() function. You will notice that the f$getjpi() function itself may be used as an argument to f$edit():

```
$ MY_USERNAME = F$EDIT(F$GETJPI(0,"USERNAME"),"TRIM")
$ SHOW SYMBOL MY_USERNAME
  MY_USERNAME = "MIKE"
```

Many lexical functions return information that is otherwise available via the SHOW command, but lexical functions allow specific bits of information to be assigned to symbols or to be acted on by a procedure. This makes lexical functions of considerable use inside command procedures.

For a complete list of lexical functions and their usage, use the HELP LEXICAL command.

Comparisons: The IF Command

The usefulness of symbols and lexical functions is enhanced by the ability to take some action based on their values. DCL allows you to compare the value of symbols, lexical functions, and literal data in any combination, and then take some action based on the result.

A basic comparison takes the following format:

```
$ IF expression THEN $ command
```

Comparison Operators

In order to take some action based on a comparison, you must define which two (or more) things you are comparing and what relationship you are looking for. For example, is one number smaller than another? Are two numbers equal? Is one character string longer than another?

DCL provides several comparison operators that each look for a different relationship between the values being compared. These are as follows:

- .EQ./.EQS. — Tests whether the values/character strings are equal

- .GE./.GES. — Tests whether the first is greater than or equal to the second

- .GT./.GTS. — Tests whether the first is greater than the second

- .LE./.LES. — Tests whether the first is less than or equal to the second

- .LT./.LTS. — Tests whether the first is less than the second

- .NE./.NES. — Tests whether they are not equal

Each of the above comparison operators has two variants: The first compares integer values, and the second compares character strings. Therefore, the .GT. operator compares two integers, and the .GTS. operator compares two character strings.

In addition to the comparison operators, there are a few logical operators. They are as follows:

- .AND. — Combines the values in a bitwise AND operation

- .OR. — Combines the values in a bitwise OR operation

- .NOT. — Negates the value occurring after it

- () — Specifies items within parentheses are evaluated (simplified) first

For those readers not familiar with Boolean logic, the preceding operators may require some explanation.

Every comparison, no matter how complex, is boiled down to one result: TRUE or FALSE. Under DCL, every odd value is considered TRUE. Even values and zero are considered FALSE.

To illustrate:

```
$ WRITE SYS$OUTPUT 4 .EQ. 5
0
$ WRITE SYS$OUTPUT 5 .EQ. 5
1
```

In the examples, the expression "4 .EQ. 5" is simplified to a single value, 0, meaning FALSE; 4 does not equal 5. On the other hand, "5 .EQ. 5" is simplified to 1, or TRUE.

The .AND. and .OR. operators return 0 (FALSE) or 1 (TRUE) based on the following rules:

.AND.	0 and EVEN	ODD
0 and EVEN	FALSE	FALSE
ODD	FALSE	TRUE

.OR.	0 and EVEN	ODD
0 and EVEN	FALSE	TRUE
ODD	TRUE	TRUE

Figure 6-1 DCL .AND. and .OR. Operators

You can use .AND. or .OR. to determine whether arguments are TRUE or FALSE in the following way. Parentheses are shown here to make clear the order in which expressions are evaluated. They may be used to force a certain order, but in these particular examples they make no difference.

This example illustrates the .AND. operator:

```
$ !
$ ! An AND operation requires that BOTH of its arguments be true
```

```
$ ! to produce a TRUE result:
$ !
$ rate = "normal"
$ sex = "Male"
$ age = 24
$ !
$ if (sex .eqs. "Male") .and. (age .lt. 25) then $ rate = "high"
$ !
$ write sys$output -
  "This subject will pay ''rate' car insurance rates."
This subject will pay high car insurance rates.
```

This example illustrates the .OR. operator:

```
$ !
$ ! The OR operator returns TRUE if either or both arguments
$ ! are true:
$ !
$ rate = "normal"
$ sex = "Female"
$ age = 24
$ !
$ if (sex .nes. "Male") .or. (age .ge. 25) then $ rate = "low"
$ !
$ write sys$output -
  "This subject will pay ''rate' car insurance rates."
This subject will pay low car insurance rates.
$ !
```

Bitwise Versus Logical Operators

The .AND. and .OR. operators in DCL are actually bitwise operators, but they are often used as logical operators by using only zero and one as inputs. DCL considers zero and all even values FALSE, and all odd values TRUE.

Chapter 7 — The User Environment

This chapter will discuss the OpenVMS user environment; how to work with files, directories, printers, and batch queues; and how to run programs and perform other common tasks.

As with earlier sections in this book, the DCL CLI interface will be used. Most common functions may also be carried out using a GUI interface, as described in Chapter 15.

Files

Most OpenVMS operations act on files, the primary unit of data storage. With few exceptions, all data processed by the system reside, at one time or another, in files. An understanding of files is essential to using most operating systems. Our description of the OpenVMS environment will begin with files.

Definition of a File

The *file* is the central unit of data storage. Programs, letters, memos, pictures, audio clips, and just about any other type of data are stored in files. A single file usually represents a single entity: one file per picture, one file per audio clip, etc. However, some file formats support the storage of multiple entities within a file. Examples of the latter are backup savesets, libraries, and zip files.

Compare this to a popular method of presenting data—the Web page. A given Web page may contain pictures, text, sounds, and other elements. This may give the illusion that all of these types of data are stored together as a single unit. In reality, each of these elements is stored in a separate file; they are presented together by the browser program at the time of viewing.

A file is a single logical unit on a computer storage device (e.g., a disk or tape) and is made up of *records*. A given file may consist of records of varying length (e.g., lines in a memo or letter) or each record may have a fixed length. A record may be divided into smaller units called *fields*. An employee name, a telephone number, or an identification number may be a field within a record, and all related records (say, one for each employee of a company) comprise a file.

OpenVMS supports many different file and record formats. Most other systems provide relatively few formats, so new users of OpenVMS may not be familiar with all of them. In addition, users familiar with other operating systems may be accustomed to slightly different definitions of some key terms. These terms are presented here as they are used with OpenVMS.

Within the file organizations listed below, there are many possible variations of the control information used to describe each record. These variations are not addressed in this book. They are handled automatically by OpenVMS Record Management Services (RMS) and the file system and are of little concern to the new user.

The overwhelming majority of files you will encounter will be sequential files. This is true for experienced users as well as novices. When you do come across files of other organizations, they will be for a specific purpose and will most often be managed by a particular piece of software.

As a new user, you will rarely need to know the details of a file's organization or of the record format within it. They are presented here mainly for informational purposes.

Sequential

Most files on a given OpenVMS system are sequential. As their name implies, they are suitable for sequential processing. That is, every record is expected to be processed in order from the beginning to the end of the file. Please note that they are expected, but not required, to be processed in this way.

There are two main variations of record formats used with a sequential file: variable-length and fixed-length. With variable-length records, the records within the file may differ in size from one another. This means that records in the file must usually be processed from the beginning of the file, one at a time, going toward the end of the file. Records may be added to the end of the file, but usually not inserted at an earlier point. Inserting records is usually accomplished by rewriting the entire file, but theoretically this can be done by rewriting all records from the point of insertion onward.

With fixed-length records, all of the records in the file are the same length. Even though the file is sequential, it is possible to retrieve a given record without reading the file from the beginning, because one may mathematically calculate the record's position within the file (but extra work is required of the program doing so). Nevertheless, records are usually accessed sequentially. Inserting a record still requires rewriting the file, as the remaining records must shift to accommodate the new record.

There is no key portion of a record, nor are the records required to be in any particular sorted order, as in some definitions of sequential.

Indexed

This type of file encompasses the terms *Indexed* and *indexed sequential* (ISAM), depending on what other operating systems one has used. Each record has one or more *keys*, which indicate the logical sequence of records within the file. For example, an employee's last name or identification number may serve as a key. This allows a given record to be reached quickly and allows insertions of records without rewriting the entire file. Complex pointers are automatically manipulated so that the ordering of records is maintained when inserting and deleting records. When read sequentially, records are automatically read in key order. The previous and next records may also be accessed, relative to the record most recently referenced.

Relative

In relative files, records are of a fixed length and are accessed by record number within the file, starting from the beginning. The system calculates the position of a record from the record size and record number within the file.

This type of access is similar to directly accessing a sequential file with fixed-length records. With a relative file, however, OpenVMS services automatically perform much of the necessary work.

Why Are Programs Stored As Sequential Files?

To highlight the practical similarities of relative files to fixed-record-length sequential files, note that executable images (programs) on OpenVMS are stored as sequential files with a record size of 512 bytes (a size convenient for the OpenVMS virtual memory management subsystem, as well as the size of a disk "block"). Even though program files are sequential, they are typically accessed by block number.

Disk Structure Levels

Some versions of OpenVMS support more than one disk organization. This is similar to a Windows NT system, which supports both the FAT and NTFS disk structures.

Most OpenVMS disks are structured as On-Disk Structure Version 2 (ODS-2) volumes. Some versions of OpenVMS support a newer disk organization, ODS-5.

ODS-5 is intended primarily to provide a disk environment more akin to the environments found on personal computer systems, including Microsoft Windows. ODS-5 supports longer filenames, deeper directory nesting, and a wider variety of legal characters in filenames than does ODS-2. These characteristics make it convenient to serve an ODS-5 volume to computers running different operating systems across the network.

ODS-5 is supported on Alpha beginning with OpenVMS Alpha V7.2 and has limited support on VAX beginning with OpenVMS VAX V7.2. Even so, not all OpenVMS applications directly support ODS-5.

Examples given in this book use ODS-2 filename and directory rules, which will also work under ODS-5.

Components of an ODS-2 File Specification

In order for the system to identify a particular file correctly, each file must have a name that is unique among all files on the network, the operative phrase being "on the network." Two different OpenVMS systems may have disks, directories, and files with identical names, but must be able to tell them apart.

To differentiate among these files, a full file specification is necessary. It contains enough information to identify any given file on the network uniquely.

A full file specification follows this format:

```
NODE::DEVICE:[DIR.SUBDIR1.SUBDIR2(...)]NAME.EXT;VERSION
```

Let's examine each component.

NODE:: is the computer upon which the disk and directory reside. This field is required when only accessing a file or directory on some other computer on the network. It is the nodename of the computer followed by two colons. If the other node requires user authentication, this field takes the form *NODE"username password"::*. Chapter 14, "Using DECnet" contains more information on the NODE field.

DEVICE: is the disk device on which the directory resides. It ends with a single colon. The standard format for device names is discussed elsewhere in this chapter.

[DIR.SUBDIR1.SUBDIR2] is the directory. Directories are explained in detail in the following section. A directory is contained within brackets ([ ]), and each subdirectory level (if any) is separated by a dot (.). The top-level directory has the format [DIR]. The first subdirectory level is denoted [DIR.SUBDIR1]; the second, [DIR.SUBDIR1.SUBDIR2]; and so forth. Earlier versions of OpenVMS limited subdirectories to a depth of seven, but later versions lift this restriction.

The NAME consists of up to 39 characters that identify the file. On an ODS-2 disk, all alphabetic characters are treated as if they were upper case. They will be stored and displayed in upper case, but you may use any combination of upper and lower-case when identifying the file. Valid characters are letters, numbers, the underscore (_), the dollar sign ($), and the hyphen (-).

EXT stands for extension. This is a 0- to 39-character field that identifies the type of file it is. It is preceded by a dot, which is present even with a zero-length (null) filetype. Legal characters are the same as for the NAME field. You may use any legal characters you wish, but the system automatically assumes some default extensions for various types of files. Examples include .LOG for batch log files, .COM for DCL command procedures, and .EXE for executable programs. See Appendix C for common default filetypes.

VERSION is a number from 1 to 32767 identifying a version number for the file. Version numbers are a feature not found on some other systems. When you create a new file, it is assigned a version number of 1, unless you specify a different number. If you later edit and save the file, version 2 is created, but version 1 continues to exist. This avoids a common problem of some other systems, where saving a file overwrites the old contents. Under OpenVMS, a previous version of a file can be accessed by specifying its version number. Previous versions are deleted with the PURGE command or by an optional version limit which can be different for each file.

Under ODS-2, all fields are case-insensitive. You may use any combination of upper and lower case to specify filenames. The system will display filenames in upper case only.

Differences in ODS-5

OpenVMS Alpha V7.2 and later and presumably OpenVMS Itanium support an additional disk structure: On-Disk Structure Version 5 (ODS-5). ODS-5 supports additional legal characters in filenames and a deeper directory level nesting. These extended filename rules support filenames similar to those found in Microsoft Windows 95/98 and Windows NT.

ODS-5 is provided primarily to support file-sharing capabilities for DCOM and JAVA applications and remote systems supporting file specifications that cannot be directly represented by ODS-2. General users can use ODS-5 volumes, but please be aware that many OpenVMS programs are not guaranteed to work properly with ODS-5 volumes. The number of compatible applications will likely increase over the next few versions of OpenVMS.

OpenVMS VAX Version V7.2 and later include only limited support for ODS-5. While participating in a cluster with an OpenVMS Alpha system, a VAX system may mount an ODS-5 disk, but can process only files that comply with ODS-2 rules.

Filenames under ODS-5 can be up to 236 8-bit characters in length, or 118 16-bit characters. Filenames can contain 8-bit ISO Latin-1 and 16-bit Unicode (UCS-2) characters, except for double quotes (" "), asterisks (*), backslashes (\), colons (:), angle brackets (< >), slashes (/), question marks (?), and vertical bars (|). To enter certain characters unambiguously in a file specification (such as a space), you must precede the character with a circumflex (^). Directory names can support most of the same characters as filenames. Periods and other special characters must be preceded by a circumflex.

ODS-5 file specifications are case-sensitive, and ODS-5 can support up to 255 levels of directory nesting.

See the *OpenVMS Guide to Extended File Specifications* for further information.

Working with Files

The following sections introduce the reader to commonly performed functions related to files. As stated previously, the file is the basic unit of data storage and most operations will involve files in some way.

Displaying a List of Files (the DIRECTORY command)

The DIRECTORY command displays information about one or more files contained in one or more *directories*. Directories are explained in detail later, but for now just be aware that a directory is a grouping of related files. Each user typically has a separate directory to keep his or her files separate from those of other users. Some operating systems use the term folder in place of directory.

DIRECTORY can display the names, sizes, dates of creation, and other details about files, depending on the qualifiers you use. The simplest form of the command shows only the names, types, and versions of files in the current default directory:

```
$ DIRECTORY

Directory DKA100:[MIKE.SCENE]

SCENE.C;1          SCENE.EXE;1          SCENE.OBJ;1

Total of 3 files.
```

The top line of the display indicates that the current directory is DKA100:[MIKE.SCENE] This means that the directory resides on a disk called DKA100:, on which there is a directory called MIKE, and within it, a directory called SCENE. A directory may contain subdirectories; think of such subdirectories as folders within a folder.

In this example directory, there are three files: SCENE.C, SCENE.EXE, and SCENE.OBJ. You will notice that directories automatically maintain files in alphabetical order.

The information shown by the simplest DIRECTORY command is quite basic, displaying only the names of the files. But DIRECTORY has numerous qualifiers that can display detailed information about files. For example, let's say you wish to see the date and time each file was last modified, its size, and its owner. You would use this command:

```
$ DIRECTORY/SIZE/DATE=MODIFIED/OWNER

Directory DKA100:[MIKE.SCENE]

SCENE.C;1                  23   5-NOV-2002 20:47:50.14  [MIKE]
SCENE.EXE;1               128   5-NOV-2002 20:49:02.88  [MIKE]
SCENE.OBJ;1               11    5-NOV-2002 20:48:23.61  [MIKE]

Total of 3 files, 162 blocks.
```

Note: File sizes are shown in 512-byte blocks. SCENE.OBJ is about 5,632 bytes in size.

You may use DIRECTORY to show only certain files by specifying one or more files as parameters:

```
$ DIRECTORY/SECURITY SCENE.OBJ

Directory DKA100:[MIKE.SCENE]

SCENE.OBJ;1          [MIKE]                  (RWED,RWED,RE,)

Total of 1 file.
```

The example above also includes the /SECURITY qualifier, which instructs the DIRECTORY command to show the ownership and file protection of any files displayed.

You may even examine files in another directory by specifying the directory as part of the parameter:

```
$ DIRECTORY [MIKE]*.EXE

Directory DKA100:[MIKE]

DECRYPT.EXE;8     ENCRYPT.EXE;1     FINGER.EXE;1     FIRST.EXE;1
MIKESUMM.EXE;1    MYSTIFY.EXE;3     TEST.EXE;3       UNZIP_AXP.EXE;1
ZIP_AXP.EXE;1

Total of 9 files.
```

You may have noticed that the previous example uses an asterisk (*) in place of part of a filename. This is a *wildcard* character, which means it will match any sequence of characters found at that location in a file specification. The use of wildcards is discussed subsequently.

File Sizes

OpenVMS expresses file sizes in *blocks*. A block is 512 bytes or 0.5KB. The following table shows various sizes expressed as blocks:

```
Bytes     Blocks
512       1
1K        2
25K       50
50K       100
100K      200
500K      1,000
1M        2,048
10M       20,480
100M      204,800
1G        2,097,162
```

File Specification Defaults

A full file specification can become quite long. However, you usually do not need to type all of it; OpenVMS assumes default values for almost all fields within the specification.

Every field from the nodename through directory, if omitted, will default to the current value: current node, current disk, and current directory. The version number, if omitted, will default to the highest version that currently exists. Even the file extension may assume a default value, depending on the context in which the file is referenced. Appendix C contains a listing of common default filetypes.

Let's say I have a command procedure in my home directory whose full file specification is PHOEBE::DKA100:[MIKE]TALLY.COM;34. Assuming my current disk and directory are the same, I can execute it by issuing this simple command:

```
$ @TALLY
```

Wildcards

Wildcards are special characters that match any character (or sequence of characters) in a file specification. You may use them to identify only those files in which you are interested. Wildcard characters may be used in the directory, filename, filetype, and version fields of a file specification. Using them in the node or device fields is not permitted.

Note: Wildcards as used in directory specifications will be discussed later along with directories.

The wildcard characters used to match file specifications are as follows:

- *—The asterisk wildcard character matches zero or more characters at the position in a file specification where it appears.

- %—The percent sign matches exactly one character at the position in a file specification where it appears. Some examples follow.

```
This file specification            Will match these files

*.DAT                              JUNIOR.DAT
                                   BRADY.DAT

19*.TXT                            1996.TXT
                                   19_BOTTLES_OF_BEER.TXT

*USE*.DAT                          USERGUIDE.DAT
                                   SYSTEM_USERS.DAT

TEST.*                             TEST.C
                                   TEST.EXE

199%.DAT                           1996.DAT
                                   199A.DAT
```

Some commands using wildcards might be:

```
$ DELETE *.TMP;*
```

Deletes all versions of all files in the current directory of the type .TMP.

```
$ TYPE CHAPTER*.TXT
```

Displays the contents of the most recent version of each file in the current directory whose name begins with "chapter" and that is of type .TXT.

```
$ TYPE CHAPTER*.TXT;*
```

Displays the contents of all versions of each file in the current directory whose name begins with "chapter" and that is of type .TXT.

```
$ DIRECTORY CHAPTER2.TXT;-1
```

Finds the previous version of CHAPTER2.TXT. The version ";-1" specifies the previous version, ";-2" specifies the version before that, etc. The notation ";-0" refers to the oldest version in existence. The notation ";" or ";0" specifies the highest version in existence.

Creating a File

To create a text file from scratch, you may use a text editor (see Chapter 13) or use the CREATE command. For most purposes, using a text editor is more convenient than using CREATE.

To use CREATE, enter "CREATE *filespec*" at the DCL prompt. Then, type the contents of your file. Each line you type will be placed into the file. You may fix mistakes on the current line only; once you press ENTER to end a line you may no longer make changes to that line. When finished entering lines, press CTRL/Z. This closes the file and returns you to the DCL prompt.

To create a file with the same contents as an existing file, use the COPY command, described later. You may also use a text editor on an existing file and save it under a different name.

Files other than text files are usually created by a program, not directly by a user, and are not covered here.

Displaying a File

To display the contents of a text file on the screen, use the TYPE command:

```
$ TYPE filespec
```

The contents of the file are displayed on your terminal. Use the /PAGE qualifier to display long files one page at a time. You may use the /TAIL=n qualifier to display the last n lines of a file.

Use caution when trying to TYPE any files that are not ordinary text files. Other types of files (say, executable programs or object files) usually contain sequences of unprintable control characters that cause rapid scrolling and beeping (at best) or may cause your terminal to freeze (at worst). If this happens, you may need to reset your terminal.

Deleting a File

To delete one or more files, use the DELETE command:

```
$ DELETE filespec
```

When deleting files, you must specify a version number or use a wildcard in the version field. Use caution when using wildcards other than in the version field because you may accidentally delete more files than intended.

You may wish to consider using these qualifiers with the DELETE command:

- /CONFIRM — Displays each filespec before deletion and asks you whether you would like to delete it. Affirmative answers (which may be abbreviated) are *yes*, *true*, *1* and *all*. ALL deletes all remaining files without confirming them. Negative answers are *no*, *false*, *0*, and *quit*. QUIT exits the delete command immediately without processing any more files.

- /LOG — Displays the file specification of each file deleted and its size; displays a summary after all files have been processed.

Renaming a File

Files are renamed by using the RENAME command. It has a simple format, as follows:

```
$ RENAME original_name new_name
```

If you exclude a specific version number, the highest version will be renamed, leaving any previous versions intact. Therefore, the previous version becomes the highest version of the original file. To rename all versions of a file, include the asterisk wildcard in the version field of *original_name* (filename.type;*).

You may also use the RENAME command to move a file from one directory to another, so long as it remains on the same disk. Simply include a new directory specification in *new_name*:

```
$ RENAME [REPORTS]FEBRUARY.RPT [OLD_REPORTS]FEBRUARY_2003.RPT
```

RENAME supports the /CONFIRM and /LOG qualifiers just as DELETE does.

Copying a File

Files are copied by using the COPY command:

```
$ COPY original_name new_name
```

As with RENAME, omitting a version number causes only the highest version to be copied. You may also use COPY to combine several files into one by using a plus sign between original files or by using wildcards:

```
$ COPY CAKE.TXT+COOKIES.TXT+FLAN.TXT DESSERTS.TXT
```

or

```
$ COPY DECEMBER*.RPT DECEMBER_ALL.RPT
```

Use this feature only with simple sequential files, and avoid using it with other formats, such as indexed and relative. As usual, this command supports /CONFIRM and /LOG. The original files are not deleted.

Deleting Previous Versions of Files

When you modify an existing file, OpenVMS creates a new version of that file and retains previous versions. In a very short time, a large number of previous versions can accumulate, consuming disk space and making directory listings longer.

You may use the PURGE command to delete previous versions of existing files.

Some examples are as follows.

- To delete all versions of all files in the current directory except the highest version of each file:

  ```
  $ PURGE
  ```

- To delete all previous versions of all files with the .LOG filetype.

  ```
  $ PURGE *.LOG
  ```

- To delete all but the latest five versions of LOGIN.COM:

  ```
  $ PURGE/KEEP=5 LOGIN.COM
  ```

The /KEEP=n qualifier instructs PURGE to retain the highest n versions of each file processed.

Use /CONFIRM to verify each file to be deleted. Answering YES deletes one version at a time. Use caution when answering ALL: Some versions of OpenVMS purge all versions of that particular file only, prompting you again at the next file; other versions of OpenVMS process all remaining files with no further prompts.

You may use /LOG to show you each file deleted and provide a summary after all files have been processed.

Setting File Version Limits

There is another way to control the accumulation of multiple file versions: you may set a version limit for any file. Let's say you set a version limit of five on a particular file. When you create the sixth version of that file, the lowest version will automatically be purged.

If you set a version limit on a file, but a greater number of versions already exists, OpenVMS will not purge files to correct the difference. It will still purge one version for each version created. You must manually purge the extra versions.

You should generally avoid setting a version limit of one; this can occasionally cause problems with some applications that read a previous version in order to create the next version. A minimum value of two is recommended.

To set a version limit of six on a given file:

```
$ SET FILE filespec /VERSION_LIMIT=6
```

Use a value of zero to disable version limits.

If you wish to set an automatic version limit for all future files in a given directory, you may set a default version limit for the directory (see "Using Directories" below). This setting takes effect only for files created after the limit is set. Once set, you may override this value on a per-file basis by using SET FILE/VERSION_LIMIT for any file.

```
$ SET DIRECTORY DKA100:[MIKE]/VERSION_LIMIT=5
```

Again, use a value of zero to disable version limits.

Running a Program

Under OpenVMS, programs have the filetype .EXE. How you run them depends on the expectations of the program. Some programs are part of OpenVMS, and these generally execute automatically in response to the appropriate DCL command. Other programs, such as those you may create yourself with a language compiler or third-party software, may be invoked in different ways.

Other than normal DCL commands that execute standard system programs, there are three main ways to run a program under OpenVMS. They are the *RUN* command, foreign commands, and custom DCL verbs created by the command definition utility (CDU).

The RUN Command

The DCL RUN command is usually used to execute a program that does not need command line arguments. Its format is as follows:

```
$ RUN program_filespec
```

To execute the program COLLECT.EXE in the current directory, use this command:

```
$ RUN COLLECT
```

> **Note:** The RUN command may also be used to start a program running as a detached process (RUN/DETACH). Creating and running such programs is not covered in this book.

Foreign Commands

Native OpenVMS programs often make use of the extensive command line processing capabilities in DCL. However, some programs are written to process their own command lines, such as programs ported from UNIX or some other operating system. For these, a foreign command is usually used.

A foreign command is a special DCL symbol that runs a program and passes the command line directly to the program. Foreign commands may also be used with many programs that do not require command line arguments as an alternative to the RUN command.

Say your program TALLY.EXE should process its own command line. You would create a foreign symbol TALLY as follows:

```
$ TALLY :== $DKB400:[ALICE]TALLY
```

The dollar sign ($) just before the program's file specification is what indicates a foreign command. If you omit the disk and directory, the directory SYS$SYSTEM will be assumed.

Using the symbol TALLY as a command verb will invoke TALLY.EXE and pass the rest of the command line to it. The format of the command line parameters and switches (qualifiers) depends entirely on what TALLY.EXE expects; DCL simply passes the command line to the program. Thus, a program ported from UNIX might have a command line that looks something like this:

```
$ TALLY +iFILE1.DAT +oFILE2.DAT +v+x
```

The above command line will be passed to the program intact, leaving TALLY.EXE to process parameters and switches on its own.

DCL Paths

Later versions of OpenVMS include a way to automatically support foreign commands for executable files residing in a set of directories you define.

Ordinarily, when you enter a command verb that does not match a DCL command, you would receive an error message. With DCL paths, directories of your choice will first be searched for programs with that name. If a matching program is found, it will be invoked as a foreign command.

To define a path search list, define the logical name DCL$PATH, specifying a directory or list of directories to be searched:

```
$ DEFINE DCL$PATH DKA100:[MIKE]
```

or

```
$ DEFINE DCL$PATH DKA100:[MIKE.TOOLS],DKA0:[UTILITIES]
```

Note: logical names are described further on in this chapter.

Let's say that a program DKA0:[UTILITIES]ENCRYPT.EXE exists. Once the DCL path has been defined, you can use ENCRYPT as a command verb, and DCL will automatically locate the program and invoke it as a foreign command.

Custom DCL Commands

When a programmer writes a program specifically designed for OpenVMS, the programmer may elect to take advantage of the extensive command line capabilities of DCL using the OpenVMS CDU. Using this feature, new DCL verbs, along with qualifiers, keywords, and parameters can be created.

Digital, Compaq, and Hewlett-Packard software products, third-party software products, or programs developed by end users may use this feature. Many sites include these custom commands in the system wide DCL command tables, making them available to all users. In fact, you may never become aware that some of the commands you use on a daily basis may have been added to your system in just this way.

Your system manager may notify you about any custom commands available to you, as well as any additional steps you must take to use them.

Working with Queues

Queues are lists of jobs OpenVMS will perform on behalf of users. For example, when you issue a PRINT or SUBMIT command, a queue entry is created representing the request. The following paragraphs show you how to create, examine, and modify queue entries.

Printing a File

Use the PRINT command to submit a file for printing:

```
$ PRINT file1[,file2,file3...]
```

The PRINT command will submit a print job to the printer queue identified by the name SYS$PRINT (which may be a logical name or the name of an actual queue). Your system manager can tell you whether this queue is appropriate for you. If it is not, you may use the /QUEUE qualifier to override it or create a logical name SYS$PRINT to represent the correct printer. For example, if your normal printer is called LASER4, you could issue this command:

```
$ PRINT /QUEUE=LASER4 file
```

Or you could place the following line in your LOGIN.COM:

```
$ DEFINE SYS$PRINT LASER4
```

Once the logical name SYS$PRINT exists, your print jobs will automatically be assigned to the queue indicated by the logical name.

Qualifiers for the PRINT command you may find useful include the following:

/AFTER="time"—holds the print job until a specified time. Times may be specified in absolute format, such as /AFTER="04-JAN-2003 15:00." If you omit the day, the present day is assumed. Times may also be relative, such as /AFTER="+5-00:00:00" (five days from now) or "TOMORROW+3-10:00" (three days and ten hours from midnight tonight). Time formats are described later in this chapter.

/HOLD—holds the print job until it is explicitly released (queue entries are maintained across system reboots.)

/BURST=ALL, /BURST=ONE, /NOBURST, /FLAG=ALL, /FLAG=ONE, /NOFLAG—control whether separator pages will precede each file in the print job (ALL), only the first file (ONE), or not at all (/NOBURST, /NOFLAG). Separators are helpful with busy printers by allowing users to identify quickly where one job ends and the next begins. /BURST prints two separator pages, and /FLAG prints one. Another qualifier, /TRAILER, places a similar page at the end of a job.

/COPIES=*number*—controls the number of copies of a job (when placed after PRINT) or a file within a job (when placed after a file specification) to be printed. If omitted, one copy will be assumed.

/JOB_COUNT=*number*—specifies how many copies of the entire job will be printed. This is useful if different files within the job have different values for /COPIES.

/DELETE—causes the file(s) to be deleted after printing. Use with caution; a paper jam or other printer malfunction could cause the loss of some portion of the file.

/FORM=*form-name*—controls the type of paper stock on which the job will be printed. Forms vary from site to site; use SHOW QUEUE/FORM on your system to see what forms are available.

/CHARACTERISTICS—controls the site-defined characteristics a printer queue must possess to process this job. Characteristics may represent any arbitrary printer attributes as defined by the system manager. Use SHOW QUEUE /CHARACTERISTICS to see what characteristics, if any, are available at your site.

/NOTIFY—causes a message to be sent to your terminal when the job completes.

/PRIORITY=*n*—allows you to set the priority of the queue entry. Priorities are in the range of 0 (the lowest) through 255. On most systems, the default queue priority for most users is 100. Jobs with higher priorities are executed first. You must hold the ALTPRI or OPER privilege to raise the priority above your default priority.

Other qualifiers are available; use HELP PRINT for descriptions.

Submitting a Batch Job

A batch job is a command procedure (see Chapter 9, "Command Procedures") that you submit to the system to execute on your behalf. Since batch jobs and print jobs use the same OpenVMS queuing mechanism, submitting a batch job is quite similar to queuing a print job, as covered previously.

You use the SUBMIT command to submit a batch job for execution:

```
$ SUBMIT CLEANUP
```

This command submits the command procedure CLEANUP.COM to the batch queue SYS$BATCH for execution as soon as an execution queue is available.

Batch queues have adjustable limits to the number of jobs that may execute at once. Your job may have to wait until previous jobs complete. Once your job starts, a BATCH mode process is created on your behalf, which executes your command procedure. By default, a log file is created in your SYS$LOGIN directory, logging the activities of the command procedure. In this example, the log file CLEANUP.LOG would be created.

Useful qualifiers include the following:

/AFTER and /HOLD—work exactly as they do for the PRINT command, see above.

/QUEUE=*queue-name*—directs your batch job to a particular queue instead of SYS$BATCH.

/LOG=*filename*—controls the name of the batch log file. Use /NOLOG to disable the logfile altogether. Use SET [NO]VERIFY within your command procedure to control the verbosity of the logfile contents, as discussed below.

/PARAMETERS=(*"P1","P2",..."P8"*)—supplies parameters to batch jobs. Command procedures executed interactively accept parameters from the command line; the /PARAMETERS qualifier provides the same functionality for batch jobs.

/PRIORITY=*n*—allows you to set the priority of the queue entry. Priorities are in the range of 0 (the lowest) through 255. On most systems, the default queue priority for most users is 100. Jobs with higher priorities are executed first. You must hold the ALTPRI or OPER privilege to raise the priority above your default priority. This priority refers to the priority of the batch queue entry, not the scheduling priority of the resulting batch process.

Batch Mode Caveats

[NO]VERIFY in Batch Jobs

Depending on the contents of SYLOGIN.COM and your own LOGIN.COM, your batch jobs may have verification turned on by default. Verification causes each line of your command procedure to be recorded in the log file as it is executed. This can result in large log files with mostly uninteresting contents. Consider using the following command in your LOGIN.COM if you usually do not need to see this information:

```
$ if f$mode() .eqs. "BATCH" then $ set noverify
```

If placed in your LOGIN.COM, this will disable verification in all of your batch logs by default. You can always use SET VERIFY and SET NOVERIFY within a given procedure to enable or disable verification at will.

Modifying a Command Procedure Already Queued

If you make a change to a command procedure that is already queued for execution, your change will not be honored when the job runs. This is true even if you reset the version number of the file back to what it was when it was queued, because the file is queued by its unique file ID, not its name. Furthermore, if you make a change and then PURGE the original version, the job will fail altogether, resulting in a "file not found" message alone in the log file.

If you change a procedure, you must delete the old queue entry (shown further on in this chapter) and queue the file again. If your batch job resubmits itself to run again later, you may wait and let your change take effect on the second run, as the old version will submit the updated version.

Be Careful of Your Directories

When your batch job begins, its default directory will be SYS$LOGIN, your home directory. This is true no matter which directory contains the procedure, or what your default directory was when you queued the job.

You should take this into account when writing your procedures. You may use SET DEFAULT within your procedures (consider restoring the original directory at exit as shown below) or fully specify any files referenced within the procedure.

```
$ !
$ ! How to use F$ENVIRONMENT() to preserve your original directory
$ ! when a command procedure must work in another directory.
$ ! This may also be useful if the procedure will be used in
$ ! interactive mode.
$ !
$ original_dir = f$environment("default")
$ set default working_directory
  .
  . (intervening work)
  .
$ !
$ ! Restore our directory to what it was when the procedure started.
$ !
$ set default 'original_dir
$ exit
```

Finding Batch Queues and Printers

To locate queues on your OpenVMS system, use the SHOW QUEUE command. Use /BATCH to narrow the search to batch queues or /DEVICE to limit it to printer queues.

```
$ SHOW QUEUE/BATCH
Batch queue SYS$BATCH, idle, on PHOEBE::

  Entry  Jobname        Username          Status
  -----  -------        --------          ------
    951  CHECK_EXPIRED  MIKE              Holding until  8-APR-2003 16:33:15
    702  HOUSEKEEPING   MIKE              Holding until  9-APR-2003 00:00:00
```

In the example above, there is only one batch queue on the system. If the system or cluster has more than one batch queue, they will all be listed. If you have any jobs currently in the queue(s), each will be shown after the queue in which it resides.

```
$ SHOW QUEUE/DEVICE
Printer queue COLOR, available, on LTA157:, mounted form DEFAULT

Printer queue LASER, busy, on LTA244:, mounted form DEFAULT

  Entry  Jobname        Username     Blocks  Status
  -----  -------        --------     ------  ------
    149  REPORT3        MIKE             49  Printing
```

```
Printer queue PRINTER1, available, on LTA300:, mounted form DEFAULT

Printer queue PRINTER2, available, on LTA301:, mounted form DEFAULT

Generic printer queue SYS$PRINT
```

In the example above, there are four printer queues and one generic printer queue. Generic queues can route jobs to the next available printer queue matching the job's requirements. Printer LASER is currently printing the print job called REPORT3.

To see jobs submitted by all users, use the /ALL qualifier. If your account has suitable privileges, all jobs will be shown. Otherwise, you may be shown only the number of intervening jobs.

```
$ SHOW QUEUE/BATCH/ALL
Batch queue SYS$BATCH, idle, on PHOEBE::

  Entry  Jobname         Username            Status
  -----  -------         --------            ------
    951  CHECK_EXPIRED   MIKE                Holding until  8-APR-2003 16:33:15
    697  CLIENT          TIMESERVER          Holding until  8-APR-2003 23:43:12
    702  HOUSEKEEPING    MIKE                Holding until  9-APR-2003 00:00:00
    710  FINDHI          MIKE                Holding until  9-APR-2003 00:21:55
    426  REMINDER        LAWRENCE            Holding until  9-APR-2003 08:00:00
```

To see complete information about queues and entries, use the /FULL qualifier.

```
$ SHOW QUEUE/BATCH/FULL
Batch queue SYS$BATCH, idle, on PHOEBE::
  /BASE_PRIORITY=0 /JOB_LIMIT=1 /OWNER=[SYSTEM] /PROTECTION=(S:M,O:D,G:R,W:S)

    951  CHECK_EXPIRED   MIKE                Holding until  8-APR-2003 16:33:15
         Submitted  8-APR-2003 14:33:15.59 /LOG=DKA100:[LOGS]CHECK_EXPIRED.LOG;
         /PRIORITY=100
         File: _PHOEBE$DKA100:[LOGS]CHECK_EXPIRED.COM;10
```

To examine only a single queue, specify it as the parameter:

```
$ SHOW QUEUE queue_name [/all] [/full]
```

Examining a Queue Entry

A single entry (job) may be examined using the SHOW ENTRY command:

```
$ SHOW ENTRY 951
  Entry  Jobname         Username      Blocks  Status
  -----  -------         --------      ------  ------
    951  CHECK_EXPIRED   MIKE                  Holding until  8-APR-2003 16:33:15
         On idle batch queue SYS$BATCH
```

You may add the /FULL qualifier to see more information:

```
$ SHOW ENTRY 951 /FULL
  Entry  Jobname         Username      Blocks  Status
  -----  -------         --------      ------  ------
    951  CHECK_EXPIRED   MIKE                  Holding until  8-APR-2003 16:33:15
```

```
      On idle batch queue SYS$BATCH
      Submitted  8-APR-2003 14:33:15.59 /LOG=DKA100:[LOGS]CHECK_EXPIRED.LOG;
      /PRIORITY=100
      File: _PHOEBE$DKA100:[LOGS]CHECK_EXPIRED.COM;10
```

Modifying a Queue Entry

You may use the SET ENTRY command to change the characteristics of a job already in a queue.

```
$ SET ENTRY entry_number [/qualifiers]
```

Common qualifiers include the following:

/AFTER="time"—changes the time at which the job should execute. Use "dd-mmm-yyyy hh:mm:ss.cc" format—for example, "23-MAY-2003 15:00" or "18:30". If you omit the day, the current day is assumed.

/HOLD—causes the job to be held indefinitely. Use /RELEASE to release a holding job for immediate execution.

```
$ SHOW ENTRY 951
   Entry  Jobname          Username      Blocks  Status
   -----  -------          --------      ------  ------
     951  CHECK_EXPIRED    MIKE                  Holding until  8-APR-2003 16:33:15
          On idle batch queue SYS$BATCH
$ SET ENTRY 951/HOLD
$ SHOW ENTRY 951
   Entry  Jobname          Username      Blocks  Status
   -----  -------          --------      ------  ------
     951  CHECK_EXPIRED    MIKE                  Holding
          On idle batch queue SYS$BATCH
```

Use HELP SET ENTRY for more information about modifying entries.

Deleting a Queue Entry

To delete an entry, whether or not the job has already started, use DELETE /ENTRY=entry-number:

```
$ SHOW ENTRY 951
   Entry  Jobname          Username      Blocks  Status
   -----  -------          --------      ------  ------
     951  CHECK_EXPIRED    MIKE                  Holding
          On idle batch queue SYS$BATCH
$ DELETE/ENTRY=951
$ SHOW ENTRY 951
%JBC-E-NOSUCHENT, no such entry
```

Queue Entry Numbers

Normally, OpenVMS queue entry numbers start at 1, increase by 1 until reaching 1,000, and then start over from 1. If more entry numbers are needed, OpenVMS will automatically use larger numbers. Some older versions of OpenVMS incremented entry numbers by values other than 1.

The special DCL symbol $ENTRY contains the number of the queue entry you created most recently. If you have not created a queue entry since logging in, the symbol will not exist. This feature is particularly helpful for command procedures that submit jobs and then need to examine or manipulate them or record their numbers. Some older versions of OpenVMS do not include the $ENTRY symbol.

```
$ SUBMIT CLEANUP
Job CLEANUP (queue SYS$BATCH, entry 952) pending
     pending status caused by queue busy state
$ SHOW SYMBOL $ENTRY
  $ENTRY = "952"
```

Using Directories

The concept of directories has been alluded to earlier in this book, and the DIRECTORY command was introduced (see "Displaying a List of Files (the DIRECTORY command)" above).

Directories provide a convenient way to organize related files into a hierarchical structure. If you imagine a file as a single sheet of paper, then the directory would be the folder containing the related papers. Papers that are related to one another are usually placed in the same folder for easy access. A folder usually has an external label on it, indicating its contents. Similarly, a directory has a name that should indicate which files it contains.

A directory may contain not only files, but other directories as well. A directory called 2003 may contain some individual files, as well as other directories called January, February, etc. Those directories may themselves contain files and yet more directories.

When your account is created, your system manager will create a top-level directory for you, sometimes called your root or home directory. When you log in, your default directly will automatically be set to your own top-level directory.

Default Versus Home Directory

Your default directory is always your current directory. When you move around directories, each one in turn becomes your default directory. On the other hand, your home directory does not change. It is the one created for you by the system manager. When you log in, your default directory is set to your home directory.

Construction of a Directory Specification

A directory specification is the following portion of a full file specification:

```
[DIR.SUBDIR1.SUBDIR2(...)]
```

Here are some examples:

```
[MIKE]
[PAYROLL.2001.NOVEMBER]
[PAYROLL.1999.AUGUST]
[USERS.FRANK.HOBBIES.FISHING.GREAT_LAKES]
[USERS.FRANK.HOBBIES.BASKETBALL]
```

> **Note:** While accessing an OpenVMS system through TCP/IP services such as FTP, it is often acceptable, and sometimes required, to use UNIX format, wherein [USERS.FRANK.HOBBIES]FILE.TXT would be expressed as /users/frank /hobbies/file.txt.

SHOW DEFAULT and SET DEFAULT

The SET DEFAULT *directory* command changes your current directory to the one you specify. It is equivalent to the CD or CHDIR commands of other operating systems. The SHOW DEFAULT command tells you your current device and directory:

```
$ SET DEFAULT DKA100:[MIKE]
$ SHOW DEFAULT
  DKA100:[MIKE]
$ SET DEFAULT [JAMES.REPORTS]
$ SHOW DEFAULT
  DKA100:[JAMES.REPORTS]
```

When you issue the SHOW DEFAULT command, DCL responds with your current disk (DKA100: above) and directory ([MIKE] and [JAMES.REPORTS]). When you issue a command that performs a file operation, your current directory will be assumed. Unless you specify another directory in a file specification, the activity will occur in that directory.

Let's say users MIKE and MURPHY each have a command procedure called SETUP.COM that performs some task for them. Even though the files share the same name, there is no confusion because each user has his own directory containing his own version of SETUP.COM.

When MIKE logs in, his current directory is DKA100:[MIKE], so his references to SETUP.COM refer to DKA100:[MIKE]SETUP.COM. When MURPHY logs in and references SETUP.COM, DKB400:[MURPHY]SETUP.COM is used.

If user MIKE wishes to use MURPHY's SETUP.COM, he may either use the DCL command SET DEFAULT DKB400:[MURPHY] to change to MURPHY's directory before using the file, or specify the file by its full name, DKB400:[MURPHY]SETUP.COM.

What the Command SET DEFAULT Really Means

While it is conceptually correct to think of yourself as being "in" a certain directory, that's not how it actually works. Your current directory is little more than an illusion. It is really only a text string used to fill in missing pieces of a full file specification. Let's say your current default directory is DKA100:[MIKE]. If you issue the command EDIT LOGIN.COM, the OpenVMS file system applies the default directory DKA100:[MIKE] to your file specification, resulting in DKA100:[MIKE]LOGIN.COM. The SET DEFAULT command sets your default directory string, giving the command it's name.

Moving Around Directories

Earlier in this book, directories were compared to folders within folders. There is another way of looking at the same setup: the directory tree. Figure 7-2 and Figure 7-3 present both ways of looking at the same directory organization:

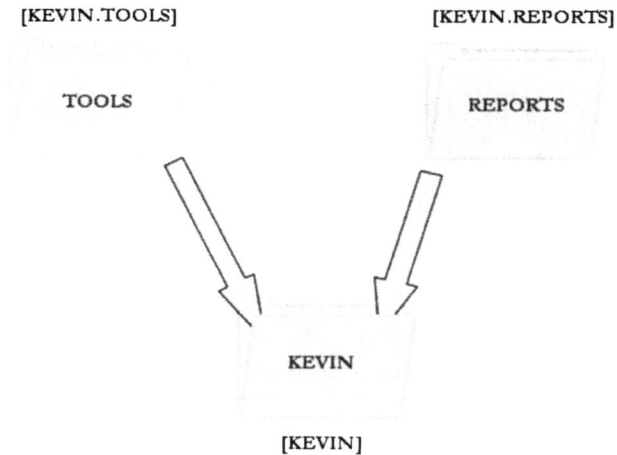

Figure 7-1 Directories As Folders

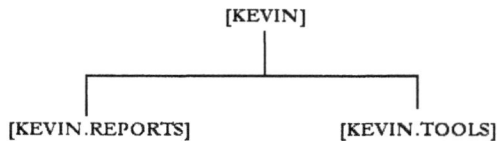

Figure 7-2 Directories As a Tree Structure

For moving around various directories, many users may find the tree concept more intuitive. There are three ways of dealing with directories. They are:

1. Staying in one directory and using full file specifications for files in other directories

2. Moving directly from one directory to another

3. Moving up and down the directory tree

All three of these methods are typically used in combination. Moving around directories is discussed in the following paragraphs.

Moving Directly to Another Directory

This is accomplished by using an absolute directory specification with the SET DEFAULT command:

```
$ SHOW DEFAULT ! see our initial directory
  DKA100:[KEVIN]
$ !
$ SET DEFAULT [KEVIN.TOOLS]
$ SHOW DEFAULT
  DKA100:[KEVIN.TOOLS]
$ !
$ SET DEFAULT [KEVIN.REPORTS]
$ SHOW DEFAULT
  DKA100:[KEVIN.REPORTS]
$ !
$ SET DEFAULT [KEVIN]
$ SHOW DEFAULT
  DKA100:[KEVIN]
```

Moving Around Relative to Your Current Directory

You may move around a directory tree using the relative notations "-" to move up one level and "." to move down one level. They may be used in combination. For example, to move to the TOOLS subdirectory of the current directory (down one level), specify [.TOOLS]. To move back from the TOOLS directory to the original directory (up one level), use [-]. To move over to an adjacent directory—for example REPORTS,—use [-.REPORTS] (this means to first move up one level and then down into the REPORTS subdirectory.)

The following performs the same steps as the previous example, but uses the relative notations:

```
$ SHOW DEFAULT   ! our original directory
```

```
   DKA100:[KEVIN]
$ !
$ SET DEFAULT [.TOOLS]
$ SHOW DEFAULT
   DKA100:[KEVIN.TOOLS]
$ !
$ SET DEFAULT [-.REPORTS]
$ SHOW DEFAULT
   DKA100:[KEVIN.REPORTS]
$ !
$ SET DEFAULT [-]
$ SHOW DEFAULT
   DKA100:[KEVIN]
```

With long directory names, relative notations can save considerable effort:

```
$ SET DEFAULT [MIKE.REPORTS.2002.MARCH.NORTHEAST]
$ SHOW DEFAULT
   DKA0:[MIKE.REPORTS.2002.MARCH.NORTHEAST]
$ !
$ SET DEFAULT [-.NORTHWEST]
$ SHOW DEFAULT
   DKA0:[MIKE.REPORTS.2002.MARCH.NORTHWEST]
$ !
$ SET DEFAULT [---.2003.MARCH]
$ SHOW DEFAULT
   DKA0:[MIKE.REPORTS.2003.MARCH]
```

Wildcards for Directory Operations

The wildcards already discussed (see "Working with Files: Wildcards," above) can be used with directories. In addition, directories support an additional wildcard consisting of an ellipsis (...), which means "from this point downward in the directory tree."

Some examples of wildcard directory specifications follow.

- To search all top-level directories for each users LOGIN.COM:

```
$ DIRECTORY [*]LOGIN.COM
```

- To search all directories on the disk for any files called ERROR.LOG:

```
$ DIRECTORY [*...]ERROR.LOG      ! Excludes MFD
$ DIRECTORY [000000...]ERROR.LOG ! Includes MFD
```

- To search all the subdirectories immediately below this one for files called BARRY.RPT:

```
$ DIRECTORY [.*]BARRY.RPT
```

- To find all logfiles from this point downward (the current directory, all subdirectories of the current directory, all their subdirectories, etc.):

```
$ DIRECTORY [...]*.LOG
```

- To perform the same search, but exclude the current directory:

```
$ DIRECTORY [.*...]*.LOG
```

- To find all files in the directory above this one:

```
$ DIRECTORY [-]
```

Creating and Deleting Subdirectories

This section describes how you may create and delete subdirectories under your own directory. Creating top-level directories for a new user or under someone else's directory tree usually requires privileges not available to the general user and is shown here for information only.

Creating a Directory

To create a directory, the general command format is

```
$ CREATE/DIRECTORY directory [/OWNER=user]
```

The /OWNER qualifier should be used if the owner of the directory should differ from the owner of the parent directory. This is generally used for top-level directories.

Some examples follow:

```
$ CREATE/DIRECTORY DKA100:[JONES]/OWNER=JONES   ! Top-level directory
$ CREATE/DIRECTORY [.REPORTS]                   ! Under current directory
$ CREATE/DIRECTORY DKB400:[BARRY.ARTICLES.JAN]
```

Intervening directory levels need not already exist. In the last example above, the directories DKB400:[BARRY] and then DKB400:[BARRY.ARTICLES] would be created first, if necessary.

Creating a Subdirectory

Creating a subdirectory is a special case of creating a directory in general.

To create a subdirectory of the current directory, use the CREATE/DIRECTORY command. If you wished to create a subdirectory called REPORTS, you would use the following command:

```
$ DIRECTORY ! To see the current directory first
Directory DKA100:[MURPHY]

LOGIN.COM;45

Total of 1 file.
$ CREATE/DIRECTORY [.REPORTS]
$ DIRECTORY

Directory DKA100:[MURPHY]

LOGIN.COM;45          REPORTS.DIR;1

Total of 2 files.
```

You can see from this example that a directory is itself a file that can be seen using the DIRECTORY command. However, it is not an ordinary file, and you cannot manipulate it as you would other files. Changes to directory files are made automatically by the system as needed. The only time a user directly manipulates a directory file is while deleting it, which is shown next.

Deleting a Subdirectory

Deleting a subdirectory is not quite as straightforward as creating one because two conditions must first be met. First, the subdirectory must be empty. If a directory contains any files, OpenVMS will not delete it. Doing so would cause its files to be orphaned, meaning the files would still exist, but would not be listed in any directory.

> **Note:** The system manager can detect and recover orphaned files using built-in OpenVMS tools should the need arise. This occurs infrequently—usually when a directory file is somehow damaged.

Second, you must set the file protection of the directory so that you may delete it. (File protections are explained in detail later.) Directory files automatically have a higher level of protection than ordinary files. To delete a directory file, you must take the following steps:

```
$ ! Delete the files within it, if any.  If [.REPORTS] itself has any
$ ! subdirectories, those must be emptied and deleted first.
$ !
$ delete [.reports]*.*;*
$ !
$ ! Now change the file protection on the REPORTS directory file so
$ ! that we may delete it (this requires CONTROL access to the directory)
$ !
$ set file/protection=(o:d) reports.dir ! (o:d) means "Owner may Delete"
$ !
$ ! Now delete the directory file
$ !
$ delete reports.dir;*
```

The Directory Structure of a Files-11 ODS-2 Disk

To show how the general concepts of directories are carried out in practice, this section will briefly describe the actual layout of an OpenVMS disk. A little history is necessary to understand the terminology.

Files-11 is the *file system* used by OpenVMS. As one might imagine, the file system is that part of an operating system that controls the storage and manipulation of files.

ODS-2 stands for On-Disk Structure, Version 2. It describes the actual layout of files on the disk, including all control information needed to interpret the contents of the disk. Later versions of OpenVMS Alpha (and presumably, the upcoming Itanium version) also support a newer Files-11 structure level, ODS-5. ODS-2 and ODS-5 volumes may exist on the same system, so long as the system is running a compatible version of OpenVMS.

On ODS-2 disks, the top-level directory is called [000000]. This top-level directory is also known as the "MFD," or "Master File Directory."

New users may find it curious that directory listings of the [000000] directory include the file 000000.DIR. This is because the MFD includes an entry for itself, making it appear that the MFD "contains itself."

Why Call It 000000?

The unlikely-sounding name 000000 has a historical basis. On much older Digital systems, the directory name for each user took the form [gggmmm], where ggg was the UIC group number for that user, and mmm was the member number. So, [000000] (also denoted [000,000]) represented the MFD. (Try it: as of OpenVMS V7.3, the command DIRECTORY [0,0] still works as a substitute for DIRECTORY [000000] if you have the appropriate privileges.)

The MFD of an ODS-2 disk contains some reserved files. These are files with specific names and purposes that the OpenVMS file system uses to maintain information on disk. Among these are the following:

- 000000.DIR—the MFD directory file. This file contains entries for all files in the top-level directory of the disk. Directories contain little information about files, mostly just their names and file IDs, which are used to locate the complete file information located in INDEXF.SYS.

- BITMAP.SYS—a file containing information about which areas of the disk are in use and which are free. Used to locate space for newly created files.

- INDEXF.SYS—also known as the Index file, this file stores all attributes (name, size, owner, location on disk, etc.) for each file on the disk. It is central to the management of files.

- SYSx.DIR—the top of the directory tree in which OpenVMS resides if the disk contains a copy of the OpenVMS operating system (as opposed to a data-only disk). On standalone systems it is called SYS0. VMScluster disks have directories for each member of the cluster: SYS0, SYS1, SYS2, and so on. These directories do not duplicate the entire OpenVMS operating system in each cluster member's directory.

- VMS$COMMON.DIR—also part of the directory tree containing OpenVMS. VMScluster systems need a mechanism to keep track of system-specific files versus cluster-common files. This directory is part of that mechanism. When a VMScluster system accesses a file in these directory trees, it looks first for that file in the system-specific directory. If one does not exist, it then looks in the common directory. In this way, more than one system can share a system disk, but still maintain member-specific files.

- SYSLOST.DIR—contains orphaned files recovered by the ANALYZE /DISK_STRUCTURE command. Should a directory file be damaged, its files can be found and placed in this directory. It is rarely needed, but it provides insurance against data loss.

There are some other reserved files, mostly of lesser importance; some of them are obsolete or unused. They include BACKUP.SYS, BADBLK.SYS, BADLOG.SYS, CONTIN.SYS, CORIMG.SYS, SECURITY.SYS, and VOLSET.SYS. Some disks might have additional reserved files depending on whether they are part of a multi disk set.

The MFD contains entries for any other top-level directories as created by the system manager or users. They may include user directories or directories containing a particular software product, database, or any other files desired.

This example shows the top-level directory of a small AlphaStation disk used by the author. The author's user directory is shown in boldface:

```
$ DIRECTORY DKA0:[000000]
```

```
Directory DKA0:[000000]

000000.DIR;1        BACKUP.SYS;1       BADBLK.SYS;1        BADLOG.SYS;1
BITMAP.SYS;1        CONTIN.SYS;1       CORIMG.SYS;1        DECC052.DIR;1
ENGINEERING.DIR;1   INDEXF.SYS;1       MIKE.DIR;1          MMK.DIR;1
SECURITY.SYS;1      SYS0.DIR;1         SYSLOST.DIR;1       TAR.DIR;1
TEMP.DIR;1          TIMESERVE.DIR;1    VMS$COMMON.DIR;1    VOLSET.SYS;1

Total of 20 files.
```

Depending on your privileges and site security policy, you may or may not be able to view the top-level directory of a given disk. Many users will be able to view or modify only the contents of their own directories and any subdirectories below it. The inability to view the MFD will not interfere with your use of the system; simply continue as though your login directory is the top-level directory of your own tree.

File Protection

Each file on the system has an associated protection level. This controls who may use the file and in what ways. You may protect your files to allow or prevent other users from reading or modifying them. Keep in mind that the system manager and perhaps certain other users are able to override any protections you place on your files. This is a necessary feature; the system manager must be able to read your files in order to create backup copies to be used in the event of a disk failure or accidental deletion.

Please be aware that access to files is determined in part by protections placed on the directory containing the files in question. Directories may have the same types of protections placed on them as the files they contain. However, since it is possible to access files without using a directory, an expert user may be able to bypass directory protections in some circumstances. It remains important to protect files themselves, without relying totally on directory protections.

Files may be protected by two methods: UIC-based protection codes normally associated with every file created and optional access control lists (ACLs). ACLs provide finer-grained file protection than UIC-based protections and can allow or disallow access to individual users or holders of certain identifiers.

ACLs are used somewhat infrequently but, if present, are checked before normal UIC-based protections. Processing stops and access is granted as soon as an item is found that grants the requested type of access, even if a later item would have explicitly denied access.

ACLs are described after the discussion of UIC-based protection.

File Protection Bits

A set of protection settings is associated with every file. They control who may access the file for various kinds of operations. Accesses are broken down into four categories: read, write, execute, and delete. Users attempting access to a file are grouped into four categories: system, owner, group, and world. Each class of user may be allowed or disallowed each type of access. The classes of users are as follows:

System: Any entity running under a system User Identification Code (UIC). A system UIC is one whose group number is less than or equal to a changeable system setting called MAXSYSGROUP, whose default value is 10 (octal). The OpenVMS operating system itself, the system manager, system operators, and backup operators usually have UICs in this range.

OWNER: Any user whose UIC exactly matches the file owner. This is usually the creator of the file, but sometimes it is the owner of the directory in which the file resides or some other user.

GROUP: Any user whose UIC group number matches that of the file owner.

WORLD: This includes all system users.

When the requestor belongs to more than one of these categories, the most permissive match prevails.

The following are the types of access that may be granted to each class of user above:

READ: The ability to examine the contents of a file. If the file is a program or DCL command procedure, READ access also grants the ability to execute it.

WRITE: The ability to modify the contents of a file, append information to it, or create a new version. If you grant write access to a class of users, you should also grant read access. Otherwise, attempts to use DCL commands, such as EDIT, APPEND, OPEN /APPEND, or OPEN/WRITE, will fail.

EXECUTE: The ability to run a program or execute a DCL command procedure. With EXECUTE access alone, a user may execute a program or command procedure but may not TYPE, COPY, PRINT, or otherwise examine the file. When applied to a directory, EXECUTE access allow users to look up a file in the directory if they explicitly specify the file name.

DELETE: The ability to delete the file.

There is a fifth type of access, CONTROL, which is not included in the protection bits, but which is granted or denied automatically. CONTROL is the ability to change the protection codes of a file or directory. It is granted automatically to users in the SYSTEM and OWNER categories, but never to GROUP or WORLD users. Because CONTROL access allows changes to protections, SYSTEM users can always gain full control over the file, as can the OWNER. Control access can also be granted to others via an access control entry (ACE).

Examples of UIC-Based File Protections

When a file is created, it is generally created with the following protections:

- System: RWED

- Owner: RWED

- Group: RE

- World: none

The next few examples show how to change those default settings.

If you wanted to disallow anyone beside yourself access to a file SECURE.TXT, you would use this command:

```
$ SET FILE/PROTECTION=(S:R,O:RWED,G,W) SECURE.TXT
```

SYSTEM is still granted READ access so that backups may be performed on the file. Remember that a SYSTEM user can gain access to any file, but it would require an extra step. Therefore, disallowing SYSTEM access will not protect the file from SYSTEM users, but may cause it to be skipped during system backups. Generally, SYSTEM should be allowed at least READ access.

If you wanted to allow members of your UIC group to view and modify the file and any user to view it:

```
$ SET FILE/PROTECTION=(S:R,O:RWED,G:RW,W:R) SECURE.TXT
```

And if you wanted to allow full access to everyone:

```
$ SET FILE/PROTECTION=(S:RWED,O:RWED,G:RWED,W:RWED) SECURE.TXT
```

Please be aware that setting file protections on directory files does not necessarily protect the files in those directories. Under OpenVMS, it is possible to access a file directly without using a directory. You should protect the files themselves.

Access Control Lists

Access Control Lists (ACLs) supplement the standard UIC-based protection. ACLs grant or deny access to an object to holders of specific identifiers. If an object has an ACL, it is checked before the normal UIC-based protection mechanism.

An ACL is composed of one or more Access Control Entries (ACEs), which are evaluated in the order in which they appear. When an ACE that grants the requested access is found, processing stops at that point and access is granted. This is true even if a later ACE would have explicitly denied access. For this reason, you should place ACEs that deny access first.

You may add an ACE to a file with the following command:

```
$ SET FILE filespec -
   /ACL=(IDENTIFIER=ident_name,ACCESS=type_of_access) [/DELETE]
```

The /DELETE qualifier deletes an existing ACE matching the one you specify.

Note that *ident_name* is the name of an identifier, which is a credential that can be held by one or more users. You may also specify the username of individual users because OpenVMS creates a separate identifier for each user by default. For example, user MIKE holds the identifier MIKE, and user HERMAN holds the identifier HERMAN. Other identifiers, such as the hypothetical PAYROLL identifier discussed earlier, may be held by more than one user.

Example:

```
$ DIRECTORY/ACL ZZZ.TXT

Directory DKA100:[LOGS]

ZZZ.TXT;1

Total of 1 file.
$ SET FILE ZZZ.TXT /ACL=(IDENTIFIER=MIKE,ACCESS=NONE)
$ SET FILE ZZZ.TXT /ACL=(IDENTIFIER=HERMAN,ACCESS=READ+WRITE)
$ DIRECTORY/ACL ZZZ.TXT

Directory DKA100:[LOGS]

ZZZ.TXT;1
         (IDENTIFIER=[HERMAN],ACCESS=READ+WRITE)
         (IDENTIFIER=[MIKE],ACCESS=NONE)

Total of 1 file.
$ SET FILE ZZZ.TXT /ACL=(IDENTIFIER=MIKE,ACCESS=NONE) /DELETE
$ DIRECTORY/ACL ZZZ.TXT
```

```
Directory DKA100:[LOGS]

ZZZ.TXT;1
          (IDENTIFIER=[HERMAN],ACCESS=READ+WRITE)

Total of 1 file.
```

Notice that ACEs are added at the top of the ACL by default. Use /AFTER=ace if you want to control the point at which it is inserted.

Note that SET FILE/ACL is technically obsolete in OpenVMS V7.3, but it still works. It is shown here because it works on older versions as well. On newer version of OpenVMS, use SET SECURITY *object* /ACL.

You may also choose to use the ACL editor to manage ACLs:

```
$ EDIT /ACL ZZZ.TXT
```

The OpenVMS ACL editor will start, allowing you to add, remove, or change ACEs using a full-screen editor. Use CRTL/Z to exit the ACL editor, and save the ACL. Press PF2 on the keypad for help ("/" on PC-style keyboards.)

Privileges That Override File Protections

Users holding certain privileges can bypass file protections as described below. The system manager grants these privileges to specific users and is responsible for granting them to users who have a legitimate need. Always remember that the judgment of the system manager in assigning UICs and privileges determines whether a given user can gain access to your files.

The relevant privileges are as follows:

SYSPRV—users who hold SYSPRV can access a file as if they were members of the SYSTEM category.

GRPPRV—if the holder of GRPPRV is in the same UIC group as the file owner, access is granted through the SYSTEM category.

BYPASS—a holder of BYPASS totally bypasses all file protections and is granted all types of access.

READALL—a holder of READALL is granted read access to the file, even if it is denied in ACL- and UIC-based protections.

OpenVMS Device Names

OpenVMS uses a standard format for the names of terminals, disks, tape drives, network adapters, and other devices.

The general format of device names is *ddcu*: where dd are letters representing the device type, c is a letter indicating which controller (adapter) the device is attached to, and u is the unit number on that adapter. The trailing colon is part of the device name.

So, TTB4: represents a terminal (TT) connected to port 4 on the second terminal adapter (B). TTA6: is port 6 on the first adapter, etc. Note that the first actual device on a given adapter may be either unit 0 or 1.

Some of the more common device types are as follows:

```
DI - Disk
DK - SCSI Disk
DP - Disk
DU - Disk
DQ - IDE Disk
DS - Disk Stripe Set

ES - Ethernet Network Device
ET - Ethernet Network Device
EZ - Ethernet Network Device
EF - Ethernet Network Device
EX - Ethernet Network Device
EC - Ethernet Network Device
XQ - Ethernet Network Device
XE - Ethernet Network Device

FC - FDDI Network Device
FX - FDDI Network Device

FT  - Network Terminal
LT  - LAT network Terminal
NTY - Network Terminal
OP  - Operators Console (OPA0:)
TT  - Terminal
TX  - Terminal
RT  - DECnet Terminal (SET HOST)
VT  - Virtual Terminal

MK  - SCSI Tape Drive
MT  - Tape Drive
MU  - Tape Drive
```

SCSI devices usually have unit numbers that are multiples of 100. The first SCSI disk will be DKA0:, the second DKA100:, then DKA200:, and so forth.

You may see a device name preceded by an underscore, as in _DKB400:. The underscore signifies that the name is a physical device name, not a logical name.

Some systems, including VMScluster members, sometimes have slightly different device names. Some devices may be preceded by the name of the VMScluster node to which the device is attached. Say, for example, that nodes PHOEBE and WILLIS each have a disk device DKA100:.

The disk attached to node PHOEBE may be shown as PHOEBE$DKA100: and the disk attached to WILLIS as WILLIS$DKA100:.

Depending on system configuration, you may instead see an allocation class associated with certain devices. An allocation class is a number identifying the primary data path to a device that has more than one possible path. This mechanism is designed to provide failover transparently should one path fail.

An allocation class is represented by the string n preceding the device name, where n identifies the allocation class. A system manager may assign a number in the range 1 through 255 as the allocation class for a given cluster node or storage controller. A different number may be used for disk versus tape devices.

So, a disk device may be shown as 1DUA4: rather than simply DUA4:. Should you find allocation classes in use at your site, simply consider the allocation class to be part of the device name and pay no further attention to them.

Specifying Dates and Times

When specifying dates and times, you will use one of two time formats: absolute or delta.

Absolute times are displayed in the format DD-MMM-YYYY HH:MM:SS.CC by default, as in 12-APR-2002 11:30:00.00. Please note that your system manager may choose some other format, but this is fairly uncommon.

When referring to the current day, you may omit the date, as in 11:30:00.00. This expression may be simplified further to 11:30. Examples of this time format are shown in the following DIRECTORY commands, which search for any files created after a certain time:

```
$ DIRECTORY /CREATED/SINCE="01-JAN-2000"
```

```
$ DIRECTORY /CREATED/SINCE="14-AUG-2000 14:30"
$ DIRECTORY /CREATED/SINCE="09:00"
```

Delta times are offsets from the current time and are expressed by d-hh:mm:ss. So, one week ago would be specified as -7-00:00:00 or -7-. Two days and five hours from now would be +2-05:00:00 or +2-05.

```
$ DIRECTORY /CREATED/SINCE="-7-"       ! 7 days ago
$ DIRECTORY /CREATED/SINCE="-3-02:30" ! 3 days, 2 hours, 30 minutes ago
```

You may also use the keywords YESTERDAY, TODAY, and TOMORROW to specify midnight on each of those three days:

```
$ DIRECTORY /CREATED/SINCE="YESTERDAY"   ! Midnight yesterday.
$ DIRECTORY /CREATED/SINCE="YESTERDAY+3" ! 3 A.M. yesterday.
$ DIRECTORY /CREATED/SINCE="TODAY"       ! Since midnight.
$ SUBMIT CLEANUP/AFTER="TOMORROW"        ! Run job at midnight.
$ SUBMIT CLEANUP/AFTER="TOMORROW+0-03"   ! 3 A.M. tomorrow.
$ SUBMIT CLEANUP/AFTER="TOMORROW+5-"     ! Five days from midnight.
```

Logical Names

A logical name is a name that can be substituted for a file specification, directory specification, device name, or even another logical name. They may be used as shorthand for long file or directory names or to achieve a level of abstraction not otherwise possible.

The string to which a logical name equates is referred to as its equivalence name, a concept that will be illustrated shortly.

Abstraction Provided by Logical Names

Let's say that several users, BILL, MARY, FRANK, and BOB, all use a certain command procedure. This hypothetical command procedure uses a file called SAVED-DATA.DAT in each user's login directory. That is, BILL's file is called DKA400:[ACCOUNTING.BILL]SAVED-DATA.DAT, MARY's is DUA3:[PAYROLL.MARY]SAVED-DATA.DAT, and so forth. How can the command procedure correctly identify which file to use?

One solution might be to design the procedure to determine which user is running it and look up the user's default directory in a table. But OpenVMS has already provided a simple, more foolproof solution: the logical name SYS$LOGIN.

For each process, OpenVMS automatically defines a logical name SYS$LOGIN, which translates to the name of the login directory of that user. Try it now:

```
$ SHOW LOGICAL SYS$LOGIN
  "SYS$LOGIN" = "DKA100:[MIKE]" (LNM$JOB_80DCBA00)
```

In the example above, the logical name SYS$LOGIN has an equivalence name of
DKA100:[MIKE]. Whenever user MIKE refers to SYS$LOGIN, the system
automatically interprets this as DKA100:[MIKE]. All users have their own equivalence
names for SYS$LOGIN, indicating their own directories.

So, our hypothetical command procedure can merely refer to SYS$LOGIN:SAVED-
DATA.DAT, which will automatically use the correct directory for each user.

Because of the flexibility inherent in logical names, they are used extensively under
OpenVMS.

Logical Names as Shorthand Notations

Another primary use of logical names is to represent long file or directory
specifications by shorter names. If you use a directory called
PAYROLL$DISK:[ALBUQUERQUE.ENGINEERING.2002.SEPTEMBER], you might
wish to use a short logical name to replace it in your commands:

```
$ DEFINE THISMONTH PAYROLL$DISK:[ALBUQUERQUE.ENGINEERING.2002.SEPTEMBER]
$ DIRECTORY THISMONTH

Directory PAYROLL$DISK:[ALBUQUERQUE.ENGINEERING.2002.SEPTEMBER]

ARTHUR.RPT      BOYD.RPT

Total of 2 files.
$ PRINT THISMONTH:ARTHUR.RPT
Job ARTHUR (queue SYS$PRINT, entry 138), started on LASER2
```

When using a logical name as part of a file specification, such as with ARTHUR.RPT,
separate the logical name from the file name with a colon as shown in the PRINT
command above.

To assign a new value to a logical name that already exists, issue another DEFINE
command:

```
$ DEFINE THISMONTH PAYROLL$DISK:[ALBUQUERQUE.ENGINEERING.2002.OCTOBER]
%DCL-I-SUPERSEDE, previous value of THISMONTH has been superseded
```

To delete a logical name, use the DEASSIGN command. Do not terminate the logical
name with a colon:

```
$ SHOW LOGICAL THISMONTH
  "THISMONTH" = PAYROLL$DISK:[ALBUQUERQUE.ENGINEERING.2002.SEPTEMBER]
(LNM$PROCESS_TABLE)
$ DEASSIGN THISMONTH
```

```
$ SHOW LOGICAL THISMONTH
%SHOW-S-NOTRAN, no translation for logical name THISMONTH
```

Predefined Logical Names

OpenVMS maintains a number of logical names equating to process- and job-specific devices and files, including, among others, the following:

- SYS$COMMAND—the device or file from which DCL accepts input data. For interactive processes, this is your terminal.

- SYS$ERROR—the device to which the system writes all informational and error messages. For interactive processes, this is your terminal. For batch jobs, this is the log file.

- SYS$INPUT—the device from which commands and data input are accepted. For interactive processes, it is usually your terminal. An exception is during execution of a command procedure, when it is temporarily assigned to the disk containing the procedure.

- SYS$OUTPUT—the device or file to which output data are written. For interactive processes, it is your terminal. For batch jobs, it is the log file.

- SYS$SYSDEVICE—the system disk, the disk from which OpenVMS was booted.

Logical Name Tables

All of the logical names described above are specific to your process or job. OpenVMS provides process wide, job wide, group wide, and system wide logical names by means of the PROCESS, JOB, GROUP, and SYSTEM logical name tables.

By separating logical names into separate tables, logical names may be created for the use of all system users or only those in a certain UIC group, or by individuals.

If you define a logical name in your process table with the same name as a system wide logical name, the value you define will take precedence over the system-defined value. It will not affect the value seen by other users of the system; they will continue to use the system wide value. When you deassign the process-level logical name, you will revert back to using the system wide value:

```
$ !
$ ! Show the value of logical name UTIL_DIR as defined system wide.
$ ! Any references I make to UTIL_DIR will reference this value.
$ !
```

```
$ show logical util_dir
    "UTIL_DIR" = "DKA100:[UTILITIES]" (LNM$SYSTEM_TABLE)
$ !
$ ! Now define my own UTIL_DIR as a process-private logical name
$ !
$ define util_dir dka400:[users.janet.utilities]
$ !
$ ! Any references I make to UTIL_DIR now will use my process-private
$ ! definition, although the system wide definition still exists:
$ !
$ show logical util_dir
    "UTIL_DIR" = "DKA400:[USERS.JANET.UTILITIES]" (LNM$PROCESS_TABLE)
    "UTIL_DIR" = "DKA100:[UTILITIES]" (LNM$SYSTEM_TABLE)
$ !
$ ! Deassign my process-private value
$ !
$ deassign util_dir
$ !
$ ! And now I have reverted to the system wide value:
$ !
$ show logical util_dir
    "UTIL_DIR" = "DKA100:[UTILITIES]" (LNM$SYSTEM_TABLE)
```

Logical Names with Concealed Translations

When a system message would include a logical name, its equivalence name is
usually shown instead. However, this translation can be concealed with the
/TRANSLATION_ATTRIBUTES=CONCEALED qualifier:

```
$ DEFINE MYDISK DKA100:
$ DIRECTORY MYDISK:[000000]

Directory DKA100:[000000]
(...)

$ DEFINE/TRANSLATION_ATTRIBUTES=CONCEALED MYDISK DKA100:
%DCL-I-SUPERSEDE, previous value of MYDISK has been superseded
$ DIRECTORY MYDISK:[000000]

Directory MYDISK:[000000]
(...)
```

Your LOGIN.COM File

You will probably come to appreciate your LOGIN.COM file as a very valuable
feature of OpenVMS as it can handle many tedious tasks and save many keystrokes.
You use it to customize your OpenVMS environment, define custom commands, or
perform other tasks automatically.

When you log into the system, OpenVMS locates the command procedure
LOGIN.COM in your home directory and executes it automatically.

Any commands you wish to execute each time you log in should be placed in your LOGIN.COM file. This may include commands to set up any software you use, the creation of symbols and logical names, or whatever else you desire.

For example, the author's LOGIN.COM assigns some command symbols, defines some logical names, performs setups for other software, such as language compilers, checks the amount of free space on disks, sets terminal characteristics, and checks the system for any device errors that may have occurred.

Aside from its automatic execution, LOGIN.COM is a normal command procedure in all respects and can be modified by any ordinary text editor. (See the sections on command procedures, symbols, logical names, and text editors elsewhere in this book.)

Here is a very simple LOGIN.COM to illustrate some possible uses.

```
$ !
$ ! A simple LOGIN.COM procedure.
$ ! This procedure is executed automatically whenever
$ ! its owner logs into the system.
$ !
$ ! The following line will cause LOGIN.COM to exit
$ ! without performing any work if this is a BATCH,
$ ! DETACHED, or NETWORK login.
$ !
$ if f$mode() .nes. "INTERACTIVE" then $ exit
$ !
$ ! The following commands will be executed when
$ ! the user logs onto the system interactively.
$ !
$ ! Set my terminal to insert rather than
$ ! overstrike mode.
$ !
$ set terminal/insert
$ !
$ ! Define some command symbols
$ !
$ del*ete :== delete/confirm/log
$ dsd     :== directory/size=all/date=modified
$ !
$ ! See how much of my disk-space quota I've used
$ !
```

```
$ show quota
$ !
$ exit
```

Keep in mind that a login does not mean only that a user logs in interactively at a terminal. Logins also include the initiation of batch jobs and processes created by OpenVMS to provide network services (e.g., FTP and POP3). These types of logins may not need all the functions your LOGIN.COM provides. In this case, executing LOGIN.COM would only waste time.

The example procedure above contains as its first non-comment line the following:

```
$ if f$mode() .nes. "INTERACTIVE" then $ exit
```

This line uses the f$mode() lexical function to discontinue the execution of LOGIN.COM for anything other than interactive logins (see Chapter 6 "The Digital Command Language", "Lexical Functions" and Chapter 9, "Command Procedures").

In many instances, non interactive logins can safely skip any commands you may have in LOGIN.COM, but there are exceptions. Suppose you have created a command procedure that uses symbols defined in LOGIN.COM in the place of DCL commands. Skipping LOGIN.COM would cause those symbols not to be recognized while in BATCH mode.

To avoid such problems, you may wish to use a format similar to the following for your own LOGIN.COM:

```
$ if f$MODE() .EQS. "INTERACTIVE" then $ goto INTER_ONLY
$ if f$MODE() .EQS. "BATCH" then $ goto BATCH_ONLY
$ if f$MODE() .EQS. "NETWORK" then $ goto NETWORK_ONLY
$ if f$MODE() .EQS. "OTHER" then $ goto OTHER_ONLY
$ !
$ INTER_ONLY:
$ !(commands appropriate to INTERACTIVE mode)
$ goto ALL_MODES
$ !
$ BATCH_ONLY:
$ !(commands appropriate to BATCH mode)
$ goto ALL_MODES
$ !
$ NETWORK_ONLY:
$ !(commands appropriate to NETWORK mode)
$ goto ALL_MODES
$ !
$ OTHER_ONLY:
$ !(commands appropriate to OTHER mode)
$ goto ALL_MODES
$ !
$ ALL_MODES:
```

```
$ !(commands appropriate for all modes)
$ exit
```

Preventing LOGIN.COM from Running

You may prevent LOGIN.COM from running during a login, or specify a different command procedure to run in its place. This is helpful if you have made some mistake in LOGIN.COM and would like to log in without executing it.

To do so, append the /[NO]COMMAND qualifier to your username while logging in:

```
Username: JONES                    Use LOGIN.COM by default

Username: JONES/COMMAND=ALT.COM  Uses ALT.COM rather than LOGIN.COM

Username: JONES/NOCOMMAND          Prevents any procedure from running
```

The system wide login procedure SYS$MANAGER:SYLOGIN.COM (or another file as specified by your system manager) will be executed even if you use /NOCOMMAND during login.

Broadcast Messages

OpenVMS sends short messages to your terminal under a variety of circumstances: when a batch or print job completes, when someone sends you mail, or when the system will be shut down, to name a few.

This general type of message is known as a *broadcast message*, even when there is a single recipient. If such a message is sent while you are at the DCL prompt, the message will be displayed on the next line after the prompt, and the prompt will be reissued below it.

The following example shows a broadcast message sent upon the completion of a batch job submitted earlier:

```
$
Job CLEANUP (queue SYS$BATCH, entry 78) completed
$
```

You may sometimes receive broadcast messages while running a full-screen program such as a text editor. The message will appear at the current location of the cursor, disrupting the display and making it appear as if the message is now part of your display.

Do not be concerned. Most programs, other than those specifically designed to catch and handle broadcast messages, are not aware that the message has been sent and are unaffected by them. The display has merely been disrupted by the appearance of the message.

Almost all full-screen programs have a refresh screen function, generally invoked by pressing CTRL/W or CTRL/R. Should a broadcast message appear in the middle of a full-screen display, simply refresh the display and continue working.

Disabling Broadcast Messages

You may disable broadcast messages via the SET TERMINAL/NOBROADCAST command. Be aware that you may miss important messages, such as system shutdown messages, if you disable broadcasts. To enable broadcast messages, use the DCL command SET TERMINAL/BROADCAST.

Using Subprocesses: The SPAWN Command

Since OpenVMS can support an arbitrary number of concurrent processes, you can create a temporary subprocess to perform time-consuming commands without tying up your terminal.

The SPAWN command creates a subprocess and optionally causes it to execute the command you specify.

The SPAWN command with no arguments creates a subprocess and attaches your terminal to it. Your original process hibernates while you use the subprocess:

```
$ SPAWN
%DCL-S-SPAWNED, process MIKE_1 spawned
%DCL-S-ATTACHED, terminal now attached to process MIKE_1
$
```

Any commands you issue will be carried out by the subprocess. To end the subprocess and return to your original process, log out:

```
$ LOGOUT
  Process MIKE_1 logged out at  7-OCT-2002 12:22:31.29
%DCL-S-RETURNED, control returned to process MIKE:
$
```

One might wonder how that feature alone is a benefit. The answer is that the SPAWN command does not disturb the process program (P0) region. Put another way, you can interrupt a long program by pressing CTRL/Y, then SPAWN a subprocess, enter some commands, log out, and continue the original program with the DCL CONTINUE command.

While the subprocess exists, you can switch your terminal between the parent process and the subprocess by using the ATTACH command:

```
$ SPAWN
%DCL-S-SPAWNED, process MIKE_1 spawned
%DCL-S-ATTACHED, terminal now attached to process MIKE_1
$ ATTACH MIKE
%DCL-S-RETURNED, control returned to process MIKE
$ ATTACH MIKE_1
%DCL-S-RETURNED, control returned to process MIKE_1
$ LOGOUT
  Process MIKE_1 logged out at  7-OCT-2002 12:38:59.78
%DCL-S-RETURNED, control returned to process MIKE:
```

The SPAWN command can also be used to pass a command to the subprocess. Let's say that you wanted to compile a very large C program, which might take a long time. You could create a subprocess to compile the program, as follows:

```
$ SPAWN/NOWAIT CC MYPROGRAM.C
%DCL-S-SPAWNED, process MIKE_1 spawned
$
```

When the compilation finishes, the subprocess will terminate.

The /NOWAIT qualifier specifies that your terminal should remain attached to your original process and not wait for the subprocess to finish. The subprocess compiles the program, while you are free to enter other commands. In this example, any output produced by the subprocess, such as compiler error messages, will be delivered to your terminal. To direct subprocess output to a file, add the /OUTPUT=*file* qualifier:

```
$ SPAWN/NOWAIT/OUTPUT=COMPILER.LST CC MYPROGRAM.C
```

You can discard subprocess output by directing it to the NULL device. The NULL device is an OpenVMS construct that acts like an I/O device, but discards any data sent to it. It is represented by the device name "NL:".

```
$ SPAWN/NOWAIT/OUTPUT=NL: PURGE [...]*.*
```

Use caution when discarding output in this way. Any useful messages will be permanently lost.

The PIPE Command

More recent versions of OpenVMS include a UNIX style PIPE command. PIPE allows you to perform multiple commands, command pipelining, and other functions.

You may perform multiple commands by separating them using semicolons:

```
$ PIPE command ; command
```

Command pipelining allows you to use the output of one command as the input for another. You specify PIPE command elements by separating then using vertical bars (pipe symbols). This example performs a SHOW SYSTEM command and then searches the output for the word server:

```
$ PIPE SHOW SYSTEM | SEARCH SYS$INPUT "SERVER"
0000008A AUDIT_SERVER     HIB    9  120421  0 00:26:08.43  1642266  174
0000008D SECURITY_SERVER  HIB   10   18124  0 00:28:48.99  5434137  110
0000008E TP_SERVER        HIB    9  535733  0 01:34:08.81  1818106  158
00000098 NAMED_SERVER     HIB    6  918580  0 00:40:35.06  1292097  659
0000009C WWW server 80    HIB    6  914949  0 01:30:22.63   765716  722  N
0001ED9D WEBSERVER_1      LEF    6      41  0 00:00:01.27    54170   43  S
000268AC SERVER_001A      LEF    6    4583  0 00:00:52.33    36800   43  N
00028633 SERVER_0013      LEF    6     803  0 00:00:06.49     3960  154  N
00027F36 SERVER_0010      LEF    6     303  0 00:00:02.58     1886  126  N
0001E3B8 SERVER_000E      LEF    6     321  0 00:00:02.51     1943  115  N
000001BC SERVER_000A      LEF    6  192107  0 00:39:33.46  1216898   43  N
```

Use HELP PIPE for further information about the capabilities of PIPE.

A Word About TCP/IP

Your OpenVMS system may be running a TCP/IP networking product. If so, you may take advantage of common TCP/IP utilities and functions such as FTP, Telnet, SSH, rlogin, SCP, RSH, and more.

Your OpenVMS system may be running one of three popular TCP/IP products, or one of several more obscure ones. The availability and usage of TCP/IP functions differs somewhat from product to product. Your system manager will be able to provide usage instructions for your particular product.

In addition to the normal TCP/IP utilities, you may be able to take advantage of the DIRECTORY/FTP and COPY/FTP commands. These commands perform DIRECTORY and COPY operations on a remote system via FTP without the need to use a dedicated FTP client program. See HELP COPY and HELP DIRECTORY for information on their use.

A Word About PERL

Your system may be equipped with PERL, a scripting language familiar to users of UNIX and certain other operating systems. Consult your system manager to determine whether PERL is installed on your system.

A complete description of the PERL language is beyond the scope of this book. However, many such books may be found at your local bookstore or online bookseller, and numerous PERL-related Web sites may be found with your favorite Internet search engine.

Adjusting Your Process Priority

Use SET PROCESS/PRIORITY=n, where n is a number between 0 and 15. This sets the base scheduling priority of your process, determining the amount of CPU attention it will receive. Processes with higher priorities are scheduled first. The default scheduling priority for most interactive processes is 4. You must hold the ALTPRI privilege to raise your priority above its default level, although anyone may lower his or her own priority. If you hold ALTPRI, you should nevertheless use caution when raising your priority, and you should never attempt to raise it above 15.

A user may choose to lower his priority if he were about to run a long, CPU-intensive program that might interfere with the CPU response of his other processes or those of other users.

You may also adjust the priority of your batch processes by placing a SET PROCESS /PRIORITY command in your batch command procedures, but this is not necessarily recommended. Batch processes usually have lower base priorities than interactive processes carefully determined by the system manager.

Please note that the system will respond sharply to even small changes in a process priority. Also, increasing the scheduling priority of a process that performs frequent I/O operations or generates large numbers of page faults will not result in as much benefit as one might expect. These processes are constrained by factors other than CPU performance and so will not respond to the same degree as other processes.

Adjusting Your Process Privileges

If your system manager has granted you elevated privileges, you should take care to use them responsibly. Your system manager can grant privileges in such a way as to be enabled by default (default privileges) or so that you must specifically enable them (authorized privileges).

Possessing elevated privileges implies that you can, by misuse of the privilege, interfere with the operation of the system. To avoid any accidental damage, it is recommended that you enable privileges only when needed, if practical.

Privileges are enabled and disabled with the following command:

```
$ SET PROCESS/PRIVILEGE=([NO]privilege_name,...)
```

Let's say that your system manager has granted you the GRPPRV privilege. This privilege allows you to access files belonging to other members of your UIC group through the SYSTEM category and to affect their processes. When the need arose to perform that type of file access, you could enable and disable the privilege in this way:

```
$ SET PROCESS/PRIVILEGE=GRPPRV
   (perform the necessary work)
$ SET PROCESS/PRIVILEGE=NOGRPPRV
```

Under normal circumstances, most users need only the TMPMBX and NETMBX privileges. To return to that state no matter what privileges are currently enabled, you may use the following command:

```
$ SET PROCESS/PRIVILEGE=(NOALL,TMPMBX,NETMBX)
```

NOALL first disables all privileges; then, TMPMBX and NETMBX are enabled. If your system manager has granted you default privileges that you do not always need, consider placing a command such as the one above in your LOGIN.COM file, enabling only the privileges you need at all times.

The OpenVMS PHONE Facility

The PHONE facility is a communications tool. It allows real-time text communication among users on the local OpenVMS node or other nodes on the DECnet network. You may find it similar to some of the messaging facilities popular on the Internet today, but OpenVMS PHONE predates them and has remained virtually unchanged since the early 1980s.

OpenVMS PHONE supports sessions among more than two users, but is used in that manner relatively infrequently. This section will describe how to use PHONE to communicate with one other user.

Starting PHONE

OpenVMS PHONE is started with the DCL command PHONE or PHONE *user*. If you include a username, PHONE immediately tries to reach that user. A broadcast message is sent to the user every 10 seconds announcing that you are calling. If the user is logged in at more than one terminal, a message is sent to all of his terminals.

If you do not specify a user, PHONE starts and presents you with the PHONE prompt, (historically known as the switch-hook character), which is a percent sign (%).

> **Note:** If your session is likely to include the default switch-hook character as part of the conversation, you may change the switch-hook character by starting PHONE with the /SWITCH_HOOK="*character*" qualifier. Pressing the switch-hook key during an active session will return you to the switch-hook prompt.

The display will look like the following:

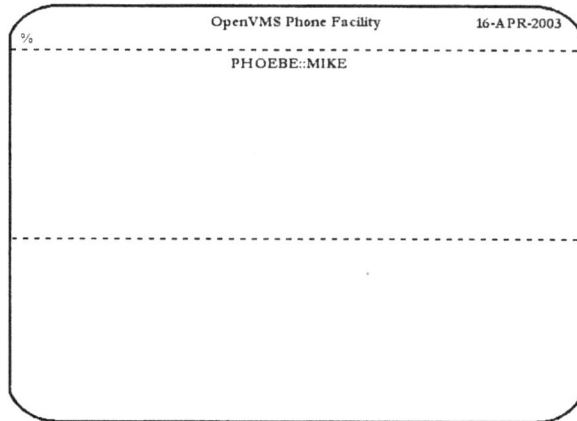

```
        OpenVMS Phone Facility          16-APR-2003
 %
- - - - - - - - - - - - - - - - - - - - - - - - - - -
                    PHOEBE::MIKE



- - - - - - - - - - - - - - - - - - - - - - - - - - -
```

Figure 7-3 OpenVMS PHONE

At the top is the command line. While PHONE is awaiting commands, your cursor will be located here, at the switch-hook character (%).

The rest of the screen is divided into two large fields. When a call is underway, your cursor will appear in the upper of the two fields. Keystrokes you type will appear there. Keystrokes the other party types will appear in the lower field.

Placing a Call

If you started PHONE specifying a username to call, a call attempt is made immediately.

While at the switch-hook prompt, you may enter DIAL *username* for a user logged into the same node, or DIAL *node::username* for a user on another DECnet node. For most usernames, you may omit DIAL and simply enter the username.

When a username is entered, PHONE will attempt to place the call. This consists of sending broadcast messages to that user's terminal(s) at 10-second intervals. If you receive no answer after some time, press CTRL/Z to cancel the call.

When the other party answers your call, his nodename and username will appear in the lower window. Anything typed by either party will now appear in the appropriate area of the screen.

Answering or Rejecting a Call

When someone is placing a PHONE call to you, you will see messages like the following every 10 seconds (your terminal must have BROADCAST enabled):

```
NODE::USER is phoning you on NODE      (hh:mm:ss)
```

These messages are repeated until you answer the call, reject the call, or the other party gives up.

To answer the call, enter PHONE ANSWER at the DCL prompt. Your cursor will be placed in the upper field, and you may begin typing immediately.

To reject the call, enter PHONE REJECT.

Terminating a Call

You may terminate a call by pressing CTRL/Z or the switch-hook character. This returns you to the switch-hook prompt. Entering EXIT at the switch-hook prompt or pressing CTRL/Z exits PHONE.

Chapter 8 — The OpenVMS HELP Facility

OpenVMS comes equipped with an extensive online HELP facility that you may use to learn what commands are available, what they do, and how to use them.

> **Note:** Third-party software that introduces new commands onto an OpenVMS system may or may not update the OpenVMS HELP database to include descriptions of its own commands.

Learning How To Use HELP

To learn about the HELP facility, enter HELP INSTRUCTIONS at the DCL prompt. A short tutorial appears describing how to find information about DCL commands.

Obtaining a List of Available Help Topics

To use the HELP facility to list the available commands, enter HELP at the DCL prompt. After a brief introduction, a list of topics appears from which you may select a particular command verb or topic. At the Topic? prompt, you may enter the name of a command, a listed topic, or the word HINTS if you are not sure of the command or topic you're seeking.

Obtaining HELP About a Particular Command

There is more than one way to get help about a particular command. Take the MOUNT command as an example. You may enter HELP MOUNT at the DCL prompt, or you may enter HELP and then enter MOUNT at the Topic prompt. A display similar to the following appears:

```
$ HELP MOUNT
MOUNT

     The Mount utility (MOUNT) allows you to make a disk or magnetic
     tape volume available for processing.

     Format

       MOUNT  device-name[:][,...] [volume-label[,...]]

             [logical-name[:]]


  Additional information available:
```

```
Parameters Usage_Summary          /ACCESSED  /ASSIST    /AUTOMATIC /BIND
/BLOCKSIZE /CACHE      /CLUSTER    /COMMENT   /CONFIRM   /COPY
/DATA_CHECK           /DENSITY    /EXTENSION /FOREIGN   /GROUP     /HDR3
/INCLUDE   /INITIALIZE=CONTINUATION          /LABEL     /MEDIA_FORMAT
/MESSAGE   /MOUNT_VERIFICATION    /MULTI_VOLUME          /OVERRIDE
/OWNER_UIC /PROCESSOR /PROTECTION            /QUOTA      /REBUILD
/RECORDSIZE           /SHADOW     /SHARE     /SUBSYSTEM /SYSTEM
/UCS_SEQUENCE         /UNDEFINED_FAT         /UNLOAD    /WINDOWS    /WRITE
MOUNT_Examples

MOUNT Subtopic? _
```

The preceding display shows the first HELP screen for the MOUNT command. A brief
description of the MOUNT command is followed by its general command line format.
Finally, a list of subtopics is shown, from which you may select descriptions of each
qualifier or example of MOUNT command usage. Enter the name of any item to see
additional information. The following example requests information about the
/SYSTEM qualifier:

```
MOUNT Subtopic? /SYSTEM

MOUNT

  /SYSTEM

      Makes the volume public, that is, available to all users of the
      system, as long as the UIC-based volume protection allows them
      access.

      Format

        /SYSTEM

    Additional information available:

    Examples

MOUNT /SYSTEM Subtopic?
```

The HELP database consists of multiple levels of detail, each topic having its own tree
of subtopics. Note that the following example ends with another subtopic prompt,
offering the viewer the opportunity to see examples of the MOUNT/SYSTEM
command:

```
MOUNT /SYSTEM Subtopic? Example

MOUNT

  /SYSTEM

    Examples

        1.$ MOUNT/NOMESSAGE/SYSTEM DUA1: SLIP SACH
```

```
        This command mounts the volume labeled SLIP on DUA1 with mount
        messages disabled. The volume is made available systemwide.
        MOUNT also assigns the logical name SACH.

   2.$ MOUNT/SYSTEM/BIND=MASTER_PAY -
     _$ DB1:,DB2:,DB3:    PAYVOL1,PAYVOL2,PAYVOL3

        This command creates the volume set named MASTER_PAY consisting
        of the initialized volumes labeled PAYVOL1, PAYVOL2, and
        PAYVOL3. These volumes are mounted physically on the devices
        named DB1, DB2, and DB3, respectively. The volume PAYVOL1 is
        the root volume of the set.

        The volumes are mounted as system volumes to make them
        available to all users.

MOUNT /SYSTEM Subtopic?
```

Returning from Subtopics

You may return to the previous level by pressing ENTER. At each level, you may
select a topic appropriate to that level or press ENTER to travel up another level.
Pressing CTRL/Z at any time exits HELP. Pressing ENTER from the top level also
exits the HELP facility:

```
MOUNT /SYSTEM Subtopic? [ENTER]
MOUNT Subtopic? [ENTER]
Topic? [ENTER]
$
```

Chapter 9 — Command Procedures

Command procedures are text files containing DCL commands that DCL executes sequentially. Much like a program, command procedures provide for branching, subroutines, comparisons, and variables (in the form of symbols).

Command procedures may be executed directly by an interactive user, or they may be submitted to a batch queue for execution at a specified time.

```
$ !
$ ! EXAMPLE1.COM, an example command procedure.
$ !
$ show time        ! Display the system time
$ wait 00:00:10    ! Wait for 10 seconds
$ show time        ! Display the time again
$ exit             ! And we're done.
```

This procedure, called EXAMPLE1.COM, displays the current time, waits 10 seconds, and then displays the time again. When executed, this procedure produces output like the following:

```
$ @EXAMPLE1
  29-OCT-2002 17:15:42
  29-OCT-2002 17:15:52
```

Note that only messages generated by the commands are shown. To cause each line of your procedure to be echoed (displayed) as it is executed, place the SET VERIFY command in your procedure or issue the SET VERIFY command at your terminal before executing the procedure. Use SET NOVERIFY to suppress it.

```
$ SET VERIFY
$ @EXAMPLE1
$ !
$ ! EXAMPLE1.COM, an example command procedure.
$ !
$ show time        ! Display the system time
  29-OCT-2002 17:15:42
$ wait 00:00:10    ! Wait for 10 seconds
$ show time        ! Display the time again
  29-OCT-2002 17:15:52
$ exit             ! And we're done.
```

The first example of a command procedure most users will see is their personal LOGIN.COM procedure. As discussed earlier, each user has her own LOGIN.COM that is executed automatically at each login. LOGIN.COM can perform almost any function, but most users use it to adjust the OpenVMS environment to their own personal preferences. Such customizations include setting terminal characteristics, defining symbols for common commands, and so on.

Command procedures can range from the very simple to the very complex. One procedure might have two or three commands that define symbols, whereas another might be several hundred lines in length and perform complex software builds. Even the simplest command procedures can save time by grouping frequently used sequences of commands together.

Command procedures allow the use of flow-control commands, such as GOTO, GOSUB/RETURN, and CALL, allowing you to create a command procedure that has many of the features of a compiled program. These commands allow the execution of different parts of the procedure in response to conditions you specify.

The following sections will show you how to create and use command procedures, both interactively from your terminal and as batch processes.

Creating a Command Procedure

A command procedure can be created by using any text editor (e.g., EDT or EVE). Place one DCL command per line except when splitting long commands onto multiple lines, placing input data into the procedure, or including comments. Each of these variations is shown subsequently.

Naming Your Procedures

Command procedures (as with all files) should be given names that indicate their functions. The default file type is .COM. Although it is possible to create a command procedure with a different file type, it is strongly recommended that you do not do so, because you would have to include its type when you execute the file. Examples of command procedure names are TERMINAL_SETUP.COM and COMPILE.COM.

Entering Commands

In command procedures, each new command must begin with a dollar sign ($).[1] The only lines that should not begin with a dollar sign are the continuations of long commands and input data lines. Many users include a space between the dollar sign and the command. This practice is optional, but is shown in this book.

---

1. It is technically possible to omit the dollar sign, but only under a strict set of circumstances. It is not good practice and should be avoided.

After the dollar sign, enter the DCL command as if you were typing it at the DCL command prompt. It is recommended that you type out each command verb, parameter, keyword, and qualifier in its entirety. Command procedures often remain in use for years. During that time, additional commands may be added to OpenVMS, some of which may cause earlier acceptable abbreviations to become ambiguous. Using complete commands also aids in the readability of your procedures. For these reasons, it is considered good form to avoid abbreviations in command procedures.

To split a command line onto multiple lines, follow the normal rule of ending the incomplete line with a hyphen. Do not precede continuation lines by a dollar sign.

As with interactive DCL commands, anything after an exclamation mark is a comment and will be ignored by DCL.

The following example shows commands (1), comments (2), and a command split across multiple lines (3):

```
$ directory /date=(created,modified) data.lst            (1)
$ !                                                       (2)
$ ! Sort the file                                         (2)
$ !                                                       (2)
$ sort data.lst * - ! A comment may be placed here too    (3)
  /key=(position:1,size:10)/key=(position:12,size:3,descending) -  (3)
  /key=(position:28,size:2)/key=(position:16,size:10)     (3)
$ exit                                                     (1)
```

Making Your Command Procedure Self-Documenting

As a professional software engineer, the author can tell you with great conviction that you should take the time to place comments into your procedures. Some of your procedures will be in use for a long time. A few concise comments placed in your procedure will benefit you greatly six months later when you wish to modify it. A few months after you write a poorly commented program or procedure, your memory of it may be dim enough to cause some difficulty in reading your own code. Good commenting is also a courtesy to anyone else who may eventually need to modify your procedure.

To make your command procedures clear, one good approach is to break your procedure down into small units, about 20 lines or fewer per unit. Before each unit, place one or two comment lines that describe in plain language what the unit does. Later, when you must come back to modify the procedure (as always happens), you will not have to spend as much time deciphering what the code does.

The command procedures presented in this book illustrate this guideline.

Executing a Command Procedure Interactively

To execute a command procedure, precede its name with an at sign (@) as the first element on a command line:

```
$ @COMPILE
```

The example above executes the procedure COMPILE.COM in the current directory. Some other examples are:

```
$ @DKB400:[JONES]ACCOUNT
$ @[.REPORTS]SUMMARY.COM
$ @[-]SETUP
```

The at sign (@) has a special meaning in DCL. Its actual meaning is "begin accepting input from this location." DCL opens the file and reads its contents, interpreting each line as a command. When the end of the procedure (or an EXIT command) is reached, DCL reverts back to its previous input source, your terminal.

A command procedure may itself execute a command procedure. Consider this example:

```
$ !
$ ! This command procedure executes other command procedures
$ !
$ @procedure1
$ @procedure2
$ exit
```

When the command procedure above executes, it will first execute PROCEDURE1.COM, then PROCEDURE2.COM.

Command Levels

Command levels are environments defining the scope of local symbols.

While typing commands at your terminal, you are at command level 0. When you execute a command procedure directly from the DCL prompt, it executes at command level 1. If that procedure executes another procedure, the second procedure will be at command level 2, and so forth. When each procedure ends, you return to the previous command level. So, when you arrive back at the DCL prompt, you are back at command level 0. There are 32 command levels.

Using the CALL command in a command procedure (discussed later in this chapter) also increases the command level for the duration of the subroutine.

Remember that each command level has a separate set of local symbols, but global symbols are accessible from all command levels. Within a command level, local symbols take precedence over global symbols of the same name. (See "DCL Symbols", "Symbol Scope" in Chapter 6, "The Digital Command Language.")

Local symbols defined at one command level are visible at higher-numbered command levels, but modifications to them are restricted to that command level. For example, if you create a local symbol at the DCL command level and then execute a procedure, the symbol will be present in the command procedure. If you modify the value of the symbol from within the procedure, it will revert to its original value when the procedure ends.

In the following example, the DCL prompt has been changed to DCL> to differentiate commands typed at the DCL prompt from the lines in the command procedure:

```
DCL> SET VERIFY ! From DCL command level
DCL> TESTVAL = 10
DCL> @SHOW_TESTVAL
$ !
$ ! Command procedure SHOW_TESTVAL begins...
$ !
$ write sys$output "Testval: ''testval'"
Testval: 10
$ TESTVAL = 1000
$ write sys$output "Testval: ''testval'"
Testval: 1000
$ !
$ ! Command procedure SHOW_TESTVAL ends...
$ !
$ exit
DCL> write sys$output "Testval: ''testval'" ! Back at the DCL prompt
Testval: 10
```

Executing a Command Procedure As a Batch Job

Command procedures may be submitted to a batch queue for immediate or delayed execution. When the batch job executes, it will run under your username and, by default, it will produce a log file recording its execution.

The SUBMIT command is used to create a batch job.(See "Working with Queues" in Chapter 7, "The User Environment," for information on submitting batch jobs.)

Reading and Writing Files From a Procedure

You may use command procedures to read existing text files and create new ones. Although it is possible to process indexed files with command procedures, only text files will be discussed in this book.

The following DCL commands are used to process files. Note that these commands may also be used from the DCL prompt.

OPEN *logical_name file*. Before you can read or write a file, you must open it. OPEN /READ opens an existing file for read access. OPEN/WRITE creates a new file. OPEN/APPEND allows you to add data to the end of an existing file. The /SHARE or /SHARE=WRITE qualifier specifies that other users may open the file for read or write access. If you specify /SHARE=READ, other users are allowed to read the file while you have it open, but not to write to it. The /ERROR=*label* qualifier branches to the specified label if a problem occurs. The logical name is used to identify the file in subsequent READ, WRITE, and CLOSE commands.

CLOSE *logical_name*. This closes a file you had previously opened.

READ *logical_name symbol*. This reads the next record from the file specified by *logical_name* and assigns it to the symbol *symbol*. Use /END=*label* to branch to the specified label on reaching the end of the file. Use /ERROR=*label* to branch to the specified label if a problem occurs.

WRITE *logical_name symbol*. This writes the value specified by *symbol* to the file specified by *logical_name*. Use /ERROR=*label* to branch to the specified label if a problem occurs.

The following example creates a file, writes a few lines to it, and then reads the file back again:

```
$ !
$ ! First, create a file and populate it
$ ! with a few records.
$ !
$ write sys$output "creating file..."
$ open/write testfile demo.txt /error=CANT_OPEN_WRITE
$ write testfile /error=writeerror -
        "This is the first line in the file"
$ write testfile /error=writeerror -
        "This is the second line in the file"
$ write testfile /error=writeerror -
        "This is the third and last line in the file"
$ close testfile
$ !
$ ! Now open the file and read its contents
```

```
$ !
$ write sys$output "reading file back:"
$ open/read inputfile demo.txt /error=CANT_OPEN_READ
$ READLOOP:
$   read inputfile inrecord /end=NO_MORE_DATA /error=READERROR
$   write sys$output inrecord
$ goto READLOOP
$ !
$ ! The READ command will branch here when the
$ ! entire file has been read:
$ !
$ NO_MORE_DATA:
$ close inputfile
$ !
$ exit ! End the procedure. Very important: If this
$ !      EXIT is omitted, execution will continue into
$ !      the code below, causing problems.
$ !
$ !-------------------------------------------
$ !
$ ! The OPEN/WRITE command will branch here if the
$ ! file cannot be opened.
$ !
$ CANT_OPEN_WRITE:
$ write sys$output "Cannot open file for writing."
$ exit
$ !
$ ! The OPEN/READ command will branch here if the
$ ! file cannot be opened.
$ !
$ CANT_OPEN_READ:
$ write sys$output "Cannot open file for reading."
$ exit
$ !
$ ! The WRITE command will branch here if the
$ ! file cannot be written.
$ !
$ WRITEERROR:
$ write sys$output "Cannot write the file."
$ close testfile
$ exit
$ !
$ ! The READ command will branch here if the
$ ! file cannot be read.
$ !
$ READERROR:
$ write sys$output "Cannot read the file."
$ close inputfile
$ exit
```

When executed, the procedure produces the following output:

```
$ @FILES
```

```
creating file...
reading file back:
This is the first line in the file
This is the second line in the file
This is the third and last line in the file
```

If you omit the error-handling capabilities shown in the example above, the command procedure will produce an error message and abort if an error occurs, but the example becomes much simpler:

```
$ !
$ ! First, create a file and populate it
$ ! with some text.
$ !
$ open/write testfile demo.txt
$ write testfile "This is the first line in the file"
$ write testfile "This is the second line in the file"
$ write testfile "This is the third and last line in the file"
$ close testfile
$ !
$ ! Now open the file and read its contents.
$ !
$ open/read inputfile demo.txt
$ readloop:
$   read inputfile inrecord /end=NO_MORE_DATA
$   write sys$output inrecord
$ goto readloop
$ !
$ ! The READ command will branch here when the
$ ! entire file has been read.
$ !
$ NO_MORE_DATA:
$ close inputfile
$ exit
$ !
```

Use caution if you omit the error-handling capabilities. If an error occurs and the procedure aborts, any file open at that time will remain open at the DCL command level. You should attempt to manually close any files the procedure might have opened:

```
$ CLOSE TESTFILE
$ CLOSE INPUTFILE
```

Getting Input Data into Command Procedures

Some programs you may wish to execute from within command procedures may require input from the terminal keyboard while they run. Alternatively, your command procedure may wish to solicit keyboard input for its own purposes, not to be passed to a program. These are separate issues with separate solutions.

First, input to programs will be discussed, then input to the procedure itself.

Passing Embedded Data into Programs

Some programs require keyboard input while running. So long as a program accepts data in the form of complete lines, DCL allows you to pass data to such programs. Programs that accept one keystroke at a time may or may not work properly from within a procedure.

To pass lines of text to a program, simply insert the data lines into the command procedure following the command that executes the program. Do not precede these lines with a dollar sign. When DCL encounters the next command (a line preceded by a dollar sign), it notifies the program that there is no more data by signaling an end-of-file (EOF) condition.

The following is an example using the OpenVMS MAIL facility with data embedded in a command procedure:

```
$ !
$ ! Send mail to MIKE
$ !
$ mail
send/subject="Message from a procedure" (In response to "MAIL>" prompt)
mike  (In response to "To:" prompt)
This message was sent from within a command procedure. (Line in message)
$ ! (Next line starting with a dollar sign terminates input)
$ exit
```

Passing Keyboard Data into Programs

Sometimes, you may want a command procedure to run a program that requires input directly from the terminal keyboard.

Most programs accept input from SYS$INPUT, a logical name that usually identifies your terminal. However, when running a command procedure, SYS$INPUT identifies the disk device containing the procedure. How, then, do we cause a program running from within a procedure to accept input from the keyboard?

When executing a procedure, the logical name SYS$COMMAND still identifies the terminal. In your procedure, you may temporarily assign the value of SYS$COMMAND to SYS$INPUT. This allows a program running from within a procedure to receive keyboard input:

```
$ !
$ ! This example allows keyboard input to a program running under a command
$ ! procedure.  We temporarily override the normal input stream by the
$ ! following DEFINE command, causing input to come temporarily from the
$ ! terminal keyboard.
$ !
$ define/user_mode sys$input sys$command ! make the keyboard SYS$INPUT
$ edit/edt somefile.txt ! The EDT program will receive from the keyboard
$ !
$ ! (The /USER_MODE qualifier above automatically cancels the definition
$ ! at the end of the EDT session.)
$ !
$ exit
```

Reading Keyboard Input into Procedures

Sometimes your command procedures may wish to read keyboard data for their own use, not to be passed to a program. You may use either of two methods for this: READ or INQUIRE. READ may be used to read data from a file or from the keyboard (when you specify SYS$COMMAND as the source). INQUIRE reads from SYS$COMMAND only. Each of them assigns the keyboard input to a symbol. Both are shown in the following example:

```
$ !
$ ! Show two different methods for reading keyboard data.  Both of these
$ ! methods assign the string to a local symbol.
$ !
$ ! First, INQUIRE.  INQUIRE converts your input to upper case (unless in
$ ! quotes) and compresses multiple spaces.  It supplies a colon at the end of
$ ! the prompt unless you use /NOPUNCTUATION.  If you omit the prompt,
$ ! the symbol name will be used by default; in this case, "NAME:."
$ !
$ write sys$output "The INQUIRE command:"
$ INQUIRE name "Please enter your name "
$ show symbol name
$ !
$ ! Now a READ from SYS$COMMAND is shown.  This does not convert your input
$ ! to upper case or compress it.  It preserves quotes, if present, in the
$ ! input data.
$ !
$ write sys$output "The READ command:"
$ READ sys$command name /prompt="Please enter your name : "
$ show symbol name
$ !
$ exit
```

When executed, this procedure produces the following:

```
$ @KEYBOARD_EXAMPLE
The INQUIRE command:
Please enter your name : Mike        Duffy
  NAME = "MIKE DUFFY"
The READ command:
Please enter your name : Mike        Duffy
  NAME = "Mike        Duffy"
```

Command Procedure Parameters

Just as many DCL commands accept parameters, so too can command procedures. Command procedures can accept up to eight parameters on the DCL command line. These parameters are automatically assigned to pre-defined symbols called P1 through P8.

The following procedure illustrates this point:

```
$ !
$ ! PARAM.COM, an example command procedure demonstrating parameters.
$ ! It will echo up to two parameters, and ignore the third and subsequent
$ ! parameters.
$ !
$ if P1 .eqs. "" then $ write sys$output "There are no parameters."
$ !
$ if P1 .nes. "" then $ write sys$output "P1: " + P1
$ if P2 .nes. "" then $ write sys$output "P2: " + P2
$ !
$ if P3 .nes. "" then $ write sys$output "Extra parameters ignored."
$ exit
```

When executed, this procedure produces the following:

```
$ @PARAM
There are no parameters
$ @PARAM 4
P1: 4
$ @PARAM TWO PARAMETERS
P1: TWO
P2: PARAMETERS
$ @PARAM TOO MANY PARAMETERS
P1: TOO
P2: MANY
Extra parameters ignored.
$
```

Labels

A label marks a certain line in a command procedure. These labels can be used as targets for GOTO, GOSUB, and CALL commands or certain other commands capable of branching, such as READ/END or OPEN/ERROR.

It is possible for a single command line to include both a label and a command, but for the sake of clarity, you may wish to place a label alone on a line.

A label starts at the beginning of a line, may not contain blanks, and ends with a colon (:). You should give a label a name that provides some information about why it is being used. This helps with the clarity of the code.

The author usually follows the convention of typing labels in upper case and most other commands in lower case. This is a completely personal matter, and you may choose any method that works for you.

Labels are used in branching, which is discussed next.

Branching

Branching means jumping from one place in a command procedure to another. Labels (described above) provide the destination for a branch.

There are four main ways to branch; GOTO, GOSUB, CALL, and certain other commands that allow branching when they encounter certain conditions. Each is described separately.

GOTO

The GOTO command branches directly to a label and causes execution to resume at that location. GOTO works in either direction, forward or backward, within the command procedure. Its format is as follows:

```
$ GOTO label       ! branches directly to a label
$ IF condition THEN $ GOTO label   ! A conditional branch.
```

The following example illustrates a label being used as the target of a GOTO command:

```
$ !
$ ! This command procedure illustrates the use of GOTO and labels.  Notice
$ ! that when branching to a label, you do not terminate its name with a
$ ! colon.
$ !
$ goto SKIP_SOME_LINES
$ !
$ ! These intervening lines will not be executed due to the GOTO above.
$ ! The GOTO command will work in the reverse direction as well as forward.
$ !
$ show time  ! will not be executed.
$ directory  ! will not be executed.
$ !
$ SKIP_SOME_LINES:  ! execution resumes here.
$ !
$ ! The following lines will be executed:
$ !
$ show logical SYS$LOGIN
$ show device d
$ exit
```

GOSUB

The GOSUB command is used in conjunction with RETURN to allow the execution of subroutines within a DCL command procedure. GOSUB transfers control to a label, where execution resumes. Execution continues until a RETURN command is encountered. RETURN causes control to be passed to the line following the most recently executed GOSUB command.

```
$ !
$ ! This example shows the control flow of a GOSUB/RETURN pair.
$ !
$ write sys$output "This line is the FIRST one displayed."
$ !
$ gosub DEMO_SUBROUTINE
$ !
$ write sys$output "This line is the THIRD one displayed."
$ !
$ exit  ! This EXIT command is very important...
$ !
$ ! Without the EXIT command above, execution would continue
$ ! into the subroutine below.  DCL would only detect an error upon
$ ! reaching the RETURN command for which there had been no
$ ! corresponding GOSUB command.
$ !
$ DEMO_SUBROUTINE:
$ write sys$output "This line is the SECOND one displayed."
$ return
```

CALL

The CALL command provides another method of calling subroutines within your procedures. CALL was added to DCL some years after GOSUB and is a more sophisticated method for calling subroutines. It allows parameters to be passed to the subroutine and allows subroutine output to be directed to a file.

To use CALL, you must declare a subroutine by placing a label into your procedure and marking it as the start of a subroutine. After the label, place the commands that make up the subroutine. Finally, end the subroutine by an EXIT command and then an ENDSUBROUTINE command:

```
$ label: SUBROUTINE
   .
   . (commands)
   .
$ EXIT
$ ENDSUBROUTINE
```

Your subroutine may be declared before or after the CALL commands that invoke it.

To use the subroutine, use the CALL command, specifying any parameters you may wish to pass to the subroutine.

Within the subroutine, the symbol names P1 through P8 refer to the parameters passed by the CALL statement, not to the overall procedure parameters:

```
$ CALL [/output=file] [param1, param2, ... param8]
```

The following example illustrates the passing of parameters to a subroutine as well as redirecting subroutine output to a file:

```
$ !
$ ! First, declare a subroutine.  It will not actually be executed
$ ! until a CALL statement references it.
$ !
$ SUB1: SUBROUTINE
$ write sys$output "''p1'"
$ EXIT
$ ENDSUBROUTINE
$ !
$ ! Now invoke the subroutine SUB1 twice.
$ ! The first time, its output will be displayed to
$ ! the terminal.  The second time, its output will be
$ ! written to the file SUB_EXAMPLE.TXT
$ !
$ call SUB1 "This is the first call"
$ !
$ call SUB1/output=sub_example.txt "This is the second call"
$ !
$ exit
```

When executed, it produces the following output. Note that the second CALL statement directs output to the file SUB_EXAMPLE.TXT:

```
$ @CALL
This is the first call
$ TYPE SUB_EXAMPLE.TXT
This is the second call
```

Remember, using CALL results in a higher-numbered command level for the duration of the subroutine. Local symbols already in existence can be seen, but if you modify them, they will revert back to their original values at the end of the subroutine. Use global symbols if you must modify symbols from within subroutines.

Other DCL Commands That Branch

Certain DCL commands (e.g., OPEN, READ, WRITE, and CLOSE) have the ability to branch when they detect a certain condition. For example, OPEN can branch to a label if it is not able to open the requested file. READ can branch on reaching the end of the input file or on an error reading the record:

```
$ !
$ ! This example shows the branching ability of certain DCL commands
$ !
$ records_read = 0
$ !
$ open/read infile payroll.txt /error=CANT_OPEN
$ READLOOP:
$   read infile inrecord /end=NO_MORE_DATA  ! reads the next record
$   records_read = records_read + 1         ! keep track of records read
$ goto READLOOP                             ! goes back for the next record
$ !
$ ! The following label will only be reached when the READ instruction
$ ! detects the end of the input file.
$ !
$ NO_MORE_DATA:
$ write sys$output "End of file reached. Records read: ''records_read'"
$ close infile
$ exit
$ !
$ ! The following label will only be reached if the file cannot be opened;
$ ! perhaps the file does not exist, or you have insufficient permissions
$ ! to open it.
$ !
$ CANT_OPEN:
$ !
$ ! Save the value of the OpenVMS reserved symbol $STATUS.  This contains
$ ! the reason for the failure.  See the section "handling errors," later,
$ ! for details.
$ !
$ savestat = $status
$ if (savestat .gt. %x10000000) then $ savestat = savestat - %x10000000
$ write sys$output "Cannot open input file, status: ''savestat':"
$ !
$ ! Use SAVESTAT with the exit command.  This will generate an error message
$ ! appropriate to the exact error that occurred.  The status code will
$ ! also be passed to the next higher command level.
$ !
$ exit savestat
```

When executed, this procedure produces output like the following:

```
$ @COUNT_RECORDS
End of file reached. Records read: 329
```

Should an error occur, the error-handling capabilities built into the procedure will show you the cause of the problem:

```
$ @COUNT_RECORDS
Cannot open input file, status: 98962:
%RMS-E-FNF, file not found
```

The section entitled "Handling Errors" (discussed later) contains information about additional methods to detect errors and take appropriate action.

More Advanced IF Commands

The simple form of the IF command was introduced in Chapter 6, "The Digital Command Language." Within command procedures, more complex IF commands are available.

Command procedures allow blocks of multiple conditional commands by the use of IF, THEN, ELSE, and ENDIF. The following example illustrates several ways to execute lines of code based on the results of comparisons:

```
$ !
$ ! To execute a single command if a condition
$ ! is true (at the DCL prompt or within a command
$ ! procedure):
$ !
$ IF expression THEN $ command
$ !
$ ! To branch to another location if a condition
$ ! is true (within command procedures only):
$ !
$ IF expression THEN $ GOTO label   ! See "Branching"
$ IF expression THEN $ GOSUB label  ! See "Branching"
$ IF expression THEN $ CALL label   ! See "Branching"
$ !
$ ! To execute multiple commands if a condition
$ ! is true (available in command procedures only).
$ ! Indentation is optional, but shown for clarity:
$ !
$ IF expression
$ THEN
$   one or more commands...
$ ENDIF
$ !
$ ! To execute one set of commands if a condition
$ ! is true, and another if it is false (in command
$ ! procedures only):
$ !
$ IF expression
$ THEN
$   one or more commands...
$ ELSE
$   one or more commands...
$ ENDIF
$ !
```

Handling Errors

DCL provides several mechanisms for detecting and handling errors that may occur during the execution of a command procedure. This section describes the $STATUS and $SEVERITY symbols and the SET ON and ON commands.

In addition, certain DCL commands including OPEN, READ, and WRITE can branch to a label upon certain conditions (see the section "Other DCL Commands That Branch," above).

The ON Command

This command directs DCL to take action depending on the severity of an error or interruption encountered during the execution of a command procedure. It takes effect at the point in the procedure at which it is encountered and is overridden by any subsequent ON commands as they are encountered.

The general format is

```
$ ON condition THEN $ action
```

You may specify actions depending on whether a WARNING, ERROR, or SEVERE_ERROR occurs, or when the user types CTRL/Y (interrupt).

Following the occurrence of an error with equal or greater severity than the level specified, the requested action will be carried out.

Some examples are as follows:

```
$ on warning then $ continue
$ on warning then $ goto ERROR_HANDLER
$ on error then $ exit
$ on control_y then $ goto CTRLY_HANDLER
```

The SET ON Command

During the execution of a command procedure, you may sometimes wish to ignore certain kinds of errors. For example, one line of a command procedure might delete a temporary file generated by a previous run. Suppose no such file exists?

The absence of that file may be perfectly normal, but DCL will not automatically know that. DCL would normally consider it an error and terminate the execution of your command procedure. Thus, DCL needs some method to suspend detection of errors for a short time.

The SET ON command enables error detection; SET NOON (set no on) disables it. The portion of our command procedure devoted to deleting temporary files would look like this:

```
$ !
$ ! Delete temporary files from yesterday's run.
$ !
$ set noon              ! Temporarily disable detection of errors.
$ delete/log []*.TMP;*  ! Delete the files, if any.
$ set on                ! Re-enable error detection.
$ !
```

$STATUS and $SEVERITY

For even finer-grained control over DCL error handling, DCL maintains the built-in symbols $SEVERITY and $STATUS. After each DCL command, these symbols contain information about the success or failure of the command that just finished.

$SEVERITY will hold one of the following values:

1—The command finished with NORMAL status (was successful).

3—The command finished with INFORMATIONAL status (was successful).

0—The command finished with WARNING status.

2—The command finished with ERROR status.

4—The command finished with SEVERE_ERROR status.

$STATUS will contain the exact status value from the command. Odd values indicate success, and even values indicate failure. The information contained in $SEVERITY is duplicated in the low three bits of $STATUS. You may check $STATUS against specific return values or simply for a severity level.

For example, place one of these lines directly after the DCL command you wish to check. "Action" can be almost anything, including GOTO or EXIT. This list does not contain all possible combinations:

```
$ IF .NOT. $SEVERITY THEN $ action  ! WARNING or worse
$ IF $SEVERITY .EQ. 4 THEN $ action ! $severity = 4: SEVERE_ERROR.
$ IF .NOT. ($STATUS .AND. 1) THEN $ action  ! Any WARNING or worse
$ IF $STATUS .EQ. exact_value THEN $ action ! Checks for specific status.
```

Chapter 10 — System Security

This chapter explains some of the ways OpenVMS attempts to ensure system security. It is important to note that implementing perfect security is impractical, if not impossible. A system with minimal security is the easiest to use, but also the easiest to misuse. On the other hand, a system with very strict security is difficult to misuse, but also makes it difficult for authorized users to perform their work. Furthermore, authorized users who either accidentally or intentionally misuse the system cause the majority of security problems.

This chapter will introduce some of the features of OpenVMS that try to provide a secure, yet usable environment.

What Is System Security?

When asked that question, many people envision teenage "crackers" spending late nights attempting to break into systems halfway across the world. This is certainly part of the story, but by no means all of it.

Hackers Versus Crackers

The word *hacker* is currently being fought over (although the war may already be lost.) It has historically meant a particularly skilled user and hardly ever meant someone with harmful intentions. A useful program, often of the quick-and-dirty type, was referred to as "a nice hack." During the past two decades, it has come to mean, in the minds of many, only those individuals seeking to penetrate system security. To those familiar with the history of the terms, *cracker* is a more appropriate term for these individuals.

In the past, the present, and likely well into the future, system security has faced more danger from authorized users of a system than from strangers, Internet access notwithstanding. Authorized users have already cleared many hurdles a cracker faces: obtaining the name and/or network address of a system, a username, a password, knowledge about its operating system, and, perhaps, what kinds of data it contains.

A well-designed computer system must take many things into account. It is impossible to provide total security, and systems attempting to do so typically make it difficult for legitimate users to do their jobs. Even so, unscrupulous users may intentionally compromise data to which they are allowed legitimate access.

An authorized user might intentionally violate system security, for instance, by selling medical records or drivers-license information stored on a computer at that user's place of employment. On the other hand, an honest user might accidentally issue a command that could erase important data.

To its credit, OpenVMS has a more solid security system than most commercial operating systems, comparing quite favorably with the systems against which it competes.

That being said, good system security still depends greatly on an informed user community. The remainder of this chapter explains some of the OpenVMS security features. This knowledge may help you notice suspicious activities and allow you to contribute to a secure system environment.

Logging out of the System

When you are finished using the system or when you leave your terminal unattended, log out. Logging out is an essential aspect of system security. Leaving a terminal unattended is a frighteningly efficient way to defeat many of the carefully designed security features of OpenVMS. Seeing an unattended terminal, someone could easily approach your terminal and steal or destroy sensitive information. The intruder could examine sensitive files, e-mail them around the world, or damage or delete them.

Many users may think, "I don't have any access to sensitive information, so leaving my terminal unattended can't hurt," but it's not as simple as that. A skilled intruder may be able to take advantage of seemingly innocuous information, such as learning the names of other machines on the network, usernames of other users, or an almost unimaginable number of other details.

Your system manager may have installed software that automatically logs users off after a certain period of inactivity. If so, you should not attempt to defeat this software by making your idle process appear to be attended.

To log out of the system, use the LOGOUT or LOGOUT/FULL command. Note that the terms *log off* and *log out* may be used interchangeably, but the OpenVMS terminology is *log out*:

```
$ LOGOUT
   MIKE           logged out at 12-DEC-2002 19:07:39.58
```
or
```
$ LOGOUT/FULL
   MIKE         logged out at 12-DEC-2002 19:08:52.31
   Accounting information:
   Buffered I/O count:            127      Peak working set size:    1771
   Direct I/O count:               50      Peak page file size:      5955
   Page faults:                 10417      Mounted volumes:             0
   Charged CPU time:       0 00:00:04.80   Elapsed time:     0 00:00:48.02
```

Passwords

Your password, associated with your username, is the primary means of proving your identity to the system. In the future, there will be an increasing use of biometrics-based identification systems, but for the foreseeable future, passwords will continue to be one of the primary means of user authentication.

Anyone who learns your password will have access to the full range of services available to you. Further, any security incidents occurring from your account will probably be traced back to you, an uncomfortable position in which to find yourself.

Don't reveal your password to anyone. A stolen or guessed password is an easy way for a cracker to gain access to a system. Crackers have been known to place telephone calls to employees of a company, pretending to be members of the system operation staff or a repair organization, and simply ask users for their passwords. It works an alarming number of times.

Don't make your password easy to guess. Passwords based on your birthday, name, make of car, favorite food, or anything identifiable with you in any way make poor passwords.

How OpenVMS Protects Passwords

OpenVMS takes a number of steps to minimize the risks associated with stolen or guessed passwords. It is the responsibility of every individual to protect his or her password, but OpenVMS attempts to help that process by preventing easily guessed passwords.

Most modern systems, including OpenVMS, store passwords in an encrypted form. They cannot be decrypted. When a user enters a password, the system encrypts it and compares it with the encrypted password stored in the user authorization file. If the encrypted values match, the password is accepted.

Many attacks on system passwords rely on stealing a copy of the user authorization file and then using another computer to encrypt many possible passwords and look for a match with any user account. Note that this implies that an attacker already has access to at least one account in order to steal a copy of the authorization file.

The following are some of the features of OpenVMS that attempt to prevent successful attacks:

Password lifetime. Passwords can be set to expire after a certain amount of time, at the end of which the password must be changed. If a password is stolen, it will be valid only for a finite time. At login, OpenVMS will notify you if your password will expire in the next few days. At your next interactive login after expiration, a password change will be required.

Password dictionary. OpenVMS maintains a dictionary of common words that it will not allow to be used as passwords. Some password attacks check against most words in a given language. The password dictionary attempts to make this type of attack impractical.

Minimum password length. It is relatively easy for an attacker to try every possible short password. Longer passwords force attackers to try many more combinations, making the attack impractical, except on very fast computer systems to which relatively few attackers have easy access. This step is made stronger by combining it with the rules of the system password dictionary. Typical minimum password lengths are currently six or eight characters. Please note that this mainly refers to attacks on stolen authorization files; it is not possible to try a large number of passwords rapidly against a live OpenVMS system.

Password histories. OpenVMS maintains a list of passwords previously used by a given account and prevents anyone from reusing a previous password. This feature is in place because reuse of previous passwords could effectively defeat the password lifetime feature.

Break-in detection and evasion. While some attacks are carried out on a stolen copy of the User Authorization File, other attacks occur directly on the system under attack. An attacker may try common account names (e.g., SYSTEM or GUEST) or try to determine the username of a legitimate user.

The attacker may then try to log in using the selected account with various likely passwords. Names of the user's family members, pets, make of car, favorite sport, and the like may be tried. Crackers know that many people use such poor passwords because they are easier to remember.

OpenVMS includes a mechanism to combat such password guessing. First, it tries never to give the attacker any clues as to how close his guess was. When an invalid username is entered or a valid username is entered with an incorrect password, OpenVMS responds with the same message, "User Authorization Failure." This prevents an attacker from learning whether the username was valid.

Each time an incorrect username or password is entered, OpenVMS makes note of it. After a certain number of unsuccessful attempts occur within a short time, typically three to five such attempts, break-in evasion is triggered. While break-in evasion is in effect, even the correct username and password will be rejected, with the same "User Authorization Failure" message.

Break-in evasion remains in effect for a random amount of time. This prevents attackers who are familiar with the mechanism from knowing exactly how long they must wait between attempts. Continued attempts during the evasion period result in it's being extended for an additional amount of time.

An attacker unfamiliar with the mechanism will never realize whether he stumbled on the right password, and even knowledgeable attackers will not know exactly how many attempts it takes to trigger break-in evasion or how long it will last.

Finally, OpenVMS records the physical location or network address of the attacker while sending security alarms to the system operators.

Changing Your Password

You may change your password at any time using the DCL command SET PASSWORD, but if you allow your password to expire, you will be required to change it at your next interactive login. Both cases will be described next.

Changing Your Password with SET PASSWORD

When you issue the SET PASSWORD command, you will be asked to answer three prompts. First, you will be asked for your old password, to confirm your identity. Next, you will be asked to enter a new password. Finally, you will be asked to enter the new password again for verification.

While answering these prompts, your keystrokes will not be displayed. You are asked for your new password twice to ensure that you typed it as you intended.

Once you've answered the three prompts, OpenVMS will check your new password for length, history, and dictionary requirements as described above. If any requirement is not met, you will see an appropriate message, and your old password will remain in effect.

Changing your password is shown below:

```
$ SET PASSWORD
Old password:   [respond with your old password]
New password:   [type your desired new password]
Verification:   [type your new password again]
```

You may optionally use the SET PASSWORD/GENERATE command to have OpenVMS automatically generate passwords that meet all security criteria. However, many people find generated passwords hard to remember and resort to writing them down. This is a tremendous security risk.

Using SET PASSWORD/GENERATE results in a sequence like the following:

```
$ SET PASSWORD/GENERATE
Old password:

grockily
blistord
diattact
redisrap
helegies

Choose a password from this list, or press RETURN to get a new list
New password: [enter] (I didn't like any of those...)


revisere
flebtick
toffinis
ashicart
uncestue

Choose a password from this list, or press RETURN to get a new list
New password: [new password from the list above]
Verification: [enter it again]
$
```

> **Note:** Your system manager can set an account so that its owner may not change the password or so that system-generated passwords are required.

Changing an Expired Password During Login

If your password has expired, your old password will be accepted at your next interactive login. However, you must immediately choose a new password or your login will not be allowed. The sequence is as follows:

```
Unauthorized access prohibited.

Username: mike
Password: [old, expired password]
   Welcome to OpenVMS (TM) Alpha Operating System, Version V7.1 on node PHOEBE
      Last interactive login on Saturday, 14-DEC-2002 11:37:33.46
        Last non-interactive login on Saturday, 14-DEC-2002 13:30:16.76

Your password has expired; you must set a new password to log in


New password: [enter a new password]
Verification: [enter it again]
$
```

Your login is now complete, and your password has been changed.

Access Restrictions

OpenVMS may be configured to allow logins for a particular user only from certain sources or during certain times. For example, you may be allowed to log in from any location during normal business hours, but only from directly connected terminals during night or weekend hours. Proper use of this feature can further protect a system from attacks from outside, even if a password is stolen. Your system manager can tell you if your account has any access restrictions.

If your attempt to log in is prevented by such an access restriction, OpenVMS will display an appropriate message, such as "You are not allowed to log in at this time" or "You are not allowed to log in from this source."

Protecting Your Files from Unauthorized Access

OpenVMS allows you to control access to your files based on the UIC of the user requesting access. File protections are discussed in Chapter 7, "The User Environment."

Captive Accounts

Under OpenVMS, a user account may be *captive*. This means that it is restricted to executing a certain command procedure, typically a menu application.

When the user logs in, the procedure starts immediately and stays in control for the duration of the session. When the procedure ends, the user is logged out. Captive accounts are not allowed access to the DCL prompt.

Compare this with the experience of a normal user who runs a menu program from her LOGIN.COM file. The normal user is permitted to terminate the menu program and issue arbitrary DCL commands, whereas the captive user is not.

Captive accounts may be used in situations in which the physical terminal is located in a public area, or the user performs the same function all the time, such as a terminal at a library checkout desk.

The Audit Trail

OpenVMS maintains several separate logs of user activities, among them the operator log file and the accounting log file. Collectively, they are known as the audit trail. OpenVMS can be configured to record a large number of events. These include recording user logins and logouts, batch jobs beginning and ending, every program executed by every user, security alarms generated by accessing files and other objects, which privileges were used to access those objects, account creations, login failures, and more.

Security Alarms

OpenVMS can be configured to generate security alarms on a variety of events. Security alarms are sent to the system operators, the operator log file, and the console terminal.

Alarms can be generated on successful or unsuccessful login attempts, successful or unsuccessful file accesses, and many other conditions.

File Highwater Marking

One possible threat to system security is *disk scavenging*. Disk scavenging is the attempt to read contents of deleted files remaining on disk after deletion. As a performance benefit, files are not actually erased from disk by default, but only the pointers to them are removed. The file contents are not actually destroyed until the next file to occupy the same disk blocks overwrites the storage space. One way to perform disk scavenging is to allocate some amount of disk space to a new file, but to write no data to the file. The new owner of that space can then potentially examine the old contents.

The OpenVMS file system supports *highwater marking*, a mechanism that ensures that a file owner cannot read blocks he has not written himself, but it causes a slight performance degradation. Your system manager can enable this feature at his discretion.

DELETE/ERASE and PURGE/ERASE

The DELETE and PURGE commands support an optional /ERASE qualifier. When a file is deleted, /ERASE ensures that the file contents are overwritten, preventing possible disk-scavenging attempts.

Chapter 11 — Using Your Terminal

Previous chapters explained logging in and using the system for the first time. This section will cover in more detail some aspects of your terminal session that will become increasingly helpful as you gain experience.

Terminal Settings

Many terminals today are actually software emulations, such as Telnet or SET HOST, which emulate a terminal and attach to a host via TCP/IP or DECnet. This chapter refers to these terminals under the generic heading *network terminals.*

Many readers, however, may use real, physical terminals attached directly to an OpenVMS system. This chapter refers to these terminals as *physical terminals.*

A physical terminal connected through a terminal server is somewhat of a hybrid; the connection between the terminal and the terminal server conforms to the definition of a physical terminal connection, but the connection between the terminal server and the OpenVMS system matches a network terminal. From the OpenVMS point of view, it is considered a network terminal.

Some terminal settings, such as terminal speed, may be largely ignored for network terminals. Other settings will be relevant to all users. Settings relevant to physical terminals will be shown first.

Communications Speeds for Physical Terminals

The communications speed of your physical terminal must match the speed of the terminal port to which it is attached. The port may have the *autobaud* feature enabled, meaning it can automatically detect the speed at which your terminal is trying to communicate. If so, you may begin your login session by pressing ENTER a few times, waiting a second or so in between keypresses. The system will adjust the terminal port speed to match your terminal before prompting you for your username. Pressing keys other than ENTER will interfere with the ability of the system to discern your terminal speed.

If your port does not have autobaud enabled, you must set your terminal speed to match what the system is expecting. For OpenVMS systems, 9,600 baud, 8 bits, no parity, and one stop bit are good first assumptions, particularly for the console terminal port. Check with your system manager if in doubt.

When changing the communications speed of a terminal at which you are already logged in, first set the speed of the terminal port via the SET TERMINAL /SPEED=*speed* command. Afterward, set the speed of the terminal to the same value. You should confirm that your terminal supports the desired speed before starting.

Other Terminal Settings

For network terminals, the communications speed settings are meaningless, as communication is handled by the network software. Most other settings apply equally to network terminals and physical terminals.

The majority of terminal settings automatically take on appropriate values. While logged in, use the SHOW TERMINAL command to examine your terminal settings. The display will be similar to the following, obtained from a local DECterm terminal (the DECterm application falls under our definition of a network terminal):

```
$ SHOW TERMINAL
Terminal: _FTA2:        Device_Type: VT300_Series  Owner: _FTA2:
                                                   Username: MIKE
    Input:    9600    LFfill:  0      Width:  80      Parity: None
    Output:   9600    CRfill:  0      Page:   24
Terminal Characteristics:
    Interactive       Echo              Type_ahead        No Escape
    Hostsync          TTsync            Lowercase         Tab
    Wrap              Scope             No Remote         Eightbit
    Broadcast         No Readsync       No Form           Fulldup
    No Modem          No Local_echo     No Autobaud       No Hangup
    No Brdcstmbx      No DMA            No Altypeahd      Set_speed
    No Commsync       Line Editing      Insert editing    No Fallback
    No Dialup         No Secure server  No Disconnect     No Pasthru
    No Syspassword    SIXEL Graphics    No Soft Characters Printer port
    Numeric Keypad    ANSI_CRT          Regis             No Block_mode
    Advanced_video    Edit_mode         DEC_CRT           DEC_CRT2
    DEC_CRT3          No DEC_CRT4       No DEC_CRT5       No Ansi_Color
    VMS Style Input
```

The following represents a typical Telnet terminal:

```
$ SHOW TERMINAL
Terminal: _NTY102:      Device_Type: VT100         Owner: _NTY102:
                                                   Username: MIKE
Remote Port Info: (removed from book for security reasons)

    Input:    9600    LFfill:  0      Width:  80      Parity: None
    Output:   9600    CRfill:  0      Page:   24

Terminal Characteristics:
    Interactive       Echo              Type_ahead        No Escape
    No Hostsync       TTsync            Lowercase         Tab
    Wrap              Scope             Remote            No Eightbit
    Broadcast         No Readsync       No Form           Fulldup
    No Modem          No Local_echo     Autobaud          Hangup
```

```
No Brdcstmbx       No DMA            No Altypeahd      Set_speed
No Commsync        Line Editing      Insert editing    No Fallback
No Dialup          No Secure server  No Disconnect     No Pasthru
No Syspassword     No SIXEL Graphics No Soft Characters No Printer Port
Numeric Keypad     ANSI_CRT          No Regis          No Block_mode
Advanced_video     No Edit_mode      DEC_CRT           No DEC_CRT2
No DEC_CRT3        No DEC_CRT4       No DEC_CRT5       No Ansi_Color
VMS Style Input
```

Compare the two sets of terminal characteristics above. Since both are network terminals, speed settings are meaningless. The Telnet session includes Remote Port Info, the network address and port from which the connection originates. The value has been deleted from this example for security purposes.

As for terminal characteristics, these settings indicate that the DECterm session emulates a Digital VT300-series terminal, whereas the Telnet session emulates the older VT100 terminal. The meaningful differences are the characteristics Remote, No Eightbit, No Regis, No SIXEL graphics, and No DEC_CRTx. Their meanings are as follows:

- *Remote*—Identifies a non local terminal, i.e. one attached from across the network, rather than attached directly to the OpenVMS system.

- *No Eightbit*—The system will send 7-bit control codes rather than their 8-bit equivalents. This is a safe bet with non-Digital terminals; the system can still make the terminal perform virtually all the same operations.

- *No Regis*—The system will not attempt to display graphics images using the Digital Regis graphics format. Usually, only genuine Digital terminals (including DECterm windows) understand Regis format.

- *No SIXEL graphics*—The system will not attempt to display graphics images using the Digital SIXEL graphics format. Usually, only genuine Digital terminals (including DECterm windows) understand SIXEL format.

- *DEC_CRTx*—This indicates the generation of Digital terminal the device emulates. DEC_CRT indicates emulation of the Digital VT100 series, DEC_CRT2 the VT200 series, etc. Almost all devices and programs can emulate VT100 terminals, which is widely considered the most widely compatible of terminal designs. Devices capable of emulating later models generally emulate all earlier models as well. OpenVMS can also simulate almost every function of later models on VT100-compatible devices by using combinations of VT100 functions.

Use the SHOW TERMINAL command to examine the terminal settings for your particular terminal session.

Using SET TERMINAL

The settings shown by SHOW TERMINAL indicate what OpenVMS believes to be the capabilities of the terminal. In other words, OpenVMS will behave as if the terminal possesses those, and only those, features. OpenVMS will send control codes (which control such things as line- and screen-editing functions) appropriate for such a terminal.

Should the default terminal settings be incorrect, you may adjust them via the SET TERMINAL command. The more common qualifiers are described below:

- *SET TERMINAL/INQUIRE*—This command causes OpenVMS to query the terminal about its capabilities and adjust settings accordingly. Some terminals do not respond to this query and may cause a delay of several seconds while OpenVMS waits for an answer.

- *SET TERMINAL/DEVICE=VT100*—Causes OpenVMS to adjust various settings as appropriate for a VT100 terminal. This command provides compatibility with a wide range of terminals and terminal emulators. Advanced functions will be achieved with combinations of simpler functions, which may slightly slow the terminal operation. Compare this with SET TERMINAL /DEVICE=VT200, VT300, VT400, etc., which cause OpenVMS to send advanced control functions, which simpler terminals cannot perform.

- *SET TERMINAL/DEVICE=UNKNOWN*—If a device type of VT100 is unsuccessful, you may wish to try UNKNOWN, which causes OpenVMS to use very rudimentary settings and functions. Most users will never need to resort to this.

- *SET TERMINAL/INSERT*—This sets INSERT mode. When editing a command, keystrokes will be inserted between existing characters.

- *SET TERMINAL/OVERSTRIKE*—This sets OVERSTRIKE mode. When editing a command, keystrokes will overwrite existing characters. You may switch between INSERT and OVERSTRIKE modes at any time by pressing CTRL / A. This will take effect for the current command only, and will then be reset to its previous value.

- *SET TERMINAL/[NO]BROADCAST*—Use NOBROADCAST to disable the reception of broadcast messages at your terminal. Use BROADCAST to enable their reception.

- *SET TERMINAL/PAGE and /WIDTH*—For DECterm devices, use /PAGE to set the number of lines in the display (the default is 24). Use /WIDTH to set the number of columns (default values are 80 and 132). When changing these values, bear in mind that not all applications will perform correctly at settings other than the defaults /WIDTH=80 and /WIDTH=132 can be used with many terminals, but other values are less often supported.

The qualifiers described above are the most common. For information about other qualifiers, use HELP SET TERMINAL.

The Recall Buffer

The *recall buffer* is not really a feature of your terminal, but rather a service provided by DCL. It is presented here because it is used at the DCL command line using your terminal control keys.

Each time you enter a DCL command, it is stored in a list known as the recall buffer. If you would like to issue the same command more than once, you do not need to type it again; it may be recalled from the buffer. Newer versions of OpenVMS can store 254 commands, whereas older versions can store 20.

Pressing the up-arrow key (or CTRL/B) recalls the last command you entered. Pressing up-arrow again continues backward through the list of stored commands.

When you reach the command you would like to repeat, press ENTER. You may edit the command before pressing ENTER.

To travel forward through the list, press the down-arrow.

Entering the same command twice in a row does not cause two copies of it to be stored in the recall buffer.

The recall buffer does not persist from one login session to the next.

The RECALL Command

To reach a certain stored command directly, use the RECALL command. Enter the first few characters of the command you would like to recall and DCL will display the most recent matching command. DCL does not automatically enter the command; you may optionally edit the command before pressing ENTER to execute it.

```
$ RECALL DIR   ! find the most recent command starting with "dir"
$ DIRECTORY/DATE=(CREATED,MODIFIED)/SIZE=ALL ! command appears on next line
```

You may also refer to a previous command by number. Use RECALL/ALL to see a list of stored commands, and then enter RECALL X, where X is the number of the command you wish to recall. Be aware that recent versions of OpenVMS store a large number of previous commands.

If you decide not to issue a recalled command, press CTRL/X to erase it.

RECALL commands you issue are not added to the recall buffer.

Erasing the Recall Buffer

Should you wish to erase all entries from your recall buffer, use the RECALL/ERASE command.

Freezing the Display

If information is coming to the screen too fast for you to read, freeze the display by pressing HOLD SCREEN (usually F1 on PC-style keyboards) or CTRL/S. To resume the display, press HOLD SCREEN again, or CTRL/Q. While the screen is frozen, the program will continue to execute and generate output, which will be stored in a buffer of limited size, typically a few screens. When the buffer is full, the program will be suspended until you resume the display.

Control Characters

DCL defines several control characters to perform various functions. To use them, press the CTRL key, and then press the indicated key before releasing CTRL. Some are active at the DCL prompt but may be ignored by certain programs. Among them are the following:

Major functions:

- *CTRL/A* toggles the terminal between insert and overstrike modes (controls whether keyboard characters overwrite existing characters or are inserted between them).

- *CTRL/B* moves backward through the recall buffer (see "The Recall Buffer," above.) Equivalent to up-arrow.

- *CTRL/C* cancels the current operation (such as a search in an EDT text editor session) or DCL command. A given program or command may or may not treat CTRL/C and CTRL/Y as equivalent.

- *CTRL/E* moves the cursor to the end of the line.

- *CTRL/H* sounds the terminal bell or beep under some circumstances and may be used within the PHONE utility to sound the terminal bell of the other party.

- *CTRL/J* deletes the previous word under some circumstances.

- *CTRL/L* generates a formfeed character within some text editors.

- *CTRL/M* sometimes equivalent to ENTER or RETURN.

- *CTRL/O* toggles output to the terminal on or off. It is handy when a large amount of output is coming to the screen, which you do not need to see. When output is toggled off, the program or command continues to execute (and in fact, executes faster.) The program still generates the same output; it is simply not displayed on the screen. Broadcast messages automatically enable output when received, and so will not be missed.

- *CTRL/P* gains the attention of the hardware console subsystem when issued from the console terminal of certain hardware models, and only when specifically enabled. Many hardware models do not have a separate console processor, so this has the effect of halting the execution of OpenVMS. The general user never has occasion to use this; it is mentioned only as a caution to readers who may have their own OpenVMS computer hardware.

- *CRTL/Q* resumes output to the screen that has been frozen via CRTL/S or HOLD SCREEN (usually F1 on PC-style keyboards).

- *CTRL/R* refreshes the screen under some circumstances, such as within text editors and other full-screen programs. It is not used as widely as CTRL/W.

- *CTRL/S* freezes the screen. It is equivalent to HOLD SCREEN (usually F1 on PC-style keyboards). Use CTRL/Q or HOLD SCREEN to resume.

- *CTRL/T* displays a one-line status display containing your node, process name, system time, the name of your current program, accumulated CPU time, accumulated page faults, accumulated I/O operations, and current physical memory usage. After this status line, certain programs may display a one-line summary of their own progress.

- *CTRL/U* erases from the beginning of the line to the current cursor location. In older versions of OpenVMS, it discarded the entire line and performed a RETURN (ENTER.)

- *CTRL/W* refreshes the screen in most full-screen applications. It is sometimes equivalent to CTRL/R, but more widely used.

- *CTRL/X* causes any keystrokes in the type-ahead buffer to be discarded and otherwise functions like CTRL/U.

- *CTRL/Y* interrupts the current command procedure or program and displays the DCL prompt. You may exit the program by (1) issuing the EXIT command, allowing the program exit handlers to run, (2) issuing the QUIT command, preventing the exit handlers from running (not generally recommended), or (3) issuing another command which causes a program to run, thereby executing an implicit EXIT. If you do not wish to abort the program, use the CONTINUE command. You may sometimes continue a program even after issuing other commands, but only if the intervening commands are handled internally by DCL (such as SPAWN).

- *CTRL/Z* means end-of-file or end-of-input. It is used to signal many applications, such as text editors and the CREATE command, that you are finished entering information. It may sometimes be used to abort a DCL command that you are typing (if a valid verb and all required parameters are present when you press CTRL/Z, the command will be issued).

- *Up-arrow* moves backward (toward older commands) through the recall buffer.

- *Down-Arrow* moves forward (toward more recent commands) through the recall buffer.

- *HOLD SCREEN* is a toggle to freeze or resume output. It is identical to the combination of CTRL/S and CTRL/Q. PC keyboards usually use F1 for this function.

Minor or redundant functions:

- *CTRL/D* moves the cursor one position to the left under some circumstances. The left-arrow is usually preferred.

- *CTRL/F* moves the cursor one position to the right under some circumstances. The right-arrow is usually preferred.

- *CTRL/I* duplicates the function of the TAB key under some circumstances. TAB is usually preferred.

- *CTRL/UP-ARROW* causes a DECterm window to scroll backward, showing information that has scrolled off the top of the screen. It duplicates the function of the window scroll bar.

- *CTRL/DOWN-ARROW* causes a DECterm window to scroll forward, the opposite of CTRL/UP-ARROW

Chapter 12 — E-mail

The MAIL Facility

This section introduces the OpenVMS e-mail facility. In the early days of OpenVMS, the mail facility could send messages only to users on the local node or on a DECnet network, but it has since been enhanced to allow messages to be sent to or received from any Internet e-mail address.

There are two ways to use OpenVMS mail. One is to use the MAIL facility directly on the OpenVMS system, either through a text interface or through the GUI. The GUI interface is covered in Chapter 15, "The OpenVMS GUI."

The other method is to use the OpenVMS computer system as an e-mail server for separate client systems, such as personal computers. Both approaches are described below.

Two Separate Strategies

Historically, OpenVMS MAIL was used to send text-only messages among users of one machine or of several machines connected via a DECnet network. This ability still exists and is used today by many OpenVMS users.

But today, OpenVMS can also run TCP/IP, so OpenVMS MAIL can send and receive messages to and from any Internet e-mail address. Fewer and fewer Internet e-mail messages are being sent as plain text, making the character-cell interface less desirable for many incoming messages.

Many users today choose to use PC-based e-mail clients, using an OpenVMS system as a POP3/IMAP and SMTP server. In this case, the OpenVMS mail facility serves as a storage location for incoming messages. The client system periodically checks with the OpenVMS system to see whether there are any messages waiting.

This chapter treats the two approaches separately, although it is possible to use a combination of the two. Using OpenVMS as a mail server is discussed first, and using a local interface is discussed after that.

Your OpenVMS E-mail Address

When someone sends you an e-mail message, the address to which the sender sends it can differ, depending on the location of the originating computer. Let's say your

OpenVMS username is JENNY. Different senders may express your e-mail address in
different formats, as follows:

```
These senders                  May send to this address
Internet, DECnet, Local        jenny@machine.domain.topdomain
Internet, DECnet, Local        jenny@domain.topdomain
DECnet, Local                  node::jenny
Local                          jenny
```

"Internet" senders are Internet users anywhere in the world. "DECnet" senders are
users of any node on your DECnet network. "Local" senders are users of your
particular OpenVMS machine.

The first two address formats may be interchangeable on your system.

Your system manager may also set up additional Internet addresses as needed. For
instance, the system manager may configure the system so that Internet mail sent to
"jenny," "jen," or "jennifer" are all routed to the JENNY account.

You may also configure your OpenVMS account to automatically forward any mail it
may receive to any other Internet e-mail address via the SET FORWARD command
within the MAIL utility.

SMTP, POP3, and IMAP

When configured for TCP/IP networking, an OpenVMS system can act as a POP3,
IMAP and SMTP server. Any computer system with an appropriate e-mail client
application (e.g., a personal computer running Microsoft Outlook Express) can be
used as a client system. POP3 (Post Office Protocol Version 3) is a protocol for
retrieving mail messages from the server, eventually deleting them from the server.
IMAP (Internet Message Access Protocol) is similar in function to POP3, but stores
messages on the server rather than on the client. SMTP (Simple Mail Transfer
Protocol) is used to send outgoing messages from the client.

Incoming Internet messages are received by the OpenVMS system, which places the
message in the mail file for the proper user. Each user has a mail file located in his
login directory. The primary file is called MAIL.MAI, but other files, also of the .MAI
type, are created and deleted automatically as needed.

At intervals, the client system logs in to the OpenVMS system (via POP3 or IMAP)
and checks to see whether new messages exist. The client uses the same username and
password that the user does when logging in interactively. If any new messages exist,
the client either downloads them (in the case of POP3) or stores them in the
appropriate OpenVMS message store folder (in the case of IMAP).

For outgoing messages, the client connects directly to the SMTP server software on the OpenVMS system and transmits the message. The SMTP server, in turn, forwards the message toward its eventual destination. The message is never stored in the user's .MAI files.

To configure POP3/IMAP/SMTP client software, you will need to know the following things: your username, your password, the name or network address of the OpenVMS server system, the TCP/IP port on which each service is running, and your Internet-format e-mail address as described above. Your system manager can supply each of those items.

If you use OpenVMS mail though a client system, your system manager will probably disable the new-mail notifications that would normally appear when you log in interactively.

Using the Terminal Interface

This section describes the traditional terminal-based interface to OpenVMS MAIL. This is not usually used in conjunction with the TCP/IP mail clients described above, but it is possible to do so.

Using the terminal interface (or the GUI interface described later) allows you to send messages to and receive messages from other OpenVMS users on the DECnet network. You may also send to and receive from Internet e-mail addresses, assuming your OpenVMS system is running TCP/IP.

Notification of Waiting Mail

If you have any new messages waiting, OpenVMS will notify you during login. If a message arrives while you are logged in, a broadcast message will notify you of it unless your terminal is set to /NOBROADCAST.

Notifications follow the format shown below with only minor variations, depending on whether the message was received from the Internet or from a local user (in this case, user RON on node BAXTER):

```
$
New mail on node ABBY from BAXTER::RON
$
```

Starting MAIL

The DCL command MAIL starts the OpenVMS mail utility. When you start MAIL, a count will be displayed if you have any messages waiting.

The MAIL prompt will appear, at which you may enter MAIL commands:

```
$ MAIL
MAIL>
```

The mail commands are named in an intuitive way, and some of them have synonyms, as shown below. Only certain MAIL commands are discussed in this book. They are the following:

```
SEND              Send a message
READ              Read a message
REPLY or ANSWER   Reply to the current message
FORWARD           Forward a message to another recipient
DELETE or ERASE   Move a message to WASTEBASKET
FILE or MOVE      Move a message to another folder
COPY              Copy the current message to another folder
EXTRACT           Write a message to an external file
PURGE             Empty the WASTEBASKET folder
DIRECTORY         List messages in a folder
SELECT            Select a mail folder
BACK              Read previous message or previous directory display
NEXT              Skip to the next message
SET               Change various MAIL settings
SHOW              Examine various MAIL settings

EXIT              Exit MAIL
QUIT              Exit without a PURGE
```

Exiting MAIL

To exit mail, use the EXIT command at the MAIL prompt.

Mail Folders

Mail messages are stored in an indexed file called MAIL.MAI (and additional files, which are created and deleted as needed.) Within your mail file, you may create folders to group messages according to your preferences.

Three folders are maintained automatically: MAIL, which is the default folder for all messages you have read; NEWMAIL, which holds messages you have not yet read; and WASTEBASKET, which contains messages that have been selected for deletion, but have not yet been permanently deleted. These folders, as with all folders, are automatically deleted when they become empty. However, these three will be automatically created when needed again.

You may create any additional folders you wish. Working with folders is described later.

Receiving Messages

When you start MAIL, your initial folder will be determined by whether or not you have new messages waiting. If so, you will be in the NEWMAIL folder. If not, you will be in the MAIL folder.

You may read the first message in the current folder by issuing the READ command or by pressing ENTER. The message will be displayed one screen at a time. Each time you press enter, you will advance by one screen. If you have reached the end of the message, pressing ENTER advances to the next message.

The first few lines of the display contain information about the mail message:

```
    #1            24-DEC-2002 16:00:41.73                    NEWMAIL
From:   ABBY::SCOTT
To:     MIKE
CC:
Subj:   Meeting at 11:30

There will be a meeting today in the main conference room.

-Scott
```

The first line contains the message number, the message timestamp, and the current folder name. Below those items are fields identifying the sender, recipients, and message subject. Lastly, the message itself is shown.

If the message is more than one screen in size, and you would like to start again from the beginning, use the CURRENT command. Use BACK or NEXT to move to the previous or next message. You may also display a specific message in the current folder by entering its number at the MAIL prompt (remember—the current message number is in the upper left of the screen.) If you enter a number greater than the number of messages in the folder, the last message will be selected.

When you have read all messages in the folder you will see a message to that effect. To start over from the first message, enter "1" at the prompt.

While you are reading new mail, messages in other folders are not visible. Use SELECT *folder* to switch to another mail folder. Conversely, if you receive a new message while in another folder, use SELECT NEWMAIL before trying to read your new message.

Sending Messages

Use the SEND command to begin a new mail message. You will be prompted for recipients and a subject for your message. After you have answered those prompts, you may begin entering your message. After you enter each line, you cannot go back to correct earlier lines. (This form of input is fine for brief messages, but not for longer ones; for those, use SEND/EDIT, discussed next.) When you have finished your message, press CTRL/Z to send the message or CTRL/C to quit without sending it.

If you wish to send the message to more than one recipient, separate them by commas:

```
MAIL> send
To:     mike,henry
Subj:   Too many meetings
```

Using SEND/EDIT

For longer messages, the default method for entering a message one line at a time may not be sufficient. You may elect to use a text editor for entering your messages by using SEND/EDIT (or REPLY/EDIT for answering messages).

The default editor for OpenVMS MAIL is the TPU (EVE) editor. This book contains a crash course for the EDT text editor, but not for TPU. To make EDT your editor of choice, enter the command SET EDITOR EDT at the MAIL prompt.

After you have entered the message recipients and subject, EDT will start, allowing you to use all its functionality to compose your message.

When you exit EDT with the EXIT command, your message will be sent. If you change your mind and choose not to send the message, exit EDT with the QUIT command.

Recipient Address Formats

When sending mail, you may need to use one of several address formats to identify its recipient. Users of the local OpenVMS machine may be specified simply by username, such as RON. For users on other DECnet network machines, specify the machine name (node name) and username, such as *ABBY::RON*.

Internet e-mail addresses may take one of several forms, depending on which version of OpenVMS your machine is running and what e-mail programs are installed. Your system manager will inform you of the proper format, which is likely to be among the following:

user@domain.topdomain

SMTP% "user@domain.topdomain"

MX% "user@domain.topdomain"

IN% "user@domain.topdomain"

WINS% "user@domain.topdomain"

Replying to Messages

You may reply to the current message by using the commands REPLY or ANSWER. The TO, FROM, and SUBJECT lines will be filled automatically. To reply to all recipients of the original message, use REPLY/ALL. Just as you may elect to use an editor with the SEND command, you may use REPLY/EDIT to use an editor to compose your reply.

Sending a File As a Mail Message

If you have a preexisting text file that you'd like to send as a mail message, use SEND *filespec*, where *filespec* is the name of the file you wish to send. You will be prompted for recipients and a message subject.

Note: To send files other than text files, please refer to The MIME Utility, discussed later.

Forwarding a Message

You may forward the message you are currently reading by using the FORWARD command. You will be prompted for recipients.

Sending Yourself a Copy of Outgoing Messages

The SEND, REPLY, and FORWARD commands accept the /SELF qualifier, which causes a copy of the outgoing message to be sent to you. For example, to reply to a message and receive a copy of your reply, use REPLY/SELF.

If you would like to receive copies of your outgoing messages by default, use the SET COPY_SELF *item* command, where *item* is SEND, REPLY, or FORWARD to enable a copy to yourself, or NOSEND, NOREPLY, or NOFORWARD to disable it. You may specify more than one item by separating the items by commas, as in SET COPY_SELF SEND,REPLY,NOFORWARD. Use SHOW COPY_SELF to examine your current settings.

Saving a Message to an External File

To save the current message to an external file, use the command EXTRACT *filespec*, where *filespec* is the name you would like to assign to the file. The contents of the current message will be saved under the specified name. The original message will be retained in MAIL.

Afterward, you may use the MIME command to extract portions of extracted MIME-format messages. The MIME command is introduced later.

Deleting Messages

You may delete the current message by issuing the DELETE command.

You may also delete a range of messages by number. For example, to delete the first four messages in the current folder, use this command:

```
MAIL> DELETE 1-4
```

You may also specify nonsequential ranges by using commas to separate them—for example:

```
MAIL> DELETE 1-4,6,12-15
```

Deleted messaged are not destroyed immediately; they are instead moved to the WASTEBASKET folder. The messages are actually deleted only when you exit MAIL or issue the PURGE command.

To retrieve messages from the WASTEBASKET folder, first use SELECT WASTEBASKET to switch to that folder. Then move through the messages until reaching the desired message and use FILE *folder* where *folder* is the desired destination folder.

To prevent the automatic emptying of the WASTEBASKET folder when you exit MAIL, use the SET NOAUTO_PURGE command. To enable automatic purging, use SET AUTO_PURGE. Use SHOW AUTO_PURGE to see your current setting.

You can also exit mail without emptying the WASTEBASKET, even if AUTO_PURGE is enabled, by using QUIT instead of EXIT.

Distribution Lists

You may send messages to multiple users by using distribution lists. Distribution lists are text files containing lists of recipients. First, use a text editor to create a distribution list with one e-mail address per line, as in the following file called FRIENDS.DIS:

```
JAKE
ABBY::SCOTT
JOE@SOMEDOMAIN.TOPDOMAIN
```

Then, when sending your message, specify the name of the distribution list in the recipient field:

```
MAIL> send
To: @friends
```

Your message will be sent to each address in the distribution list.

Moving Around Folders

You can see a list of folders using the DIRECTORY/FOLDER command:

```
MAIL> DIRECTRY/FOLDER
Listing of folders in DKA100:[MIKE]MAIL.MAI
     Press CTRL/C to cancel listing
MAIL
MEETINGS
WASTEBASKET
```

To move to another folder, use "SELECT folder," which is synonymous with "SET FOLDER *folder*."

Note: The SELECT command can also be used to select a group of messages within the current folder— for example, by date or recipient. These messages can then be acted on as a group. Within mail, use HELP SELECT for more information.

Listing the Messages in a Folder

To list the message in the current folder, use DIRECTORY:

```
MAIL> DIRECTORY
                                                                    MAIL
# From                 Date         Subject
1 PHOEBE::MIKE         24-NOV-2002  You missed the meeting again
2 ABBY::RON            24-NOV-2002  Let's reschedule
3 PHOEBE::MIKE         25-NOV-2002  RE: Let's reschedule
4 ABBY::RON            26-NOV-2002  Tomorrow at 10:30
5 SMTP%"Gail@somedoma  18-DEC-2002  Bring home some milk
```

Moving a Message to Another Folder

To place the current message in another folder, use FILE *folder*, where *folder* is the name of the desired folder. If the folder specified does not exist, you will be asked if you would like to create it.

You may also copy the current message to another folder, leaving a copy in the original folder. Use COPY *folder*.

Folders are automatically deleted when they become empty.

Creating a Folder

Folders are created when you attempt to move a message to a folder that does not exist. You will be prompted as to whether the new folder should be created.

Deleting a Folder

Folders are automatically deleted when they become empty.

Setting and Examining Options

The SET and SHOW commands are closely related; SET changes an option, and SHOW examines its current value. For example, use SET AUTO_PURGE or SET NOAUTO_PURGE to control this setting and SHOW AUTO_PURGE to display its current setting.

The following is a summary of most options and their purposes:

- SET AUTO_PURGE, SET NOAUTO_PURGE—This controls whether the WASTEBASKET folder is emptied when you exit mail with the EXIT command.

- SET CC_PROMPT, SET NOCC_PROMPT—This controls whether you will be prompted for CC ("carbon copy" or "courtesy copy") recipients when sending mail. Use the SEND/CC or SEND/NOCC (or REPLY/[NO]CC or FORWARD/[NO]CC) command to override this setting on a case-by-case basis.

- SET COPY_SELF *item*—This controls whether a copy of your outgoing message is sent back to you. "Item" may be SEND, FORWARD, REPLY, NOSEND, NOFORWARD, or NOREPLY.

- SET EDITOR *item*—This selects your default text editor. *Item* may be any callable text editor on your system, typically EDT or TPU (EVE).

- SET FORWARD *address*, SET NOFORWARD—This allows you to automatically forward all mail to another address. This may be another OpenVMS account or an Internet e-mail address.

- SET PERSONAL_NAME *name*, SET NOPERSONAL_NAME—This establishes a personal name to be shown in the FROM field in outgoing mail, along with your e-mail address. It is customary to provide a personal name field for outgoing Internet mail:

```
MAIL> SET PERSONAL_NAME "Mike Duffy"
```

Other OpenVMS users receiving this message will see the personal name on the FROM line:

```
    #1          25-DEC-2002 17:23:46.30                    NEWMAIL
From:    PHOEBE::MIKE         "Mike Duffy"
To:      MIKE
CC:
Subj:    personal name demo.

This message demonstrates the PERSONAL_NAME mail setting.

MAIL>
```

- SET SIGNATURE_FILE *file*, SET NOSIGNATURE_FILE—This allows you to specify a file to be appended onto outgoing messages. An example is a text file simulating a business card, including your name, company name, and telephone number.

The MIME Utility

The OpenVMS MIME utility is a standalone application that can encode and decode MIME–(Multipurpose Internet Mail Extension) formatted messages. MIME format is commonly used to include non text file types (e.g., graphic images, audio files, and spreadsheets files) and is understood by a wide variety of e-mail clients.

If you do not use a MIME-capable mail client, you may use the MIME utility to decode any MIME-formatted messages you receive or to encode MIME messages you wish to send to others.

To decode a MIME message, use the EXTRACT command in OpenVMS mail to save the message to an external file. Then use the MIME utility to extract and decode the various parts of the message.

For information about the MIME utility, enter HELP MIME at the DCL prompt, or start the MIME utility and enter HELP at the MIME prompt.

To start the MIME utility, enter the following commands:

```
$ MIME :== $SYS$SYSTEM:MIME.EXE  ! May not be necessary on your system
$ MIME
```

Chapter 13 — Text Editors

Text editors are programs that enable the creation and manipulation of text files. Text editors are useful in many situations where word processors or certain markup programs may not be suitable: when creating program source files, command procedures, when manually manipulating HTML or XML source files, or when the resulting file will be processed by a program, rather than viewed by a person.

Word processing programs include special formatting instructions, macros, and other items in their document files that are not compatible with the purposes listed above. Further, word processing programs often perform unwanted text formatting even when creating files in text-only mode.

OpenVMS comes with several general-purpose text editors and various other specialized editors and text processors. EDT and EVE are the most popular of the editors that can be used via the terminal interface. For GUI users, there are three main text editors: the GUI version of EVE, the CDE text editor, and DECwindows notepad.

This chapter describes the EDT text editor, a powerful, but uncomplicated, editor well suited to many tasks.

Many experienced users of OpenVMS prefer the EVE (TPU) text editor, often for its extensive macro capabilities and its ability to be customized. Because space constraints do not permit a discussion of both EVE and EDT, the more straightforward EDT is the editor introduced.

A Crash Course in EDT

This chapter provides the reader with enough information to use the EDT text editor. It is not a complete description of all of EDT's features, but it contains enough information to perform most tasks quickly.

EDT Caveats

Please be aware that EDT cannot process lines longer than 255 characters. Longer lines will be truncated.

For lines longer than the display width (80 or 132 characters), EDT will display only the number of characters that will fit on the display. You will not be able to see the remaining characters unless you use the line mode SET NOTRUNCATE command. This causes the remainder of the long line to be wrapped to the next line of the display.

This is for display only; the line is not actually broken into pieces. To restore the default behavior, use SET TRUNCATE.

Starting EDT

From the DCL command line, issue EDIT/EDT *filename*, where *filename* is the file you would like to edit. If no file with that name exists, it will be created.

EDT is compatible with hardcopy terminals (a terminal that has no video screen, but prints directly on paper). By default, EDT starts in line mode for compatibility with such devices, unless your system manager or LOGIN.COM causes it to start in screen mode. This chapter describes the full-screen mode, but includes a few useful line-mode commands.

Why Hardcopy Terminals?

Although they may seem obsolete, hardcopy terminals are very useful as *console* terminals. System-event messages, security alarms, and other important messages are always displayed upon the system console terminal, which is also known as the *operator's console*. Hardcopy terminals print a record of all console activity and system messages, preserving a security auditing record that cannot be falsified without physical access to the logs.

When you start EDT in line mode, it will display either the first line of the file or the message "Input file does not exist," followed by the line-mode prompt, a single asterisk (*).

```
$ EDIT/EDT NOSUCHFILE.TXT
Input file does not exist
[EOB]
*
```

Switch to full-screen mode by entering C or CHANGE at the line-mode prompt and pressing ENTER. EDT will switch to full-screen mode and will display the first 22 lines of the file—or the [EOB] (End of Buffer) marker if the file does not exist. Your cursor will be positioned at the first character of the file.

Your system manager may have configured EDT to automatically start in full-screen mode. If so, the instructions above are unnecessary.

The EDT Journal File

While you are editing a file, EDT automatically keeps a log of all modifications you make to the file. Every few seconds, your most recent keystrokes are saved to the journal file. In the event of a network problem, system failure, power failure, or some other event that disrupts the system, the journal file is saved. Later, you may use the EDIT/EDT/RECOVER command to reload the original file and apply all of your changes to it. The journal file is given the same name as your original file, but with the extension .JOU. So, if you edit your LOGIN.COM file, the journal file will be called LOGIN.JOU. When you successfully save your file, the journal is automatically deleted unless you exit EDT with the /SAVE option.

Working with Your Text

In the strictest sense, all you need are your four keyboard arrow keys and the BACKSPACE key. Characters you type will be inserted, meaning that characters to the right of the cursor position will be shifted to the right to make room. The BACKSPACE key deletes the character before the cursor position.

The remainder of this section describes the functions of other keyboard keys and provides helpful line-mode commands. The first important item is a warning that you might not be able to trust the labeling on your keyboard keys.

Why You Should Not Trust Your Keyboard

One thing a new user to OpenVMS does not need is a keyboard whose keys do not do what they say they do. However, if you are using something other than a genuine VT-series terminal, your keyboard is almost certainly labeled incorrectly for use with EDT.

The EDT text editor was designed for the keyboards of the Digital VT-series terminals, such as the LK201 and LK401 keyboards. The function keys of those keyboards were in different locations from those on a PC-style keyboard. Most VAXstations and AlphaStations come with PC-style keyboards whose function keys are labeled incorrectly for use with EDT. Presumably, the Itanium-based machines will also have PC-style keyboards.

Compare the function key layouts and labeling on a PC-style keyboard with those on an LK201/LK401:

Find	Insert	Remove
Select	Pg Up	Pg Dn

↑	
←	↓	→

Gold	Help	FNDNXT / FIND	DEL L / UND L
PAGE COMMAND	SECT FILL	APPEND REPLACE	DEL W UND W
ADVANCE BOTTOM	BACKUP TOP	CUT PASTE	DEL C UND C
WORD CHNGCASE	EOL DEL EOL	CHAR SPECINS	ENTER
LINE OPEN LINE		SELECT RESET	SUBS

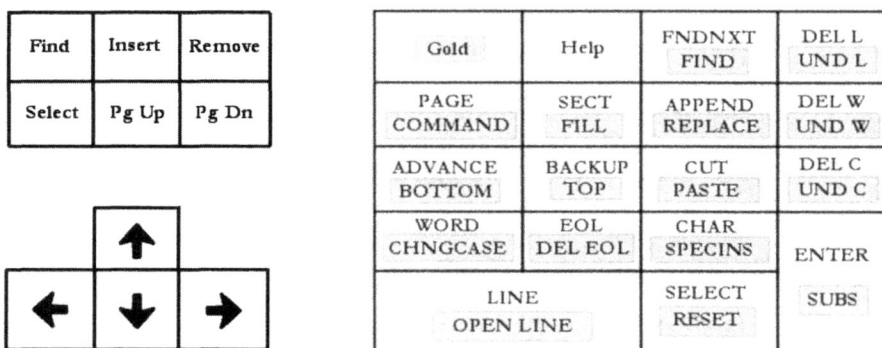

Figure 13-1 LK-Style Keyboard Layout

EDT uses the LK-style keyboard layout, even with a PC-style keyboard. This means, for example, that the PC key labeled "Page Up" will actually perform a "Remove." The PC key labeled "End" will perform "Page Up" (Prev Screen), and so on.

If you have a PC-style keyboard layout, you may wish to affix some small handwritten adhesive labels to your keys while you learn their layout.

In the remainder of this chapter, certain conventions are used to describe keyboard keys. Keys on the keypad (the block of keys on the extreme right of the keyboard) are identified in this way: the top row (NumLock, /, *, -) are referred to as PF1 through PF4. The remaining keys are identified with the prefix "KP-." So the key labeled "1" will be referred to as "KP-1," and the dot (.) will be identified KP-DOT.

PC-keyboard users will note that they have no KP-COMMA key because the PC-style "+" key takes up two positions. This will not interfere with using EDT.

Each keypad key has two functions. The first function is activated by pressing the keypad key. The second function is activated by first pressing PF1, also known as the GOLD key on LK-style keyboards, and then pressing the keypad key.

Use the HELP (PF2) key from within EDT to obtain additional information about each keypad function.

Using Line-Mode Commands

This book concentrates on using EDT in full-screen mode. However, there are certain instances in which line-mode commands are more efficient for a given task. When instructed to use a line-mode command, use one of the following two methods:

1. The first method consists of the following steps:

   i. Enter line mode by pressing CTRL/Z. The line mode prompt (*) will be presented.

   ii. Enter the line-mode command and press ENTER. This executes the command.

   iii. Enter C or CHANGE to return to full-screen mode.

2. The second method is to use the COMMAND key (PF1,KP-7). When you issue COMMAND from screen mode, a command: prompt appears at the bottom of the screen. You may issue your line-mode command at this prompt, but when finished, you must use the ENTER key on the keypad, not the main keyboard ENTER key.

The normal ENTER key would be interpreted as an instruction to insert CTRL/M (shown as "^M") into your command. If you accidentally use the keyboard ENTER key, simply use the DELETE key (BACKSPACE on PC-style keyboards) to erase the "^M" and use the keypad ENTER key instead.

Why "^M" Sometimes Appears When ENTER or RETURN Is Pressed

In the ASCII standard (see the Glossary), a carriage return is denoted by the value 13. Lower numbers of the ASCII table represent unprintable control codes, historically generated by pressing the CTRL key in combination with another key. Since the letter M is the thirteenth letter of the English alphabet, CTRL/M and RETURN (ENTER) both represent the ASCII value of 13. This trick is sometimes used to insert an extra carriage return into the middle of a line.

Moving Around Your File

You may move around your file by using your 4 arrow keys, PrevScreen, NextScreen, or SECT (KP-8). Your arrow keys move the cursor one character at a time in the direction you indicate. PrevScreen and NextScreen move 16 lines in the direction indicated and move the cursor to the first column. SECT moves the cursor 16 lines in the current direction. The current direction is set to forward by pressing ADVANCE (KP-4) or backward by pressing BACKUP (KP-5).

You may move to the beginning of the file by pressing TOP (PF1,KP-5). You may move to the end of the file by pressing BOTTOM (PF1,KP-4).

You may move one word at a time using WORD (KP-1). This moves the cursor one word in the current direction.

You may move to the next page by using PAGE (KP-7). This actually means moving to the next form-feed character in the current direction and so may not be useful for some files.

To move by large amounts, line-mode commands may be more efficient. You may move to a certain line number within the file by entering the line number and pressing ENTER. To move to line number 10, enter "10" at the line-mode prompt.

To move by a given number of lines, you may indicate a direction and amount by using the "+" or "-" sign followed by the number of lines you'd like to move. To move 1,000 lines up in the file, enter "-1000" at the line mode prompt.

> **Note:** In the course of editing the file, line numbers may be deleted or extra line numbers added between existing numbers as you add, remove, and move text. To reset the line numbers, use RESEQUENCE at the line mode prompt.

Adding Text

To add text to your file, you may position the cursor at the point you would like to insert text and begin typing. EDT is automatically in insert mode, meaning existing text will be shifted to the right as you type. Pressing ENTER in the middle of a line breaks the line and moves the portion to the right of the cursor to the next line.

To add the contents of another file, you may use the line-mode INCLUDE command. Position your cursor at the place you intend to insert the external file and issue the line-mode command INCLUDE *filename*, where *filename* is the specification of the file you'd like to include.

To add text currently in your paste buffer (see, "Moving or Copying Text") move the cursor to the desired position and use PASTE (PF1,KP-6).

Removing Text

To remove text, you may position the cursor at the next character after the one you would like to delete and use the DELETE key (BACKSPACE on PC-style keyboards). This deletes one character at a time.

LK-style keyboard users may use DEL-W to delete the current word. PC-style keyboard users have no such key; the oversized KP-PLUS key takes up two positions.

To remove a large amount of text, use the CUT function. Position your cursor at the first (or last) character you'd like to remove. Press SELECT (either the SELECT key or KP-DOT). This places an anchor at the current location. Now move your cursor to the other end of the text you'd like to remove. Intervening text will be shown in reverse video, highlighting the text you've selected. Press CUT (KP-6) to remove your text. To cancel a select range without removing any text, press RESET (PF1,KP-DOT).

Moving or Copying Text

To move or copy text, use a combination of the CUT and PASTE functions. There is no separate COPY function, but the same result can be achieved by using CUT, followed by an immediate PASTE and then a second PASTE at the appropriate target location.

To copy text into the paste buffer, position your cursor at the first (or last) character you'd like to remove. Press SELECT (either the SELECT key or KP-DOT). This places an anchor at the current location. Now move your cursor to the other end of the text you'd like to move or copy. Intervening text will be shown in reverse video, highlighting the text you've selected. Press CUT (KP-6) to remove your text. To cancel a select range without removing any text, press RESET (PF1,KP-DOT).

If you are copying text, not moving it, immediately press PASTE (PF1,KP-6). This restores the text to its original location, but leaves a copy in the in-memory paste buffer.

Now move the cursor to the place you'd like to insert the text. Use PASTE (PF1,KP-6) to insert the text at that point.

Setting Autowrap

EDT can be set to automatically wrap lines (end the current line and advance to the next line) when you approach the right-hand margin while typing.

Use the line-mode command SET WRAP n, where n is the desired right-hand margin. Most of the time, 75 is a good value for a typical 80-column display.

This feature works on one line at a time and will not justify the remainder of a paragraph when you insert text. However, you can select a block of text to fill (see "Formatting Text").

To disable this feature, use the line mode command SET NOWRAP.

Formatting Text

When inserting or removing text, you may end up with an uneven right margin. You can use the FILL command to fill text between the left and right margins (the right margin is defined by the SET WRAP command; see "Setting Autowrap").

Select a block of text to fill as follows:

1. Place the cursor at one end of the desired range of text.

2. Press SELECT (SELECT or KP-DOT).

3. Move the cursor to the other end of the desired range.

Once you have selected the appropriate range, use FILL (PF1,KP-8). This will fill the selected text between the left and right margins.

Saving Your File

Your file is automatically saved when you end your EDT session with the line-mode EXIT command. This is true even if there have been no changes to the file. You may save the file under a different name by using EXIT *filename*. (See "Exiting EDT" for more information.)

You may save your file at any time by using the line-mode WRITE *filename* command. You may save the file under an alternative name if you wish, but even if you are saving the file under its original name, you must specify a filename. The EDT session will not end after saving the file with WRITE.

Exiting EDT

When exiting the EDT editor, you may choose to save your file, save it under a name different from its original name (the original file is preserved), or exit without saving changes.

To exit EDT, the first step is to enter line mode. To enter line mode, press CTRL/Z. The line mode prompt (*) will be presented at the bottom of the screen.

To save the file under the name you specified at the beginning of the session, enter the command EXIT. A new version of the file will be saved, and any previous versions will also be preserved, according to your version-limit settings.

If you wish to save the file under a different name, use EXIT *filename*, where *filename* is the new name. If you save the file under a new name, the original file will also be preserved, unmodified, under its original name.

To exit the EDT editor without saving your changes, use the QUIT command.

You may add the qualifier /SAVE to either EXIT or QUIT, which preserves the journal file. When used with QUIT, it allows you to reapply your changes later, using EDIT /EDT/RECOVER.

Starting EDT in Full-Screen Mode Automatically

Most users will want to start EDT in full-screen mode. This may be accomplished by using an *initialization file*. This file contains commands that will be executed automatically when EDT starts. To use this feature, create a file called EDTINI.EDT in your login directory. It should consist of one line that reads SET MODE CHANGE (you may add additional commands later to suit your preferences.) Thereafter, use the command EDIT/EDT/COMMAND=SYS$LOGIN:EDTINI.EDT to start EDT (or define a short symbol to represent it in your LOGIN.COM file). When EDT starts, the commands in EDTINI.EDT will be performed automatically.

EDT Summary

This section does not provide a complete introduction to the EDT text editor; it is only a crash course in the most essential functions.

Using this basic guide, you should be able to create new text files, edit existing ones, and effectively use the EDT editor for normal tasks. EDT is not the only editor supplied with OpenVMS; your system may have additional editors or word processors installed. Your system manager can tell you if this is the case.

Chapter 14 — Using DECnet

DECnet is a suite of peer-to-peer networking software developed by Digital Equipment Corporation to work with several of its operating systems in addition to OpenVMS.

Your OpenVMS system may or may not be running DECnet or other networking products (e.g., TCP/IP). Use the SHOW NETWORK command to determine which networking products your system is running.

> **Note:** Some third-party networking products are reported by the SHOW NETWORK command, others are not.

Your system manager will provide you with the names of any other systems on your DECnet network that you are authorized to use. Node name formats may differ somewhat depending on the version of DECnet software in use at your site. Your site may be running DECnet Phase IV, DECnet Phase V (a.k.a. DECnet OSI or DECnet-Plus), or both. The node-naming and addressing rules are explained here for completeness. You will be instructed as to the names in use on your network.

DECnet Phase IV Node Names and Addresses

Computers participating in DECnet networks are known as nodes. This is synonymous with the term *hosts* used with TCP/IP networking.

> **Note:** OpenVMS machines often participate in DECnet networks and TCP/IP networks at the same time. Many system managers configure DECnet to carry private company wide traffic among local OpenVMS machines, and TCP/IP to handle both internal and Internet traffic.

As with most other types of networking schemes, nodes can be referred to by name or by network address. DECnet Phase IV node names consist of one to six alphanumeric characters, including at least one alphabetic character.

DECnet Phase IV networks are divided into *areas*, with each DECnet node being a member of exactly one area. An area can be in the range of 1 through 63, and a node can be in the range of 1 through 1,023. A DECnet Phase IV network may therefore include about 65,000 nodes. The format of a DECnet address is

```
area.node
```

Let's imagine a small DECnet network with three nodes:

```
Name      Address    Explanation
BAXTER    1.1        Area 1, node 1
ARTHUR    1.27       Area 1, node 27
PHOEBE    2.15       Area 2, node 15
```

In DCL commands, you may refer to a DECnet node by its name or by its address. For example, the following two commands are equivalent:

```
$ SET HOST ARTHUR
$ SET HOST 1.27
```

Furthermore, if you are referencing an address from a machine in the same area, you may omit the area number from the address. BAXTER (in area 1) may refer to ARTHUR as "1.27" or simply as "27." PHOEBE, however, must use "1.27" because PHOEBE is in a different area.

The address "0" always refers to the local node (the machine you are currently using). Experienced users often use the command SET HOST 0 to briefly log into the current machine under a different username.

DECnet-Plus Node Names

Whereas DECnet Phase IV node names consist of up to six straightforward characters, DECnet-Plus (if available on your system) allows longer node names with a wider range of legal characters. These are referred to as *node full names*.

A node full name can be up to 255 characters in length and can include any characters except commas, quotation marks, slashes, apostrophes, parentheses, and double colons. A single colon may not be the first or last character.

However, if a node full name is enclosed in quotation marks, it can contain any of the characters just mentioned, except unpaired quotation marks. In this case, quotation marks in the node name must each be doubled, as shown below. Some examples of valid full names are as follows:

```
TAMPA
LOCAL:.DNS4
"DALLAS:.HEADQUARTERS.""ACCOUNTING"""
```

DECnet-Plus nodes may also have Phase IV–style names and network addresses assigned to them to provide compatibility with Phase IV nodes elsewhere on the network.

Using DECnet To Access Remote Files

DECnet file access is very easy to use. It is so well integrated with the OpenVMS file system that you may be only peripherally aware that you are using it. You only need to identify the system on which a file resides and, in some circumstances, to provide a username and password for the remote system.

You will recall the full file specification format presented earlier:

NODE::*DEVICE*:[*DIR.SUBDIR1.SUBDIR2*(...)]*NAME.EXT*;*VERSION*

Notice the first element of a full specification, *NODE*::. Simply specifying a node in a file specification automatically causes DECnet to perform the file operation. If the remote node requires user authentication, this field takes the form *NODE username password*::.

Note: This is a conventional DECnet file specification. For remote file specifications that do not conform to OpenVMS filename rules, see "Foreign File Specifications" below.

Imagine a file existing on the remote DECnet node TAMPA. You may display its contents simply by specifying its location in the file specification, as in the following example:

```
$ TYPE TAMPA"username password"::CALENDAR.TXT
```

The command above causes DECnet to contact the remote node TAMPA. TAMPA will verify that the username and password you supplied match a valid user on TAMPA. If so, the DECnet software on TAMPA will act on your behalf to access the file. Of course, the username you supply must have permission to access the file exactly as if you had logged in interactively.

Since no disk or directory was specified, the login directory (SYS$LOGIN) of the username you specified will be assumed. If the file exists in some other directory, simply add that information to the file specification:

```
$ TYPE TAMPA"username password"::DKB400:[USERS.SMITH]CALENDAR.TXT
```

Virtually any DCL command can be used with DECnet file access, just as if the files were local. Here are some examples:

```
$ DIRECTORY TAMPA"username password"::DKA300:[SMITH]

$ EDIT TAMPA"username password"::LOGIN.COM

$ COPY TAMPA"username password"::DKA300:[SMITH]*.TXT []*.*
```

```
$ DELETE TAMPA"username password"::DKA300:[SMITH]JUNK.DAT;*
```

DECnet Proxies

Many OpenVMS users have accounts on several systems or must routinely access the files belonging to a particular account on a remote node. DECnet proxy access relieves you of the need to supply a username and password for each file access.

With proxy access, your system manager sets up a relationship between your local account and a given account on the remote system. When you access files on the remote system, you may omit the username and password.

While the network connection is being established, the remote system automatically recognizes that your username has a proxy relationship with an account on that node. File accesses are carried out using the remote account.

The preceding examples become much simpler when your local account has proxy access to user SMITH on node TAMPA:

```
$ DIR TAMPA::

$ EDIT TAMPA::LOGIN.COM

$ COPY TAMPA::*.TXT []*.*

$ DELETE TAMPA::JUNK.DAT;*
```

Even when your account has proxy access to a given node and account, you may still use another remote identity by specifying a valid username and password.

Your system manager will configure any appropriate proxies for you.

Foreign File Specifications

On DECnet-Plus systems, you may use a *foreign file specification* to specify remote files that do not conform to OpenVMS filename rules:

```
node::"foreign-filespec"
```

The following file specification includes a question mark, which is not legal under OpenVMS filename rules. It must therefore be enclosed in quotes:

```
MIAMI::"file?.text"
```

The filename must be in a format recognized by the operating system running on the remote node.

DECnet Tasks

DECnet tasks allow applications on different nodes to work together. For most applications, your system manager will have already configured the applications, so the general user most often has no need to be concerned with the details.

However, as a general user, you can set up your own DECnet tasks to perform work on a remote node without logging in. This section demonstrates how to set up a simple DECnet task. This example shows the bare framework, which you can expand upon later as the need arises.

To use a DECnet task, you need only two things: network access to an account on a remote node and a command procedure that performs the work.

Creating a DECnet Task

A DECnet task takes the form of a command procedure. It resides on the remote node and executes in response to a certain type of network access. The command procedure can pass information back to the originating process, perform work on the remote node, or both.

Our task will simply pass the system time on the remote node back to the node which originated the request:

```
$ !
$ ! The following DEFINE directs information which
$ ! would normally go to SYS$OUTPUT to go instead to
$ ! SYS$NET.  The logical name SYS$NET represents the
$ ! remote process that caused this procedure to
$ ! execute.  In this way, we can pass information
$ ! back to the requesting process.
$ !
$ DEFINE SYS$OUTPUT SYS$NET
$ !
$ ! Now display the system time (on the node where
$ ! this command procedure resides), which will be
$ ! directed back to the originating process on SYS$NET
$ !
$ SHOW TIME
$ !
$ ! And we're done.
$ !
$ EXIT
```

Simply place this command procedure in the SYS$LOGIN directory of the remote account under the name SHOWTIME.COM. Directories other than SYS$LOGIN are not supported.

Executing the Remote Task

To execute this DECnet task, you may use the DCL command TYPE (which displays the information returned by the task) with a special file access syntax shown below.

Replace the nodename, username, and password with those applicable to your configuration:

```
$ TYPE TAMPA"SMITH password"::"task=showtime"
  12-MAY-2003 17:26:09
```

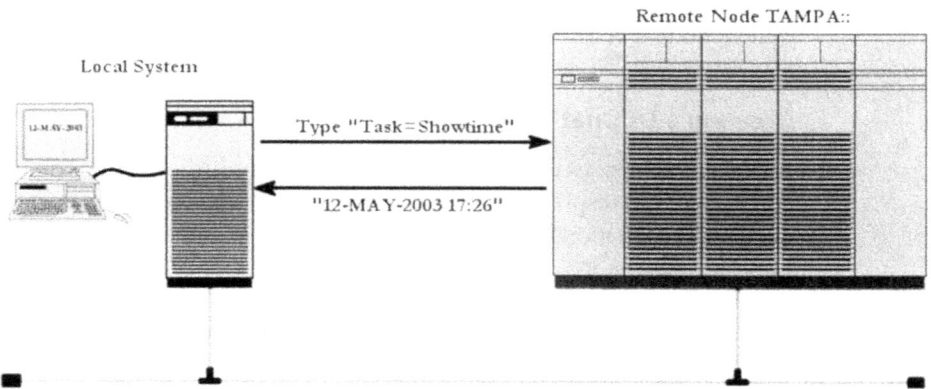

Figure 14-1 A DECnet Task

Just as with DECnet file access, TAMPA"SMITH *password*":: specifies the remote node TAMPA, using the SMITH account. This time, however, the addition of "task=showtime" causes the command procedure SHOWTIME.COM to be executed.

The command procedure executes on node TAMPA, not on your local node. Therefore, the time shown is the system time on TAMPA. Likewise, any work performed by the command procedure will be carried out on node TAMPA under the account TAMPA::SMITH. In this manner, you can maintain command procedures to perform various tasks on remote nodes simply by typing them.

If Your Task Did Not Work

If your task failed to work, there are a few likely explanations. Please compare your error message to those below:

```
%TYPE-W-OPENIN, error opening TAMPA"smith password"::"task=showtime" as input
-RMS-E-ACC, ACP file access failed
-SYSTEM-F-LINKEXIT, network partner exited
```

This probably means that your assignment of SYS$NET is missing or mistyped. Check your command procedure and compare it to the example. Other possible causes include network communications problems.

```
%TYPE-W-OPENIN, error opening TAMPA"smith password"::"task=showtime" as input
-RMS-E-ACC, ACP file access failed
-SYSTEM-F-INVLOGIN, login information invalid at remote node
```

This means that the username and password you supplied are not valid or that the account is disabled or has network access disallowed. Ensure that the username and password are valid.

```
%TYPE-W-OPENIN, error opening TAMPA"smith password"::"task=showtime" as input
-RMS-E-ACC, ACP file access failed
-SYSTEM-F-NOSUCHOBJ, network object is unknown at remote node
```

This means that the command procedure specified is not present. Did you spell its name correctly? Does it reside in the SYS$LOGIN directory of the account you specified?

```
%TYPE-W-OPENIN, error opening TAMPA"smith password"::"task=showtime" as input
-RMS-E-ACC, ACP file access failed
-SYSTEM-F-NOSUCHNODE, remote node is unknown
```

This means that the nodename you specified is unknown to the DECnet software. Check the nodename you entered.

```
%TYPE-W-OPENIN, error opening TAMPA"smith password"::"task=showtime" as input
-RMS-E-ACC, ACP file access failed
-SYSTEM-F-UNREACHABLE, remote node is not currently reachable
```

This means that the DECnet software knows of the node you specified, but there is currently no response from that node. The node may not be running, or there may be routing problems or other network problems preventing communication.

Logging into Another Node

Use the "SET HOST *node*" command to log into another DECnet node. The remote node will prompt you for a username, just as if you were logging in locally:

```
$ SET HOST BAXTER

  Unauthorized access strictly prohibited.

Username: mike
Password:
 Welcome to OpenVMS (TM) VAX Operating System, Version V7.3 on node BAXTER
    Last interactive login on Thursday, 16-JAN-2003 16:11
```

```
  Last non-interactive login on Thursday, 16-JAN-2003 17:16
$
```

You may now use BAXTER just as if you were logged in locally. In reality, your local node accepts your keystrokes and forwards them to BAXTER. Similarly, output from BAXTER is passed back to your local node to be displayed on your terminal.

When you are finished using the remote node, log out. A logout message will appear, followed by a message indicating that control has been returned to the original node:

```
$ LOGOUT
  MIKE          logged out at 16-JAN-2003 17:22:13.50
%REM-S-END, control returned to node PHOEBE::
$
```

Note: SET HOST can also be used to dial out through a modem connected to a terminal port. This command takes the form SET HOST/DTE *device*.

Aborting a DECnet Session

If, because of network communication problems, your remote session becomes unresponsive, you may abort the connection by pressing CTRL/Y twice in succession. You will be asked whether you would like to abort the connection to the remote node. Answer yes.

Summary

This chapter has shown how to access remote files, use simple DECnet tasks, and log into other nodes on the DECnet network.

Part II of this book contains some additional information about the implementation of DECnet.

Chapter 15 — The OpenVMS GUI

This chapter introduces the OpenVMS GUI.

Earlier chapters concentrated entirely on the text-only DCL interface. Many OpenVMS systems have no graphics hardware at all; others may not offer GUI services to all users, such as those connecting via Telnet.

Some readers will have direct access to a desktop OpenVMS system or to X Window System clients, which allows the execution of many components of the OpenVMS GUI. Users who have text-only access may skip this chapter if they desire.

GUI users are strongly encouraged to learn about the DCL interface, as DCL and command procedures are a central part of OpenVMS, even for GUI users.

The remainder of this chapter is designed to guide the reader through logging into the GUI interface and then to introduce its features.

Systems That Can Support the GUI

In order to use the OpenVMS GUI, you must have either an OpenVMS system with graphics hardware or an X Window System client system that can use the OpenVMS system as a server.

The GUI interface was added several years after OpenVMS was created, and some OpenVMS machines have neither a graphics monitor, nor a mouse. These machines usually have terminal ports and network connections. They often sit in dedicated computer rooms or are mounted in a rack and act only as servers. Graphics hardware is simply not required for them to carry out their work.

On the other hand, many recent OpenVMS systems come equipped with graphics hardware. They have a monitor, a keyboard, and a mouse. Certain models are even configurable with or without graphics hardware. GUI-capable OpenVMS computers are easily recognized; simply look for a graphics monitor and a mouse.

This book will concentrate on using the GUI interface directly on an OpenVMS system equipped with the appropriate graphics hardware. Most of the material is applicable to users of X Window System clients, but using such clients will not be specifically covered.

GUI Basics

There are a few terms you will need to know in order to use a GUI system. GUIs
generally use windows to display information. A *window* is a rectangular area on the
screen, generally under the control of some application. Some applications may
present many windows simultaneously.

Most windows have a uniform format, following a standard format for borders, title
bars, and controls. Windows often have a *menu bar* just beneath the title, and below
that, a *client area*. The client area usually comprises most of the window and is where
the application displays text, graphics, or both.

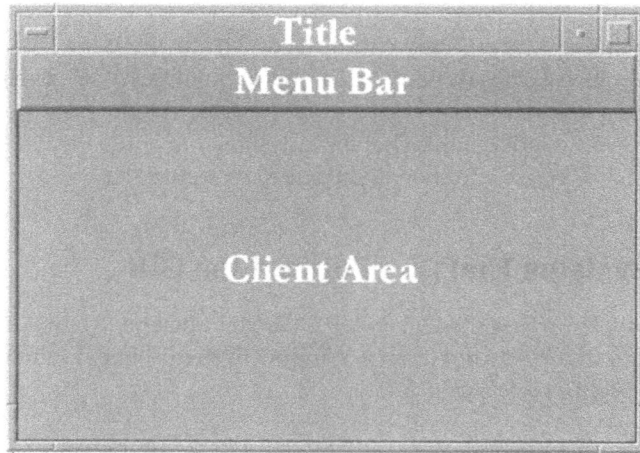

Figure 15-1 A Window

A *dialog box* is similar to a window but is used mainly for accepting data input from
the user or to notify the user about various conditions. It usually has one or more
buttons, *menus*, or *input fields*. These items allow the user to select various options or
enter data. Buttons are selected by *clicking* them (see "Using the Mouse"), and input
fields are used by first clicking on the field, then using the keyboard to enter data into
the field. The TAB key can also be used to advance from one field to the next.

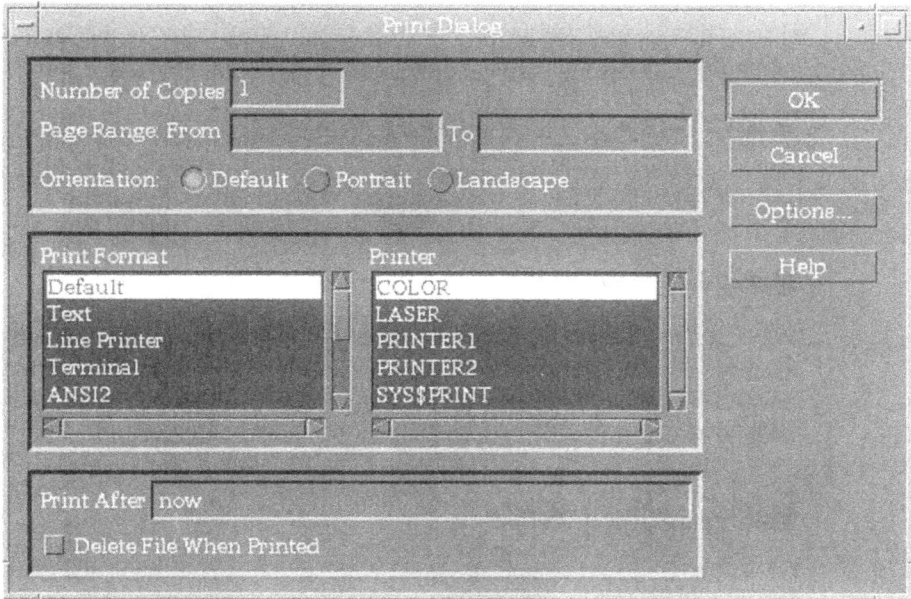

Figure 15-2 A Dialog Box

Using the Mouse

Your OpenVMS system comes with either a two- or a three-button mouse, depending on your hardware. If your mouse has three buttons, you can essentially ignore the third button for most purposes.

The terms *click*, *right-click*, *double-click*, and *drag* are used throughout this chapter. They are the basic skills required to use the mouse in the GUI environment.

Click and Right-Click

To click, press and release the left mouse button (Button 1) and release it without moving the mouse. This is used to select a window, press a button, follow a hyperlink, or choose a menu item. Clicking while your mouse pointer is directly over one of the above items selects that item.

To right-click, use the right mouse button.

Double-Click

Press and release the left mouse button twice in quick succession. This is used to restore a window that has been minimized and for other selected actions described in the following sections.

Dragging

This action is used within the File Manager to copy or move files, to move icons or other items around the screen, and to scroll the contents of a window.

Position the mouse pointer over the item, then press and hold Button 1. While holding Button 1 down, move your mouse pointer to the desired location, then release the button. The selected item will be moved or copied to that location.

Manipulating Windows

Windows can be manipulated in a variety of ways: They can be moved to a new location, minimized (reduced to an icon), restored (brought back from an icon), maximized (enlarged to take up the entire screen), or closed (destroyed), and they can usually be resized. They can also be made active or inactive.

Making a Window Active

Only one window is active at a time. When a window is made active, it is usually brought "to the front." This means that if it had been partially covered by other windows, it will now jump to the front, unobscured.

You can tell which window is active by the color of its border; all inactive windows have uniformly colored borders, while the active window will have a unique border color. An active window is also said to have "input focus." Any keyboard input will be received and processed by the active window.

A window becomes active when you click anywhere on the window. Please note that if you click on a button or menu, you will also usually activate that button or menu in addition to making the window active.

Note: You may change your system settings so that pointing to a window is sufficient to make it active. Use the Window option in the Style Manager.

Minimizing a Window

Too many open windows clutter the screen and make it difficult to work. Click the minimize control (see Figure 15-3) to reduce the window to an icon. While minimized, the program is not frozen and can continue to perform work. Icons appear in a row starting from the upper-left corner of the screen, but you may drag an icon to any location where it will remain, even if it is restored and minimized again.

Figure 15-3 The Minimize Control

Figure 15-4 Icons

Restoring a Minimized Window

When a window is minimized, it is reduced to an icon. Double-click on the icon to restore the window.

Maximizing a Window

Clicking the maximize control enlarges the window to occupy the entire screen. When the window is maximized, clicking the same control again restores the window to its original size.

Figure 15-5 The Maximize Control

Resizing a Window

Most windows may be resized at will. The borders of a window are divided into eight controls: four edge and four corner controls (three of which are highlighted in Figure 15-6 with their effects shown.) To resize a window, drag one of these eight controls to the desired position. The edge controls affect one edge, whereas the corner controls affect both adjacent edges.

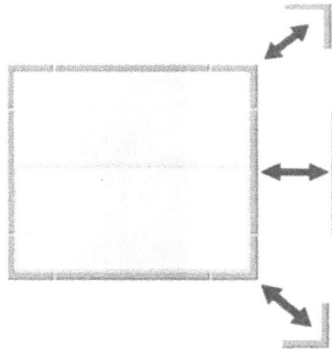

Figure 15-6 Window Resizing Controls

The Window Menu

At the upper-left corner of every window is the window menu control (see Figure 15-7). Clicking on the window menu control produces a pop-up menu containing alternative ways to perform some of the functions already discussed. Certain applications may include additional items on this menu.

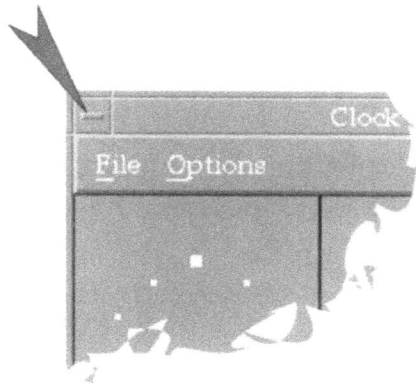

Figure 15-7 Window Menu Control

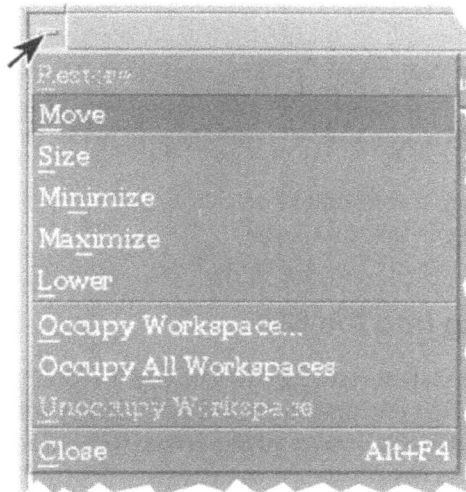

Figure 15-8 The Window Menu

This menu almost always contains a Close command that will close the window. Double-clicking the window menu control or pressing ALT/F4 while the window is active will also close it.

Note, however, that most applications provide an exit function in their own menus. Using the exit function provided by the application is generally the preferred method.

Additionally, there are Occupy Workspace and Occupy All Workspaces selections, which move the window to another workspace or make it present in all of them. Workspaces are described further on.

The Lower command pushes the window to the bottom of the stack (i.e., makes any overlapping windows obstruct the current one). To bring the current window back to the top, you must first make another window active. When you switch back to the first window, it will again be on top.

Window Menu Bars

Menus within windows are separate from the Window Menu just described. Most applications present a row of menus just beneath the window title.

Figure 15-9 A Menu Bar

When you click on one of these menu names, a pull-down menu will appear. Select an option by clicking on it. Menu items that are not currently available will appear greyed out (e.g., a Delete command will not be available if there is nothing to delete.)

If you change your mind and choose not to select any option, click outside the menu, and the menu will disappear.

Logging into the GUI

When the system starts or when no one is logged in, the GUI presents a login window while waiting for someone to log in. Different versions of OpenVMS may present slightly different versions of this screen with differing corporate logos, etc., but each of them works essentially the same way.

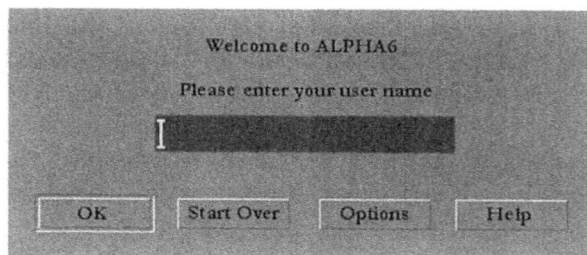

Figure 15-10 The Login Screen

The system begins by asking for your username. Type your username and press ENTER (or click OK). The system then asks for your password. Type your password and press ENTER (or click OK). Just as with the terminal interface, your password will not be displayed. Unlike the terminal interface, the password prompt will not time out in 20 seconds.

Once your password is entered, your session begins. If an error occurs (such as a mistyped password), a dialog box will display the cause of the error. After reading the message, click OK to start again.

If you make a mistake or decide not to log in, click Start Over.

Login Screen Options

This section describes the login screen Options menu. Most users rarely have a need to change any of these settings.

Options: Language

Allows you to choose the session language.

Options: Session

- *New Desktop* This is the default desktop for OpenVMS, based on the Common Desktop Environment (CDE). It is one of two desktops supported by OpenVMS, the other being DECwindows.

- *Failsafe Session* This starts a basic session with a single DECterm terminal window. This is mostly used for correcting problems that otherwise prevent your selected desktop from running. Use this option only when needed to correct a problem.

- *DECwindows Session* This causes the older DECwindows GUI to run instead of the New Desktop. The DECwindows interface is discussed later as a separate topic.

Options: Reset Login Screen

Resets the X Server, the software that coordinates and oversees the general operation of the GUI.

The New Desktop

The OpenVMS New Desktop is an implementation of the Common Desktop Environment (CDE). CDE combines the technologies of the X Window System, OSF /Motif, and other original components. CDE is supplied with several commercial systems, including a variety of UNIX systems from various vendors. Information about CDE, the X Window System, and Motif is available at

```
http://www.opengroup.org/desktop/
```

Logging out of the New Desktop

Before logging out, first save any work that has not been saved in any open applications.

There are several ways to log out of the New Desktop. You may click the exit control on the workspace switch (described later) or activate the Window menu of the Front panel (also described later) and select Log out, or right-click on an unoccupied area of the screen and select Log out from the workspace menu that appears.

Depending on your Style Manager settings, you may or may not be asked to confirm your desire to log out.

The Front Panel

The *front panel* is the bar located at the bottom of the screen with a variety of small graphical elements on it.

The front panel is present at all times under the New Desktop and is the starting point for most functions you will perform. It contains controls that perform a variety of functions. Some controls start applications. Others, such as the clock, only provide information.

A control may provide information and also start an application. For example, the mailer icon notifies you when there is new mail waiting, but it also starts the mail program when clicked. Certain controls, such as the trash can, are known as *drop zones*. For example, when you drag a file over the trash can and release it, the file is deleted.

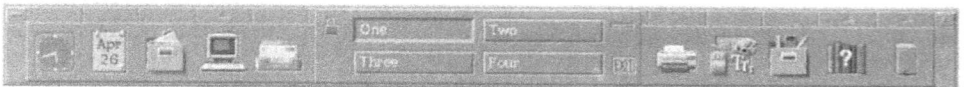

Figure 15-11 The Front Panel

Parts of the Front Panel

The front panel is divided into three main sections. In the middle is the *workspace switch*. To either side are controls for applications, utilities, and subpanels.

The Front Panel Window Menu

Just as each window has a Window menu, so does the front panel itself. It is activated by the control located in the upper-left corner of the front panel, as shown in Figure 15-12.

Figure 15-12 The Front Panel Window Menu

It contains many of the same functions as any other menu (minimize, restore, etc.), but also contains a Log Out item that can be used to end your session.

The Workspace Switch

The New Desktop supports separate *workspaces*. Conceptually, workspaces are like having several separate monitors, each with a different set of applications and windows. By default, four workspaces are provided, named One through Four, but workspaces can be added, removed, and renamed at will. Each workspace can have its own background and color scheme as well. You may wish to use multiple workspaces to avoid too much clutter in one workspace or to group tasks into separate related units.

Figure 15-13 The Workspace Switch

To switch workspaces, click on the bar containing a workspace name. To add, remove, or rename a workspace, right-click on one of the workspace names and select the appropriate item from the pop-up menu that appears.

You may move a window to another workspace or make it present in all workspaces by selecting Occupy Workspace or Occupy all Workspaces from its Window menu (see "The Window Menu").

The workspace switch also contains three other controls: the lock, the activity indicator, and the exit control.

- *The Lock* Clears the display and locks it from being accessed when clicked. To unlock the display, you must enter your password again.

> **Note:** Locking the workstation applies to the GUI only; it does not prevent such access as terminal logins or remote file access.

- *The Activity Indicator* Flashes while the system is performing an activity. It is otherwise known as a busy indicator, but that name is inaccurate. You can usually initiate other activities while it is flashing, and it flashes only while the GUI-control software (not OpenVMS itself) is working.

- *The Exit Control* Initiates a logout from the system when clicked. You may be asked to confirm your desire to log out, depending on your settings. If you confirm, all applications will be closed and your session will be ended.

Other Front Panel Controls

The rest of the front panel is divided into controls and subpanels (discussed later). The controls, from left to right, are as follows:

- *Clock* This is an indicator of the time only and performs no other function.

Figure 15-14 The Clock Control

- *Calendar* This indicates the current date. When clicked, it starts the calendar application, a combination calendar and day planner.

Figure 15-15 The Calendar Control

- *File Manager* When clicked, this starts a File Manager view of your home folder (directory). When dropped on, it starts a File Manager view of the folder that was dropped.

Figure 15-16 The File Manager Control

- *Personal Application* This position in the front panel is reserved for an application of your choice, which starts when clicked. Your personal application may differ from this example. Changing your personal application is discussed further on in the section "Adding to a Subpanel."

  The default personal application is the text editor (the CDE editor, not EDT). Dropping a file onto the text editor icon causes the editor to start with the specified file loaded.

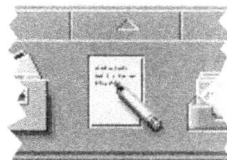

Figure 15-17 The Text Editor Control

- *Mailer* When clicked, this starts the GUI interface to OpenVMS mail. When dropped on, it starts mail with the specified file loaded. The appearance of the mailer icon changes when new mail messages are waiting.

Figure 15-18 Mailer Control with No New Mail

Figure 15-19 Mailer Control with New Mail

- *Default Printer* When dropped on, this prints the dropped file on your default printer. When clicked, it starts a dialog box that allows you to change your printer settings.

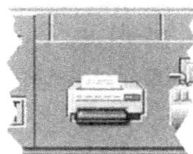

Figure 15-20 The Default Printer Control

- *Style Manager* When clicked, this starts the style manager, which allows you to change the screen background, colors, mouse settings, screen savers, etc.

Figure 15-21 The Style Manager Control

- *Application Manager* When clicked, this opens the Application Manager window, which contains controls for starting most applications and tools.

Figure 15-22 The Application Manager Control

- *Help Manager* When clicked, this opens the Help Manager. Use this application to obtain help on the New Desktop and its applications.

Figure 15-23 The Help Manager Control

- *Trash Can* When clicked, this opens the trash can window. When dropped on, it deletes the file that was dropped. The trash can window allows you to recover files previously selected for deletion, provided they have not yet been permanently deleted.

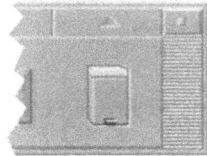

Figure 15-24 The Trash Can Control

Subpanels

A *subpanel* is a menu associated with a control slot on the front panel. You will notice that there is a small rectangular field just above each front-panel control. If this field contains an upward-pointing arrow, a subpanel is available.

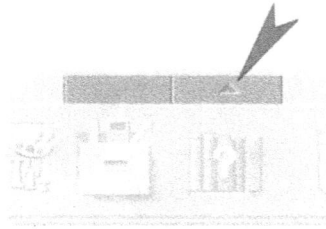

Figure 15-25 A Subpanel Control

Clicking the arrow displays the subpanel. Clicking the arrow again (now pointing downward) hides it.

Figure 15-26 A Raised Subpanel

Each subpanel contains additional controls relevant to the front-panel control with which it appears. For example, the Personal Application subpanel contains personal applications, and the help subpanel holds help controls.

Selecting from a Subpanel

Simply hold the mouse pointer over the desired option and click.

Adding to a Subpanel

You may add an icon (e.g., an icon that starts an application) by dropping the icon onto the Install Icon control on a subpanel. The following example will add the Calculator application to the Personal Applications subpanel. The steps are as follows:

1. Open the Personal Applications subpanel by clicking the up-arrow symbol over the Personal Application control.

2. Open the Application Manager window by clicking the Application Manager control.

3. Double-click DECwindows Apps to display the window containing the Calculator application.

4. Locate the Calculator icon. Drag the calculator icon directly over the Install Icon control in the Personal Applications subpanel and drop (release the mouse button).

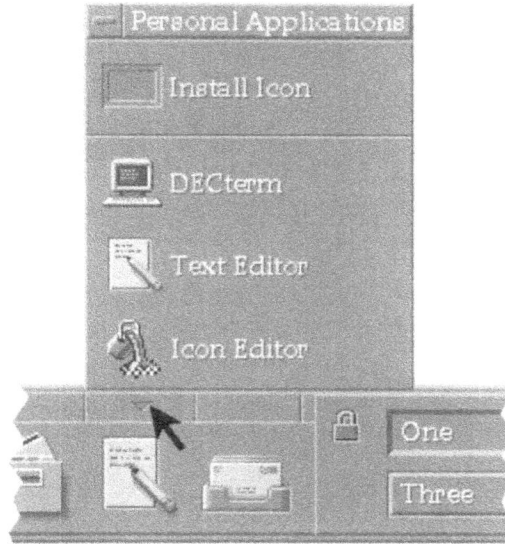

Figure 15-27 The Personal Applications Subpanel

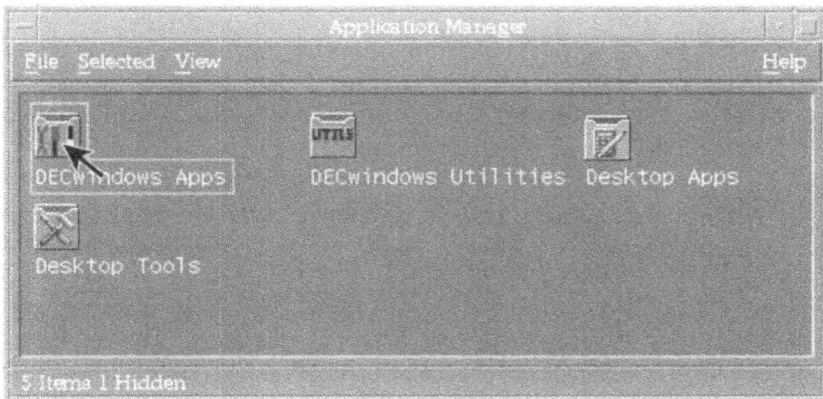

Figure 15-28 The Application Manager

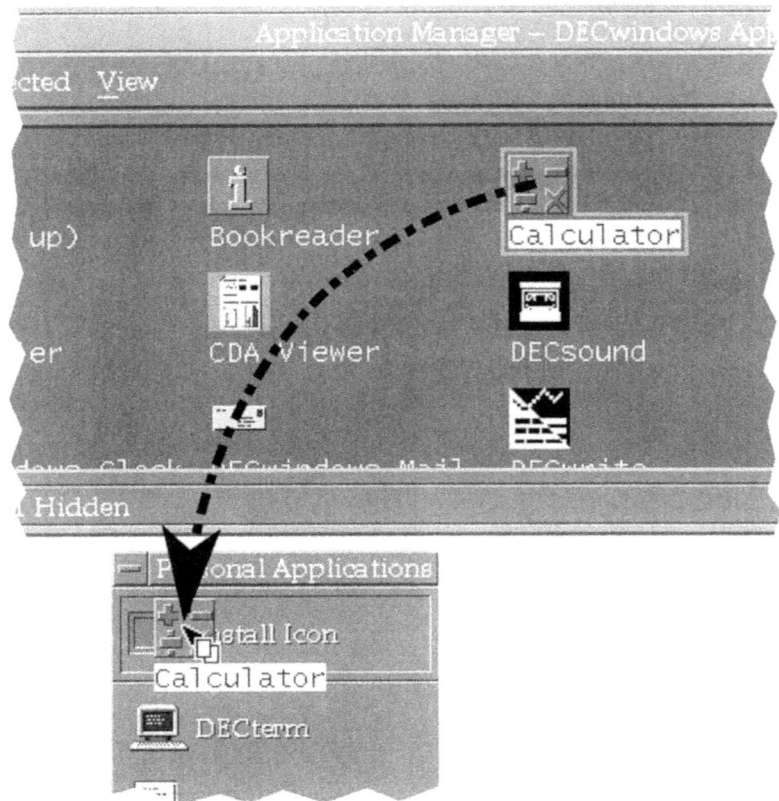

Figure 15-29 Adding an Icon to a Subpanel

The Calculator application is now added to the Personal Applications subpanel.

Setting Your Personal Application

To change your primary personal application, first add it to your Personal Applications subpanel, if necessary. This process is described above, in "Adding to a Subpanel."

While the Personal Applications subpanel is open, right-click on the application you wish to set as your default application. Click Copy to Main Panel.

Your selected application replaces the previous front panel control.

Deleting from a Subpanel

Use caution when deleting an item from a subpanel. Some items may be difficult to add again should it become necessary. In general, delete only items you have added yourself, thus ensuring that they can be replaced easily.

To delete from a subpanel, right-click on the desired control and click Delete.

Overview of Front-Panel Applications

This section briefly describes each application appearing on the front panel. It does not describe any applications in detail; instead, only major functions are briefly mentioned. Keep in mind that each application has a built-in Help menu that can answer most questions about its use.

Applications available via the Application Manager are discussed further on.

Calendar

This application is a traditional calendar as well as a day planner. It allows you to schedule events and send yourself notifications prior to their occurrences.

- *View Menu* Month and Year display calendar pages for the current month and year, respectively. Selected, Today, and Day switch to a planner page for the appropriate date (Selected refers to a day you have highlighted on the Month or Year displays.)

- *Entry Menu* The Entry menu appears only on a day-planner page. To use the items on it, you must create or select an entry on the planner page. You create an entry by clicking on a time of day and typing the name of an event. Selecting Edit from the Event menu allows you to customize the event. For example, you may elect to make the event repeat at weekly intervals or adjust how far in advance of the event you should be notified.

File Manager

The File Manager allows you to move around a directory tree and work with files. You may create files and directories (referred to as *folders*), list files by various criteria, and perform operations on them. For example, files may be dragged to the Printer, Text Editor, or Trash Can controls, which will automatically operate on the file. You may drag frequently used files directly onto the workspace for quick access.

Navigating the Directory Tree

When your view is set to By single folder, double-click on a folder shown in the view window to switch to that directory. When your view is set to By tree, click the "+/-" sign beside a folder to reveal or hide the contents of that folder.

You may view folders other than your own if you have appropriate privileges. Use the Go To option from the File menu.

File Manager Menus

- *File Menu* allows you to create files and folders, navigate the directory tree, open a DECterm window, or exit the File Manager.

- *Selected Menu* allows you to perform operations on groups of files, such as moving, copying, or setting permissions on them.

- *View Menu* allows you to customize the style in which files and folders are displayed.

Mailer

The Mailer is essentially a GUI interface to the OpenVMS mail facility, whose text interface was previously described. Operation is virtually the same, except that commands are chosen from menus as opposed to being typed at a terminal. (See Chapter 12, "E-mail")

Default Printer

When clicked, this opens a dialog box from which you can select a default printer and various printer settings. When selected directly from the front panel in this way, you select default settings only; no file is actually printed. To print a file, drag and drop the file onto the printer control on the front panel.

Style Manager

With the Style Manager, you control several options regarding the appearance and functionality of your display, keyboard, and mouse. The Style Manager options are as follows:

- *Color* selects a color scheme for your workspace windows.

- *Font* controls the size of the type font used by applications.

- *Backdrop* selects from a variety of screen backgrounds. Each workspace may have its own backdrop.

- *Keyboard* allows you to enable or disable keyboard autorepeat and set the volume of optional keyclick sounds.

- *Mouse* allows you to adjust mouse settings (e.g., left- or right-handedness and pointer acceleration).

- *Beep* allows you to set the pitch, volume, and duration of the standard beep sound.

- *Screen* allows you to select an active screen background (screen saver) to run while the display is locked or the session is idle.

- *Window* controls window behavior, including whether pointing or clicking in a window makes it active and whether an active window is automatically placed on top.

- *Startup* controls the startup action of your session—Reset to home session or Resume previous session—and whether logouts are confirmed. It also allows you to set your current session as your home session (handy for selecting which applications to automatically start at login). An example of setting your startup session is included in the section "Starting Applications Automatically."

- *Security* allows you to add or remove access control entries for access by accounts on your node or from other nodes on the DECnet network.

Application Manager

Use the Application Manager to start applications not present on the front panel or any of its subpanels. The Application Manager presents folders containing GUI applications in much the same way that the File Manager presents other files.

When started, the Application Manager presents four folders: DECwindows Apps, DECwindows Utilities, Desktop Apps, and Desktop Tools. To select a folder, double-click on it.

The four folders and their contents are listed below.

Note: Applications can be added to and removed from the Application Manager folders; the applications on your system may differ from those described here.

Application Manager: DECwindows Apps

The DECwindows Apps folder contains several DECwindows applications, which can be used under the New Desktop as well as the older DECwindows interface.

- *Bookreader* an application for viewing DECwindows "books," including certain versions of the OpenVMS documentation kit on CD-ROM. (Other versions supply PostScript and / or PDF files.) DECwindows books are similar in look and feel to documents in PDF format.

- *Calculator* an emulation of a hand-held calculator. In addition to simple arithmetic, it can perform some trigonometric functions, calculate square roots and exponents, and display decimal, octal, and hexadecimal representations.

- *Calendar* the same Calendar application available on the front panel.

- *Cardfiler* the cardfiler is an on-screen representation of a file of index cards. Cards might contain names and addresses of business contacts, for example. The Cardfiler can group and maintain separate sets of cards for different purposes.

- *CDA Viewer* CDA stands for "Compound Document Architecture." This application is a viewer for documents in Digital Document Interchange Format (DDIF), PostScript files, and text files.

- *DECsound* an application for playing sound files.

- *DECterm* a terminal emulator program that acts as a Digital VT-style terminal. When started, DECterm is automatically logged into the system without the need to enter your username and password again. A DECterm window functions very much like a physical terminal connected to the system, but with some additional capabilities.

- *DECwindows Clock* a program that simulates an analog or digital clock. It optionally displays the date and can function as an alarm clock.

- *DECwindows Mail* the same mailer application as available on the front panel.

- *DECwrite* a full-featured word processing application.

- *EVE Editor* EVE (also referred to as TPU) is a text editor that can be used through text or GUI interfaces. This control starts the GUI version.

- *Image Viewer* an application for displaying graphics files in .GIF, .JPEG, .TIFF, or .XPM format.

- *Message Window* an application specifically designed to display broadcast messages. As discussed previously, OpenVMS sends a variety of broadcast messages to user terminals. In the GUI environment, you may or may not have a DECterm terminal session with which to receive these messages. The Message Window provides a destination for them.

- *Mosaic* an HTTP client (Web browser). Future versions of OpenVMS may include the Mozilla browser instead.

- *Notepad* a text editor. This is separate from EDT, EVE, and the CDE text editor, all mentioned previously. Common functions (e.g., include, find, replace, copy, cut, and paste) are included.

- *Paint* a simple graphics program allowing you to create images in DDIF format.

- *Print Screen* a utility for capturing screen images and saving them in DDIF, PostScript, or SIXEL (a Digital-specific) format. Many of the illustrations in this book were captured using this utility.

- *Puzzle* a video representation of a simple puzzle game consisting of numbered squares that the user must put in order by sliding the pieces.

Application Manager: DECwindows Utilities

This folder contains utility programs mostly used to examine or modify the internal states of the GUI software, generally requiring a somewhat advanced knowledge of the GUI's internals to be of use. They are not discussed in this book.

Application Manager: Desktop Apps

This folder contains applications associated with the New Desktop. These are separate from the applications in the DECwindows Apps folder, many of which are associated with the older DECwindows environment.

- *Calculator* This is a separate program from the DECwindows calculator program. It is similar in most respects, but has several additional features.

- *Create Action* This is a tool with which you can create custom action icons for your desktop. You may use these icons to perform customized tasks. Further on, this chapter contains an example of creating an action.

- *File Manager* This is the same File Manager application available on the front panel.

- *Help Viewer* This is the same Help Viewer application available on the front panel.

- *Icon Editor* This allows you to create and modify icons. For example, you might use this in conjunction with the "Create Action" application to place a new icon on your desktop and associate it with a custom action.

- *Man Page Viewer* This is the viewer for UNIX-style Help entries concerning the New Desktop. These help entries are separate from the Help Viewer entries and the OpenVMS Help facility. To view a man page, start the viewer and type the name of the desired page. The available pages are located in directory SYS$COMMON:[CDE$DEFAULTS.SYSTEM.MAN]. This feature should be familiar to users accustomed to UNIX systems.

- *Style Manager* This is the same Style Manager application available on the front panel.

- *Text Editor* This is the CDE text editor. On many systems, this is the default personal application on the front panel. It is similar to the DECwindows Notepad application.

- *Trash Can* This is the same Trash Can application available on the front panel.

Application Manager: Desktop Tools

This folder contains several utilities that are GUI interfaces to normal OpenVMS commands and X Window System utilities. Some entries are duplicates of items in other folders and will not be mentioned again here.

Except where noted, each of these tasks can be performed at the DCL prompt using the command indicated.

- *Compare Files* invokes the OpenVMS DIFFERENCES command to compare two files and report any differences.

- *Delete File* invokes the DELETE command to delete a file.

- *Directory/Full* invokes the DIRECTORY/FULL command to display the complete attributes for files you specify.

- *Edit* invokes the EDIT command to edit a file. The default editor is EVE (TPU), but it may be overridden by defining a symbol EDIT in your LOGIN.COM to invoke another editor.

- *Execute DCL Command* executes an arbitrary DCL command that you supply.

- *Search Text* invokes the SEARCH command to locate certain text within files.

- *Show Device* invokes the SHOW DEVICE command to display information about disks, tapes, terminals, printers, and other devices.

- *Show Logical* invokes the SHOW LOGICAL command to show the translation of a logical name. (See Chapter 7, "The User Environment:", "Logical Names.")

- *Watch Errors* is essentially the same as the Message Window described earlier.

Help Manager

The Help Manager control starts the Help Manager with an introductory text and links for each piece of software that has registered its help materials. On a new OpenVMS system, the only topic shown will be the CDE itself.

Help on specific topics is available in the Help Manager subpanel, as well as in the Help menus within applications.

Trash Can

The Trash Can control is a drop zone; files you drag and drop to the trash can are discarded. Clicking the trash can control opens a view of files currently in the trash can, from which you may recover files before their actual deletion. You also may select "shred," which immediately deletes the selected file.

New Desktop Examples

Moving a Window Between Workspaces

You may move a window to other workspaces or make it present in all workspaces by using the Occupy Workspace and Occupy All Workspaces items from the Window menu.

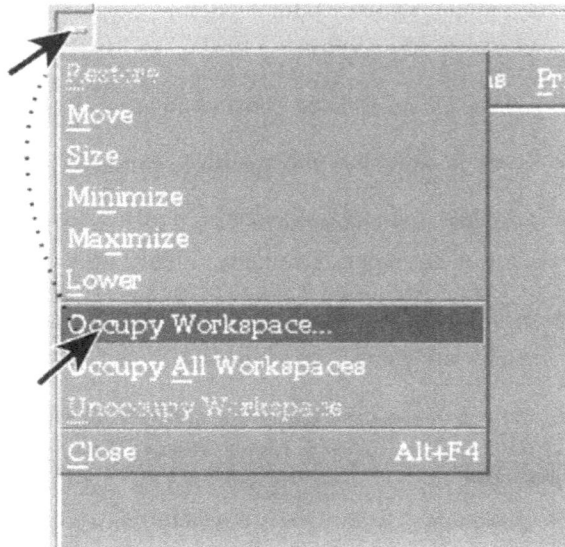

Figure 15-30 Moving a Window to Another Workspace

Copying an Application or File Directly to the Desktop

If you frequently use the same application or file, you may wish to copy it directly to the desktop. Copying an item to the desktop is easy. Simply drag the icon to the desktop and release.

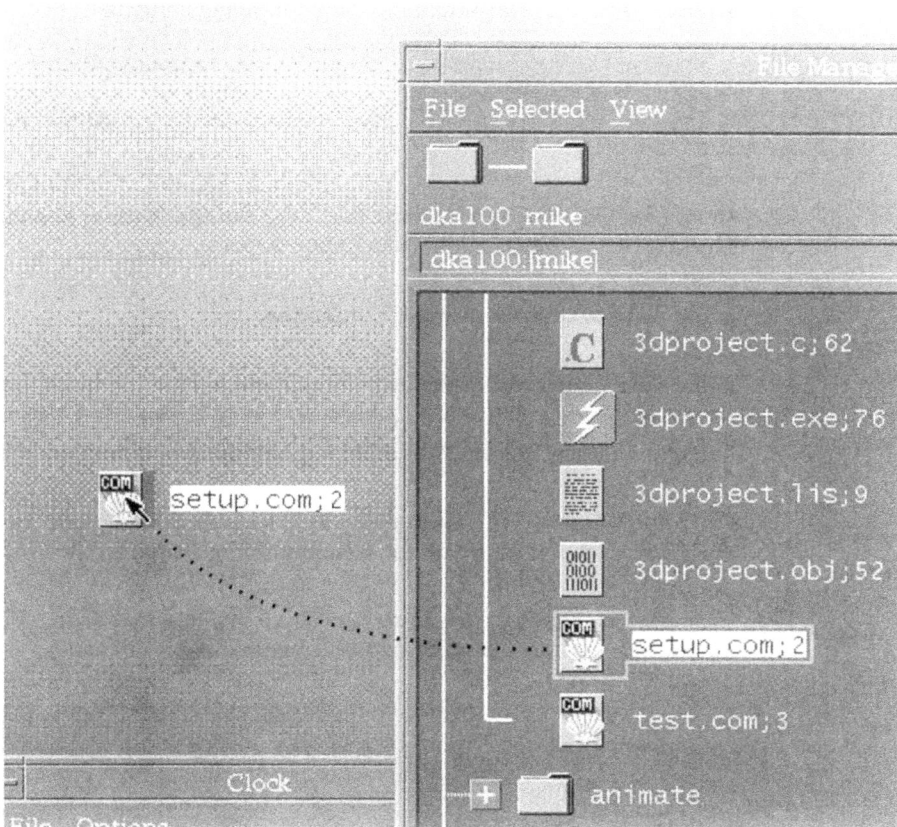

Figure 15-31 Copying an Item to the Desktop

To remove an item from the desktop, right-click in the icon and select Remove from Workspace.

Creating an Action

You can create your own icons to perform common tasks. The action performed is up to you and can be almost anything. This particular example will show you how to create an action to identify files in your home directory that have been modified during the past week.

Note: This action is implemented as a command procedure. You may wish to refer to Chapter 9, "Command Procedures," for more information.

1. The first step is to create a command procedure in your home directory called CHECK_FILES.COM. Use any text editor you like, whether it's the CDE editor on

the front panel, EDT in a DECterm window, or another editor.
CHECK_FILES.COM should have the following contents:

```
$ DIRECTORY *.* /MODIFIED/SINCE="-7-"/DATE=MODIFIED
$ WRITE SYS$OUTPUT ""
$ INQUIRE/NOPUNCTUATION YESNO "Press ENTER to close window"
$ EXIT
```

2. Once CHECK_FILES.COM is created, start the Application Manager, double-click Desktop Apps, then double-click Create Action.

3. In the field Action Name enter Check Files.

4. In the field Command When Action Is Opened, enter "@check_files".

5. In the field Help Text for Action Item, enter "Shows recently modified files."

6. From the Window-Type drop-down box, select Terminal (auto-close). (To display the choices, click directly on the box containing Graphical (X-Window)).

7. From the File menu, select Save. A message will appear saying, "The new action Check Files has been placed in your home folder."

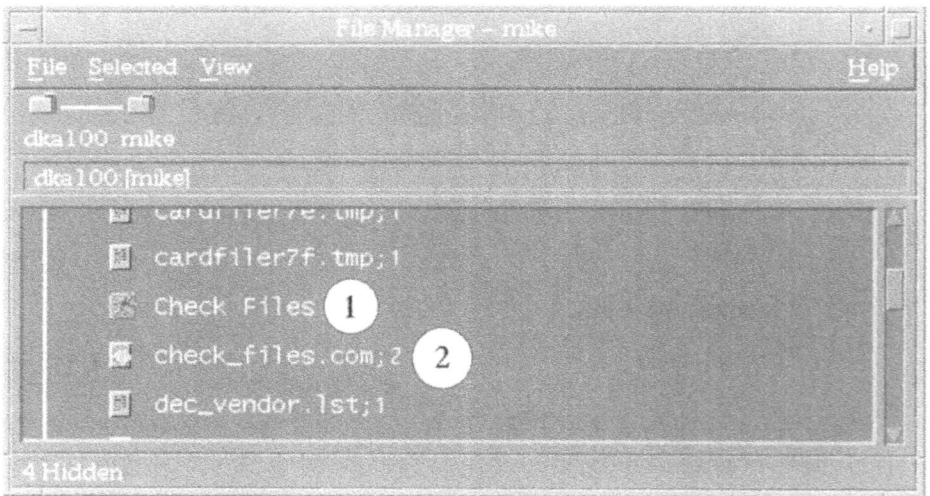

Figure 15-32 Check Files Action and Procedure As Shown in File Manager

The item Check Files now appears in the File Manager view of your home folder (1).
Double-clicking it causes the command procedure to execute, showing recently

modified files. You may execute it from the File Manager or copy it to the desktop, as described previously.

> **Note:** If the window appears briefly, but disappears too quickly to read its contents, an error has occurred. See below.

You will note that in your File Manager view, the command procedure CHECK_FILES.COM will itself appear (2). Double-clicking it will also cause it to execute, but with the following differences: you will be prompted for parameters (which this action does not need), and the window will not automatically close when the procedure is finished.

There is a further distinction to be pointed out between executing the action versus the command procedure. Let's say you were to copy each of them to the desktop, as shown in Figure 15-33:

Figure 15-33 Check Files Action and Procedure on the Desktop

There is an important distinction between these two icons: The command procedure icon executes a specific version of the procedure, whereas the action icon executes the latest version. If you modify the command procedure after creating the icons, only the action icon will automatically use the new version. The command procedure icon will continue to execute the original version.

Actions may be created for purposes other than executing command procedures. You may specify an individual DCL command or an X Window System executable program to be executed instead of a command procedure.

If the Window Disappears Too Quickly To Read

The preceding paragraphs pointed out some advantages of executing command procedures from an action icon rather than a command procedure desktop icon. However, there is at least one drawback: Some errors can occur which cause the window to appear and disappear so quickly that you cannot read the error message.

If this happens, use the Create Action program to modify the action. From the File menu, select Open and choose the CHECK_FILES.DT action. Change the Window Type to Terminal (Manual Close) and select Save from the File menu.

Now when the action is executed, the window is left open, allowing you to read any error messages and correct the command procedure error that caused the problem. Afterward, use Create Action to switch the window back to Auto Close.

Starting Applications Automatically

Rather than having a startup window containing applications to start automatically when you log in, the CDE environment provides a way to save your entire session. The next time you log in, all of the same applications will start with their windows sized and positioned just as they were when you saved them.

To establish an initial set of applications, follow the following steps:

1. First, start any applications you would like to run automatically at startup.

2. Size and position their windows according to your preferences.

3. Exit any applications you do not wish to start automatically.

4. Add any desired icons to your workspace(s), and remove any undesired ones (these can be action, file, or application icons).

5. Once your session is set up the way you would like it to be at startup, save it as follows: Start the Style Manager and select Startup.

6. From that menu, select Set Home Session. This saves the current state of your session, except for the Style Manager. Ensure that At Login: Return to Home Session is selected.

At future logins, your session will be just as it was when you saved it, without the Style Manager windows.

On the other hand, if you would like logins to restore your session to the way it was when you logged out, see the following section, "Resuming Your Session at Next Login."

Resuming Your Session at Next Login

If you would like to have each login session resume exactly as it was when you logged out, follow these steps:

1. Start the Style Manager and select Startup.

2. From that menu, select At Login: Resume Current Session.

At each logout, the state of your session will be preserved. This means that at each login, applications and icons will be restored to the way they were at the preceding logout.

The DECwindows Interface

In addition to the New Desktop (CDE), OpenVMS provides the older DECwindows interface used with previous OpenVMS versions. It is maintained partially for upward-compatibility reasons. New users may prefer to use the New Desktop exclusively and, thus, may skip this section

DECwindows Basics

The concepts of applications, windows, menus, use of the mouse, and many other topics apply to DECwindows in essentially the same way as to the New Desktop and are not repeated here.

Starting DECwindows

To start DECwindows, click Options at the login screen. From Session, choose DECwindows Session.

When you start a DECwindows session, the Session Manager starts. The session manager is the starting point for most DECwindows functions and is discussed after the Window Manager.

The Window Manager

The Window Manager is actually a separate component that handles the manipulation of windows: moving, resizing, minimizing, and so forth. Without a window manager, it is still possible to run applications and perform many essential functions, but it is cumbersome and this book assumes that a window manager is running.

If a window manager starts automatically, you may ignore this section. You can tell whether a window manager is running by the appearance of the Session Manager when DECwindows starts.

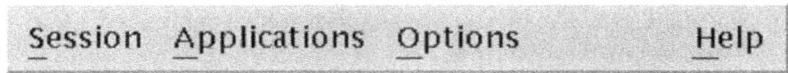

Session   Applications   Options   Help

Figure 15-34 No Window Manager

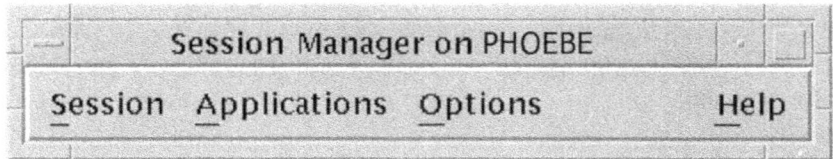

Session Manager on PHOEBE

Session   Applications   Options   Help

Figure 15-35 The MWM (New Desktop) Window Manager

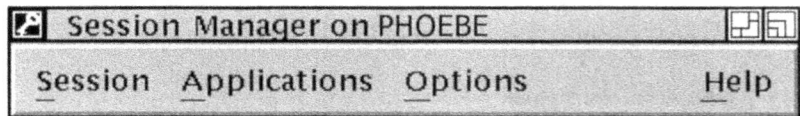

Session Manager on PHOEBE

Session   Applications   Options   Help

Figure 15-36 The DECwindows Window Manager

Note: If you are using an X Window System client, you may need to start a window manager manually. There may be more than one window manager application available, and an individual user may select one depending on his or her preferences. This book recommends the program DECW$MWM (fully specified as SYS$SYSTEM:DECW$MWM.EXE), if it is supported. If DECW$MWM is not supported, use DECW$WINMGR (the DECwindows Window Manager). The former is generally associated with the New Desktop, and the latter with DECwindows. If you need to start a window manager manually, the details are particular to the client software you are running. Consult your system or network manager for instructions on starting a window manager.

Window Manipulation Under DECW$WINMGR

In most respects, the DECW$WINMGR (DECwindows) Window Manager is comparable to the DECW$MWM (New Desktop) Window Manager. However, there are some differences with regard to resizing, minimizing, maximizing, and restoring. The following paragraphs describe some differences to be found in DECW$WINMGR.

- *The Push-to-Back Control* This control causes the window to be pasted below all other windows (all overlapping windows will now cover this one). This is useful to reveal a window that had been totally covered by other windows.

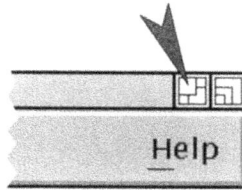

Figure 15-37 The Push-to-Back Control

- *Resizing a Window* Rather than dragging edges or corners of a window to a new size, the DECW$WINMGR Window Manager has a resize button in the upper-right corner of each window. Click the resize control (do not release) and then move the mouse pointer to touch the border you'd like to move. The border will now move along with the mouse pointer. Release the edge when it reaches the desired placement.

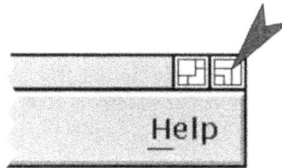

Figure 15-38 The Resize Control

The Session Manager

The starting point for most DECwindows functions is the Session Manager.

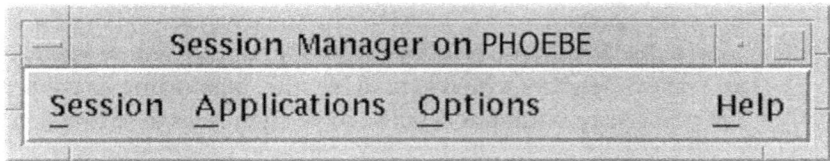

Figure 15-39 The Session Manager

Note: Depending on your configuration, the Session Manager may be displayed as an icon at the beginning of your session. If so, double-click the icon to restore the Session Manager window.

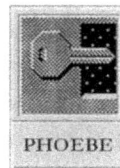

Figure 15-40 Session Manager as an Icon

The Session Manager contains four menus from which you may start applications, set options and preferences, and obtain help. Each of the four menus is described in the following sections.

Ending a DECwindows Session

From the Session Manager, click the Session menu and select End Session. Alternatively, use the window menu of the Session Manager and select Close.

The Session Menu

The Session menu contains functions that are mostly global in nature; they affect the entire session.

- *Logical Names* This window allows you to define or examine a logical name. To examine a logical name, type its name in the Name input field, select a logical name table (Any, Job, Group, System, Other), and click Show. To define a logical name, follow the same steps but click Define. To deassign a logical name, enter its name and click Deassign. If you define a jobwide logical name, keep in mind that a process created by the DECterm application may not be in the same job tree. Consider creating a groupwide logical name instead.

  Logical names are discussed elsewhere in this book.

- *Privileges* This window allows you to show which account privileges are currently enabled and to enable or disable any for which you may be authorized. For some tasks, you may need to enable a specific privilege beforehand. You may not enable a privilege your system manager has not authorized in your user authorization file record (account profile).

> **Note:** Not all of the privileges available under the latest versions of OpenVMS may be accounted for here. In addition, settings in this window will not affect processes created with DECterm; use SET PROCESS /PRIVILEGE from the DECterm window instead.

- *Work in Progress* This window shows which applications are currently running (DECterm is not represented) and allows you to stop them. However, it is recommended that you exit each application normally, from the application's own menu, unless it is impossible to do so.

- *Pause* This option causes the GUI to be locked and all information on the screen to be hidden. You must enter your password to unlock the workstation. Locking the workstation applies to the GUI only; it does not prevent such access as terminal logins or remote file access.

- *End Session* This allows you to log out of the DECwindows GUI and return to the login screen. From the login screen, you may choose DECwindows or the New Desktop.

The Applications Menu

This menu contains most of the same applications as previously discussed in "Application Manager: DECwindows Apps."

The most noticeable difference is the FileView application. This is similar in function to the New Desktop File Manager, but has a different look and feel.

For applications other than FileView, please refer to their descriptions in the section covering the New Desktop.

Applications: FileView

The FileView application performs the same basic functions as the New Desktop File Manager: navigating the directory tree and creating directories and printing files, to name a few.

However, FileView includes several menu selections that perform many of the functions that are separated under the New Desktop, such as executing a DCL command, comparing files, and examining X Window System internal information. The New Desktop has many of these functions spread out as separate applications, whereas FileView groups them together.

The following paragraphs briefly discuss how to use FileView and its menus.

FileView: Navigating Directories

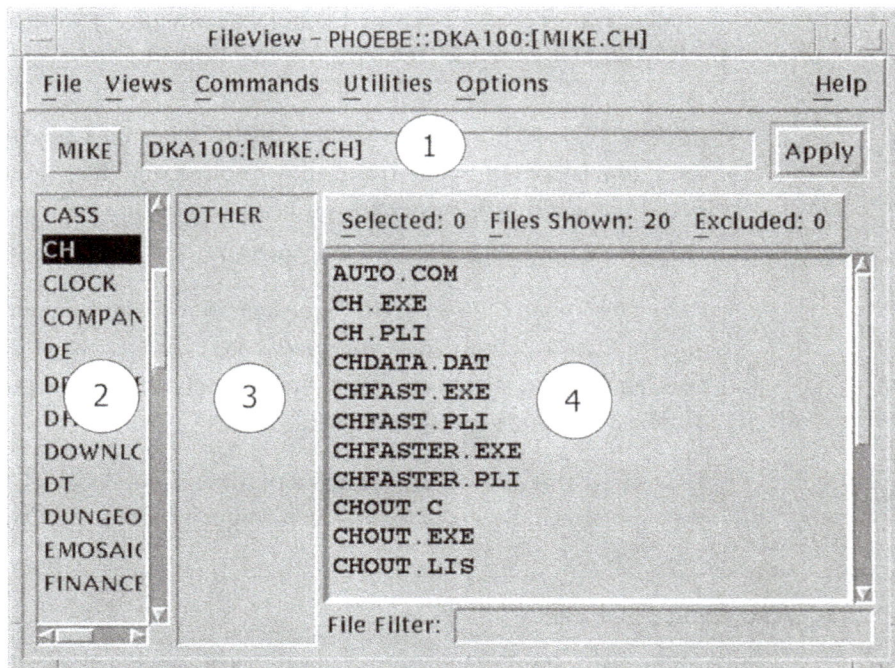

Figure 15-41 FileView

In Figure 15-41 below the menu bar of FileView is the current disk and directory (1). Any subdirectories of the current directory are shown in the narrow frame occupying the left side of the window (2). Files within the current directory are shown in the large area occupying most of the window (4).

To navigate to a subdirectory, click on its name in the left-hand pane. When you move to the subdirectory, one of two things may happen. If you are at the top or bottom of a directory tree, a single pane of directories will be present (2). If you are not at the top or bottom, there will be two panes of directory levels shown (2, 3).

To navigate to an arbitrary directory, perhaps on another disk, click on the current directory name and edit it directly. Press ENTER or click Apply to move to the new directory.

To navigate to the parent directory, click its name, which appears in a box to the left of the current directory display. If you are already at the top of the tree, no entry will appear there.

Note: The top of the directory tree may not represent the top-level directory of the disk. For example, your home directory may represent the top of the FileView tree but not of the directory tree of the disk that contains it. To establish a new top-of-tree, edit the directory name directly.

FileView: The File Menu

This menu contains two items: New View and Quit. New View opens another window identical to the first. By having multiple views open, you may work with more than one directory tree at a time.

FileView: The Views Menu

This menu provides a quick way to change some of the common view options. You may decide to show all versions or only the highest version of files, include the size and date of files, or you may select a brief view that does not include this information. You may also return directly to your login directory via this menu.

FileView: The Commands Menu

This menu contains commands that have DCL equivalents and, in fact, are GUI shells around normal DCL commands.

- *Compare* compares two files and reports any differences using the DIFFERENCES utility.

- *Copy* makes a copy of a file or copies multiple existing files into a combined output file.

- *Delete* deletes one or more files.

- *Edit* starts a text editor (you may choose among EDT, EVE, Notepad, or another editor as defined on your particular system) and loads the specified file.

- *Print* queues one or more files to a printer.

- *Protection* changes the UIC-based protection on one or more files. File protections are explained elsewhere in this book.

- *Purge* deletes earlier versions of specified files while keeping the latest version(s).

- *Read* displays the contents of text files using the editor of your choice or the TYPE command.

- *Rename* changes the name of one or more files.

- *Run* executes a program or command procedure.

- *Search* searches for text you specify in one or more files.

- *Show File* performs a DIRECTORY / FULL on one of more files.

FileView: Utilities Menu

This menu contains commands that display the internal state of the GUI software. A somewhat advanced knowledge of the GUI is required for most of these utilities to be of use, so they are not covered here.

FileView: Options Menu

This menu contains commands that allow you to customize many aspects of the way FileView operates.

- *Layout* allows you to specify which fields of a full file specification will be shown and that files be sorted by a variety of criteria.

- *Window* allows you to customize the window in which FileView runs.

- *Menus* allows you to add, remove, and reorder items in the FileView and Session Manager menus. It also allows you to add and populate new menus (see Menu Bar, next).

- *Menu Bar* allows you to specify which menus appear in the FileView Menu bar. After you create a new menu, use this option to add it to the Menu bar.

- *File Types* allows you to control what action the system takes when you double-click on files of a certain type. For example, double-clicking on a program (.EXE) file causes it to execute. This option allows you to change or add associations between actions and file types.

- *Show/Hide Work Area* controls whether the directory, subdirectory, and file panes are visible or only the menu bar is.

- *Filter by Size* allows you to exclude files from the display based on their sizes.

- *Filter by Date* allows you to exclude files from the display based on their dates of creation, modification, backup, or expiration.[1]

- *Filter by Owner* allows you to exclude files from the display based on their ownership.

The Options Menu

- *Automatic Startup* allows you to specify which applications should automatically start at login time.

- *Window* allows you to customize the window in which the Session Manager runs.

- *Menus* allows you to add, remove, and reorder items in the FileView and Session Manager menus. It also allows you to add and populate new menus (see Menu Bar, next).

- *Menu Bar* allows you to specify which menus appear in the Session Manager menu bar. After you create a new menu, use this option to add it to the menu bar.

- *Pause Screen* allows you to control what text is displayed while the session is paused (while the workstation is locked). (See Pause under "The Session Menu").

- *End Session Prompts* controls whether DECwindows asks you to confirm your desire to end a session. It also controls whether DECwindows notifies each application of the impending application shutdown. Some applications, upon receiving such a notification, automatically save unsaved data.

- *Screen Background* allows you to choose the background colors and pattern for the screen. You may also choose that the screen go blank after a period of inactivity.

- *Window Colors* allows you to choose foreground, background, highlight, and shadow colors to be used in application windows.

- *Keyboard* allows you to set keyboard options, such as caps lock versus shift lock, autorepeat, cursor blinking, and others.

---

1. Many OpenVMS systems do not employ file expiration dates. An expiration date, if set, is for identification purposes only. The system takes no action when a file expires.

- *Language* allows you to choose another language to be used by DECwindows, but requires the proper language support module to be installed on your system.

- *Pointer* allows you to choose from different mouse pointers and set options including doubleclick timeout, handedness, and acceleration.

- *Security* allows you to allow or disallow system access from other network users (typically via DECnet). This includes allowing remote logins and allowing the use of DECwindows applications by remote users.

Summary

This section has presented a brief overview of the DECwindows environment. As previously stated, DECwindows is no longer the default GUI environment for OpenVMS, but is still provided for compatibility reasons and for those users who became accustomed to it under previous OpenVMS versions.

Chapter 16 — Your Personal OpenVMS System

This chapter is intended for users who have acquired their own personal OpenVMS system. The system manager would normally perform the tasks explained in this chapter, but for personal systems the owner must perform them.

Under no circumstances should you attempt to perform any of these tasks on any other OpenVMS system besides your own.

If you do not have your own personal OpenVMS system, you may wish to skip this chapter.

System Startup and Shutdown

In years past, OpenVMS computers were almost always large machines isolated in air-conditioned computer rooms with dedicated staff. Dedicated system managers and operators handled system management functions like startup and shutdown. While this is still true of many OpenVMS systems, there are a considerable number of smaller OpenVMS machines owned by individuals, often located in their own homes. This section provides those individuals with a brief explanation of how to start up and shut down their personal OpenVMS computers properly.

If the OpenVMS system you are using is not your own personal system, do not issue any of the commands described in this section. Your system manager will not take kindly to unauthorized experimentation in these areas.

The Console Subsystem

In the old days, large computer systems often had a *console processor*, a separate small computer or a separate processor within the main computer. This processor controlled the larger computer; it turned the power on and off, initialized the CPU of the main computer, and performed other control functions.

Today, it is much less common to find a separate console processor, but the concept lives on in the form of a *console subsystem*. This usually takes the form of a program that is stored in the nonvolatile[1] memory of the main computer and runs on the same CPU that executes the operating system.

---

1. In this context, nonvolatile memory may mean any storage medium that is not erased when power is disconnected. Today, it is usually read-only memory (ROM or EPROM).

To start OpenVMS, it is necessary to give the appropriate instructions to the console subsystem. The console subsystem locates and loads that portion of OpenVMS dedicated to system startup, which, in turn, loads the remainder of OpenVMS.

OpenVMS uses the *SRM* console. If your computer is currently running ARC or some other console, you must first switch to the SRM console before using OpenVMS. This usually consists of loading a console CD-ROM and selecting the desired console from a menu. Consult your hardware documentation for details.

System Startup

When you power-on your system, the hardware will perform a series of self-tests. If no serious problems are found, it will present you with the console prompt. The SRM console prompt is three consecutive angle brackets: ">>>." You may hear it referred to as the three-arrow prompt.

The power-up sequence varies from system to system, but the following example comes from a small AlphaStation 200, which shows a display representative of typical personal systems:

```
ff.fe.fd.fc.fb.fa.f9.f8.f7.f6.f5.          (self-tests)
ef.df.ee.ed.ec.f4.eb.ea.e9.e8.e7.e6.....e5. (self-tests)
V7.0-9, built on Mar 18 1999 at 13:41:11
>>>      (the console prompt)
```

The following is an example power-up sequence from a VAXstation 3100/76:

```
KA43-A  V1.0

F...E...D...C...B...A_..9...8...7...6...5...4...3_..2_..1..

? 6  80A1  0000.4001

>>>
```

If the self-test sequence detects any errors, they will be reported here. The format and meaning of these messages varies from system to system.

> **Note:** In this example, the error message "? 6 80A1 0000.4001" is reported. On a VAXstation 3100 system, this means that the system can find no devices connected to the external SCSI bus. For the particular sample system shown here, this is normal.

If your system is set to autoboot (to automatically start OpenVMS from a certain disk), it will do so at this time. Otherwise you must enter the BOOT command, followed by the name of the disk device from which you wish to boot.

The Autoboot Console Feature

If your system autoboots and you would like to change the boot device or disable the autoboot feature, do so after a shutdown. Shutdowns are described in the next section. Different console versions and hardware models handle autoboot differently. Some use a SET BOOT command, while others use *environment variables* called auto_action and bootdef_dev. Consult the hardware documentation for your particular model.

If you enter BOOT without specifying a disk, your system may either (1) produce an error message and take no action, (2) boot from a particular prearranged disk, or (3) search for any bootable device, including requesting a downline-load of OpenVMS from another system on the network. The action taken depends on your hardware model and console settings.

A given system may have more than one disk containing an operating system, each of them a valid candidate from which to bootstrap the system.

To see available devices, use the SHOW DEVICE command (if your system is older, you may need to use a different command; consult your hardware documentation).

```
>>>SHOW DEVICE
dka0.0.0.6.0          DKA0                            RZ28M   0568
dka100.1.0.6.0        DKA100                           RZ26   392A
dka400.4.0.6.0        DKA400                           RRD43  1084
dva0.0.0.0.1          DVA0
ewa0.0.0.11.0         EWA0               08-00-2B-xx-xx-xx
pka0.7.0.6.0          PKA0                SCSI Bus ID 7
>>>
```

In the display above, devices starting with DK are disk devices (your system may use another designation, such as DU or DQ, among others; it depends on the system data bus type). On this particular system, DKA0, DKA100, and DKA400 are valid candidates. Device DKA400 is an RRD series disk, which is a CD-ROM, usually used as a boot device only during OpenVMS installations or upgrades. DKA0: and DKA100: are normal SCSI hard disks.

To boot from DKA100, issue the following command (your hardware may require a different format; see your hardware documentation):

```
>>> boot dka100
```

The console will attempt to load a boot block; certain data at a known location on disk that starts the bootstrap process. If a valid boot block is located, system startup begins (your hardware may show a somewhat different sequence):

```
>>>boot dka100
(boot dka100.0.0.1009.0 -flags 0)
block 0 of dka100.0.0.1009.0 is a valid boot block
reading 936 blocks from dka100.0.0.1009.0
bootstrap code read in
base = 1d8000, image_start = 0, image_bytes = 75000
initializing HWRPB at 2000
initializing page table at 1ca000
initializing machine state
setting affinity to the primary CPU
jumping to bootstrap code

    OpenVMS (TM) Alpha Operating System, Version V7.3

%DECnet-I-LOADED, network base image loaded, version = 05.0E.00

$! Copyright 2001 Compaq Computer Corporation.
%STDRV-I-STARTUP, OpenVMS startup begun at 19-JAN-2003 18:36:48.54
```

When the boot process is finished, the last few lines of the display will look something like this:

```
%SET-I-INTSET, login interactive limit = 64, current interactive value = 0
   SYSTEM       job terminated at 19-JAN-2003 18:38:45.55

   Accounting information:
   Buffered I/O count:            2695    Peak working set size:      5264
   Direct I/O count:              1323    Peak virtual size:        171664
   Page faults:                   2412    Mounted volumes:               1
   Charged CPU time:      0 00:00:10.15   Elapsed time:      0 00:02:31.76
```

At this time, you may press ENTER to log into text-based machines. If your system is GUI-based, the login screen will appear after a few seconds. If it fails to appear after about one minute, you may need to start the GUI software manually. Log in as user SYSTEM, as if you were logging in from a text terminal, and enter the command

```
$ @SYS$MANAGER:DECW$STARTUP
```

Customizing Your System Startup

OpenVMS can automatically perform arbitrary commands at each system startup via a command procedure called SYS$MANAGER:SYSTARTUP_VMS.COM.[1] Do not confuse this with STARTUP.COM, which you should never modify.

As one of the final steps in system startup, OpenVMS executes SYSTARTUP_VMS.COM. You may place any commands that OpenVMS should execute at each system startup in this file. You may use this file as a way to start

---

1. Older versions of OpenVMS called this file SYSTARTUP.COM or SYSTARTUP_V5.COM.

DECnet or TCP/IP, start batch and print queues, start a database product, configure devices, etc.

System Shutdown

As with any other operating system, it is important to shut OpenVMS down properly. If you simply turn off the power, a number of inconvenient side effects may occur. Any application data not saved to disk may be lost or incomplete, depending on the journaling capabilities of the application. Batch and print jobs underway at that moment will be interrupted and disk volumes will undergo a time-consuming consistency check at the next boot.

OpenVMS stands out for its ability to avoid data corruption as the result of interruptions, such as a sudden loss of power, but the problems listed above cannot be avoided. Therefore, you should shut OpenVMS down in a controlled manner.

Before Shutting Down

Before shutting down, you may wish to stop any batch, print, and server queues. At any given time, a number of jobs may be underway. Allowing those jobs to complete will avoid inconveniences later.

To stop batch and print queues, use SHOW QUEUE/BATCH/ALL and SHOW QUEUE/DEVICE/ALL to examine batch and printer queues, respectively. Use the STOP/NEXT *queue-name* command on each queue, which prevents any additional jobs from starting, but allows any jobs underway to finish. Server queues may usually be stopped in the same fashion, but whatever application is associated with a given server queue may have its own requirements; check your software documentation. You may also wish to shut down any software products that may be running. Each of these will have its own shutdown method; check your software documentation.

Finally, consider customizing the SYS$MANAGER:SYSHUTDWN.COM command procedure to include any other commands you would like to have executed at each system shutdown. This command procedure will be executed during the system shutdown, provided you answer yes to the appropriate prompt issued by the shutdown procedure (explained later).

Queues should be stopped before initiating a system shutdown because SYSHUTDWN.COM may provide insufficient time to allow jobs to finish.

Shutting Down

After you have completed any preshutdown tasks as described above, use the SYS$SYSTEM:SHUTDOWN.COM command procedure to shut down the OpenVMS operating system.

> **Note:** Do not modify SHUTDOWN.COM. Any customizations should be added to SYS$MANAGER:SYSHUTDWN.COM instead.

SHUTDOWN.COM will ask you a series of questions about how the shutdown is to proceed. They are as follows:

```
$ @SYS$SYSTEM:SHUTDOWN

            SHUTDOWN -- Perform an Orderly System Shutdown
                      on node PHOEBE

Are you sure you want to shut down node PHOEBE [NO]?
How many minutes until final shutdown [0]:
Reason for shutdown [Standalone]:
Do you want to spin down the disk volumes [NO]?
Do you want to invoke the site-specific shutdown procedure [YES]?
Should an automatic system reboot be performed [NO]?
When will the system be rebooted [later]:
Shutdown options (enter as a comma-separated list):
 REBOOT_CHECK       Check existence of basic system files
 SAVE_FEEDBACK      Save AUTOGEN feedback information from this boot
 DISABLE_AUTOSTART  Disable autostart queues

Shutdown options [NONE]:
```

Let's take these questions one at a time and explain why they are asked.

Are you sure you want to shut down node PHOEBE?

This question is asked only if you are logged in from a different machine via SET HOST. Its purpose is to ensure that you have not accidentally initiated a shutdown on the wrong node. If you are logged in at a local terminal, this question is not asked. After this point, if you wish to cancel the shutdown, press CTRL/Y.

How many minutes until final shutdown?

If the system is used by more than one user, supplying a delay will give other users a chance to save their work and log out. During the countdown, OpenVMS sends periodic broadcast messages to all users, warning them of the impending shutdown.

Reason for shutdown [Standalone]:

You may enter an explanation for the system shutdown here. This explanation will be included in the broadcast messages sent to all users. The default reason "Standalone" refers to "Standalone Backup," a program used to make backup copies of disks while no operating system is running (this ensures that no files will be in transition while they are being saved).

Do you want to spin down the disk volumes [NO]?

This question asks whether system disk drives should remain spinning after the shutdown or should be stopped. Only certain disk models honor this option; many will continue to spin as long as there is power. This question has little relevance for small personal systems.

Do you want to invoke the site-specific shutdown procedure [YES]?

This asks whether SYSHUTDWN.COM (described previously) should be executed. Normally, it should.

Should an automatic system reboot be performed [NO]?

If answered yes, this option will initiate a reboot as soon as shutdown is complete. This is synonymous with restart on some personal computer systems.[1]

When will the system be rebooted [later]:

The answer to this question will be included in the shutdown broadcast messages sent to all users. If you have selected an automatic reboot, the default message will contain words to that effect.

Shutdown options (enter as a comma-separated list):

The options are as follows:

- *REBOOT_CHECK* This will ensure that certain operating system files exist. This is a rudimentary check to ensure that the system, once shut down, will be able to start again. The author recommends always choosing this option.

- *SAVE_FEEDBACK* OpenVMS includes a tool called AUTOGEN, which attempts to automatically tune the performance of OpenVMS over time. This

---

1. *Restart* historically refers to restarting an operating system already in memory whose operation was suspended, perhaps because of a momentary power failure. *Reboot* has historically meant initializing the hardware and reloading the operating system from disk. Some personal computer systems use the term restart where reboot or reload would be more accurate.

question asks whether data collected since the last reboot should be saved (if your system has been under an unusual workload since the last boot, the data may not help tuning efforts and should perhaps be discarded). AUTOGEN is not covered in this book (see the OpenVMS documentation set).

- *DISABLE_AUTOSTART* Later versions of OpenVMS have the ability to automatically start designated queues under certain startup conditions. The autostart feature is not covered in this book (see the OpenVMS documentation set—personal systems may make little or no use of autostart queues).

After all the questions have been answered, SHUTDOWN.COM will send out a broadcast message to all users, similar to the following but based upon your answers:

```
SHUTDOWN message on PHOEBE from user MIKE at _PHOEBE$OPA0:    18:32:06
PHOEBE will shut down in 10 minutes; back up in about 1 hour
Installing a new disk drive.
```

At intervals, OpenVMS will send out additional messages, counting down the time remaining until shutdown. As the shutdown time approaches, OpenVMS will begin shutting down various system components and execute the SYSHUTDWN.COM, if appropriate.

Determining When the System Is Fully Shut Down

Various hardware models present different displays once OpenVMS has been fully shut down. What to look for depends on the exact hardware model you are using, but it should resemble the following example:

```
%%%%%%%%%%  OPCOM  22-JAN-2003 18:14:14.92  %%%%%%%%%%
Message from user MIKE on PHOEBE
_PHOEBE$OPA0:, PHOEBE shutdown was requested by the operator.

%%%%%%%%%%  OPCOM  22-JAN-2003 18:14:14.95  %%%%%%%%%%
Logfile was closed by operator _PHOEBE$OPA0:
Logfile was PHOEBE::SYS$SYSROOT:[SYSMGR]OPERATOR.LOG;291

%%%%%%%%%%  OPCOM  22-JAN-2003 18:14:15.03  %%%%%%%%%%
Operator _PHOEBE$OPA0: has been disabled, username SYSTEM
```

A series of messages like those above signals the very last steps of the OpenVMS shutdown sequence. After these messages appear, your system may behave in a number of different ways, depending on your hardware model.

Some models, mostly older VAX computers, will show this message:

```
SYSTEM SHUTDOWN COMPLETE -- USE CONSOLE TO HALT SYSTEM
```

Other models may indicate the execution of a "breakpoint" instruction:

```
Brk 0 at 8000200C
8000200C!        BPT
```

GUI-based systems will place the hardware back into text mode (white on black or white on blue) and may automatically display the console prompt, ">>>."

Your system may now be safely powered off.

If you wish to use the console subsystem (perhaps to reboot, perhaps to change some console setting), the method you use will depend on your hardware model.

If the console prompt does not appear, you must gain the attention of the console subsystem. Some systems use CTRL/P or BREAK from the console keyboard. Others have a HALT or RESET button, usually located on the front or the rear of the computer. Consult your hardware documentation for details.

When the console prompt (>>>) appears, you may then enter console commands.

Software Licenses

Many OpenVMS software products require a license to be installed before they are used. For many, you must use the OpenVMS License Management Facility (LMF) to load the licenses onto your system.

Software vendors usually supply your license in one of two formats: a paper product authorization key (PAK) or a DCL LICENSE command with the appropriate qualifiers to license the product. Some LICENSE commands may come in the form of a command procedure for easier execution.

To work with software licenses, you must use a fully privileged user account.

If you receive a DCL LICENSE command, issue it at the DCL prompt. It may be helpful to copy-and-paste the command to avoid errors.

If you receive a PAK, use the command procedure SYS$UPDATE:VMSLICENSE.COM.

```
$ @SYS$UPDATE:VMSLICENSE
     VMS License Management Utility Options:

          1. REGISTER a Product Authorization Key
          2. AMEND an existing Product Authorization Key
          3. CANCEL an existing Product Authorization Key
          4. LIST the Product Authorization Keys
          5. MODIFY an existing Product Authorization Key
          6. DISABLE an existing Product Authorization Key
```

```
 7. DELETE an existing Product Authorization Key
 8. COPY an existing Product Authorization Key
 9. MOVE an existing Product Authorization Key
10. ENABLE an existing Product Authorization Key
11. SHOW the licenses loaded on this node
12. SHOW the unit requirements for this node

99. EXIT this procedure

   Type '?' at any prompt for a description of the information
   requested.  Press Ctrl/Z at any prompt to return to this menu.
Enter one of the above choices [1]:
```

At the VMSLICENSE menu, choose REGISTER to enter a new license. You will be asked to enter the information found on your PAK. For blank PAK fields, press ENTER when prompted for that field.

Please note that a license must be enabled, not just registered, for the software product to work. Answer yes when asked if the license should be loaded.

VMSLICENSE.COM may also be used to disable or remove licenses or to list the licenses on your system.

Installing Software

Some OpenVMS software products must be installed using the SYS$UPDATE:VMSINSTAL.COM command procedure; others use the POLYCENTER Software Installation Utility (PCSI) via the DCL PRODUCT command. Yet others may have their own installation methods, such as an included command procedure.

Consult your software documentation for details about installing a particular product. Many products come with a sample installation procedure for you to examine before starting. Please note that some products may require that a software license be loaded before the product is installed.

If You're Stuck with Savesets Only

You may sometimes receive software in the form of BACKUP savesets with no additional instructions. In this case, log in as user SYSTEM and use the VMSINSTAL procedure. You must supply the name of the product and the directory that contains the savesets. Let's say you have the savesets for Bells-n-Whistles V2.0 in a directory:

```
$ DIRECTORY/SIZE

Directory DKA400:[SOFTWARE_KITS]

BELLS020.A;1      118
```

```
BELLS020.B;1    3014
BELLS020.C;1    4417
```

The general VMSINSTAL command is

```
$ @sys$update:vmsinstal product kit_directory
```

In this example, the actual command would be

```
$ @SYS$UPDATE:VMSINSTAL BELLS020 DKA400:[SOFTWARE_KITS]

        OpenVMS VAX Software Product Installation Procedure V7.3

It is 9-APR-2003 at 18:06.

Enter a question mark (?) at any time for help.
```

VMSINSTALL will invoke the installation procedure for the product and ask you a series of questions. The questions asked are entirely dependent on the software product being installed.

After you have answered all the questions, VMSINSTAL will complete the installation of the product.

If Your System Will Be Connected to the Internet

Because OpenVMS can run full-featured TCP/IP products, you can connect it to the Internet. You may host one or more domains, including Web sites and FTP sites or use your OpenVMS system as an e-mail server for your personal computers.

However, if you are planning to connect your OpenVMS system to the Internet, you should take several things into consideration before making the connection. You must realize that your OpenVMS system will, like any computer on the Internet, come under attack from malicious users around the world. Because OpenVMS can act as a full network server, it will be of particular interest to certain kinds of attackers.

This section is not intended to frighten the reader, but to point out that malicious users wishing to make illicit use of your resources will probe your systems. Before flipping the switch, you should take the appropriate precautions.

Educate yourself about TCP/IP in general and the activities of malicious network users in particular. Read books, explore Web sites, and join mailing lists or newsgroups related to Internet security. Read the documentation set for your TCP/IP product. The more you know, the better prepared you will be to handle any situation that arises.

The author would suggest doing the following before establishing connectivity. Some of the terminology will be foreign to those not familiar with TCP/IP. If necessary, use the resources suggested above to become familiar with the terminology used in these suggestions:

Disable any services you will not need. These may include Telnet, FTP and the "r" services, such as rlogin. The more unnecessary services you have running, the more opportunities you give malicious users.

For those services you plan to use, consider moving them to different network ports from the defaults. This will prevent at least some probes from finding an active service on your machine.

Consider replacing FTP with SCP and Telnet with SSH. FTP and Telnet send unencrypted data, whereas SCP and SSH provide similar services using encrypted communication. Unencrypted data stand a small, but real, chance of being intercepted by malicious users.

If you will be using your OpenVMS system as an e-mail server, ensure that your SMTP server is not configured as an *open relay*. An open relay is a system that will forward mail messages from any source, not just from internal users. Senders of unsolicited e-mail ("spam") will attempt to use your system to send their unwanted messages. If they are successful, some of the messages will be traced back to you. Some of the recipients and their e-mail managers will send you unkind messages, and your ISP may threaten to take action against you.

Do not maintain more user accounts than you need. Do not allow accounts to log in from remote locations unless necessary.

Now for the good news: As an OpenVMS network manager, you will spend much less time applying security patches than administrators of other operating systems. This is because OpenVMS is less vulnerable to "buffer overflow" attacks, a particularly popular kind. You will still need to pay attention to security alerts, particularly from the maker of your TCP/IP product.

The list of suggestions presented above is far from complete, but following these recommendations will prevent some of the common mistakes made by inexperienced network managers. Continue to monitor your system for anything out of the ordinary and continue to educate yourself about the latest threats.

Part 2 — A Technical Introduction

The following chapters introduce some important features of OpenVMS in a more detailed fashion. You do not need to read these chapters in order to use OpenVMS effectively. This material is for those readers who wish to understand a bit more about the internal workings of the OpenVMS operating system.

Chapter 17 — The Process

Part 1 defined the *process* as the basic unit of scheduling; a separate task which can be scheduled by OpenVMS, independently of other tasks.

This chapter will expand upon that definition, explaining some of the internal structure of a process. Later sections will explain how the virtual memory and scheduling mechanisms of OpenVMS act upon a process.

Expanded Definition of Process

Earlier in this book, a process was described as a separate task that could be executed by OpenVMS. This is true, but incomplete. Because many things can qualify as "tasks to be scheduled", the following paragraphs detail what a process actually is.

OpenVMS maintains a list of processes that exist at any given time. When you, a user, log in, a process is created for you. When you log out, it is destroyed. Each batch job executes as its own process, and many DECnet network operations execute as separate processes.

A CPU executes one process at a time. If your system has one CPU, only one process may actually be executing at a given time. This is probably the easiest way for a new user to envision a process. If you and user HOWARD are logged in at the same time, you each have a separate process. When HOWARD's process is executing, yours is not. When the CPU switches its attention from HOWARD's process to yours, it must take several steps: It must first save the state of HOWARD's process so that it may be resumed later. Then, it must select the next process to execute, perhaps yours. Finally, it must load your process, and begin executing it at exactly the point at which it stopped before. This sequence of events is known as a *context switch:* HOWARD's context is saved and yours is loaded. Context switches typically happen several times per second, giving the illusion that the CPU is executing HOWARD's work and your work at the same time.

A process has its own memory context. The concept of a memory context is essential to the idea of a process. One way to envision a context is to consider it to be a snapshot of the process, which can be saved while the CPU works on other things.

The concept of a process context includes more than just a snapshot of its structure, however. Under OpenVMS, each process has its own memory, separate from the memory of other processes, which cannot be directly accessed by another process. To clarify: The private memory space of one process is not merely protected from access by other processes; it conceptually does not exist from the viewpoint of the other process. This is one aspect that can help to drive home the idea of separate contexts.

Under OpenVMS, main memory starts at address zero. Each byte is numbered up to a maximum address (again using the 32-bit definition) of 4,294,967,296 (FFFFFFFF in hex format). This represents a range of 4GB that can be addressed in the context of a process (a given machine may have more or less than 4GB of physical memory—more on that topic is presented under "Virtual Memory").

OpenVMS constructs processes so that the first 2GB of each process's memory-addressing space is separate from that of all other processes. For example, two different processes can each access "memory address 1,000," but each refers to a separate place in physical memory. Process A has its own memory address 1,000, as does Process B. This memory location and the entire first 2GB of each processs's memory is effectively nonexistent in the context of any other process. OpenVMS arranges the allocation of physical memory so that each process can address its own 2GB of private memory.

Memory addresses 2,147,483,648 (80000000) through 4,294,967,296 (FFFFFFFF), though, are a different story. Those addresses are shared among all processes, so each process has 2GB of private virtual memory plus 2GB of memory shared by all processes. OpenVMS itself resides in the shared area, so that each process may use system routines from within its own context.

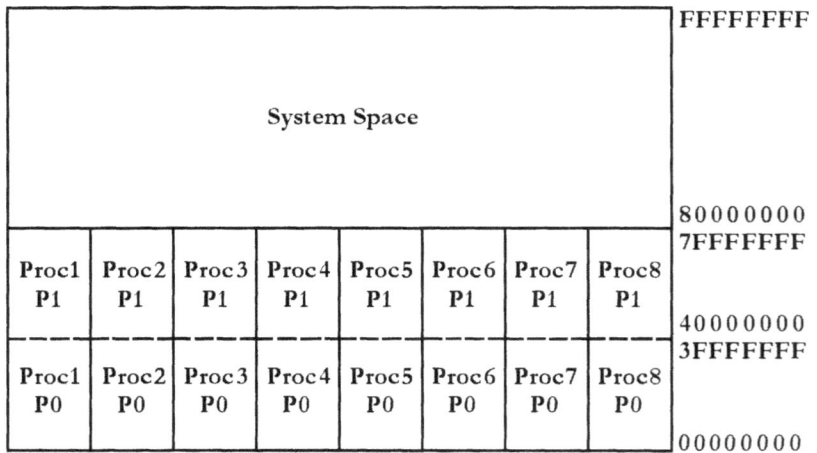

System Space								FFFFFFFF 80000000
Proc1 P1	Proc2 P1	Proc3 P1	Proc4 P1	Proc5 P1	Proc6 P1	Proc7 P1	Proc8 P1	7FFFFFFF 40000000
Proc1 P0	Proc2 P0	Proc3 P0	Proc4 P0	Proc5 P0	Proc6 P0	Proc7 P0	Proc8 P0	3FFFFFFF 00000000

Figure 17-1 Virtual Memory Regions

The two features just described represent the essence of a process; therefore, the ability to be scheduled for execution by a CPU combined with a unique memory context is a good working definition of a process.

A user may actually own several processes at once. An application may create a temporary child process (a subprocess) to perform some task, or a GUI application with several windows may create a separate subprocess to control each window. Alternatively, the user may issue a command that creates another process (e.g., SPAWN, RUN/DETACH, or SET HOST).

Batch jobs also execute in separate processes which themselves may create subprocesses. There are also *detached* processes, processes that may be semipermanent and are owned by no other process.

Use the DCL command SHOW SYSTEM to see a list of processes currently running on your system.

Memory Layout of a Process

The OpenVMS virtual memory management subsystem is responsible for the allocation of physical memory among processes and provides the illusion of a 4GB address space to each process.

This section describes the layout of memory as seen from within a process. This does not bear any resemblance to the contents of physical memory on the computer; it is the memory-addressing space as seen from process context, an illusion constructed by the virtual memory management subsystem. The process is free to use the 4GB addressing space as if it were real, physical memory. The memory management subsystem is responsible for allocating memory to the process so as to maintain this illusion.

The layout to be described here is based mostly on the 32-bit VAX layout. The earliest Alpha layouts closely resembled that of the VAX, effectively using only 4GB of the 64-bit space. Over time, the Alpha approach began moving certain items to previously unused ranges of the 64-bit space. Ignoring these details will not change the essence of this discussion.

The remainder of the discussion will express memory addresses in hexadecimal format. A primer on hexadecimal notation is included as Appendix A.

A process-addressing space is divided into two main parts: *process space*, from 0 to 7FFFFFFF, and *system space*, 80000000 and above. You will recall that process space is unique to each process and that system space is shared by all processes. Process space is further divided into two regions: the *program region,* or *P0 space,* located from 0 through 3FFFFFFF, and the *control region,* or *P1 space,* located from 40000000 through 7FFFFFFF.

Recall Figure 17-1:

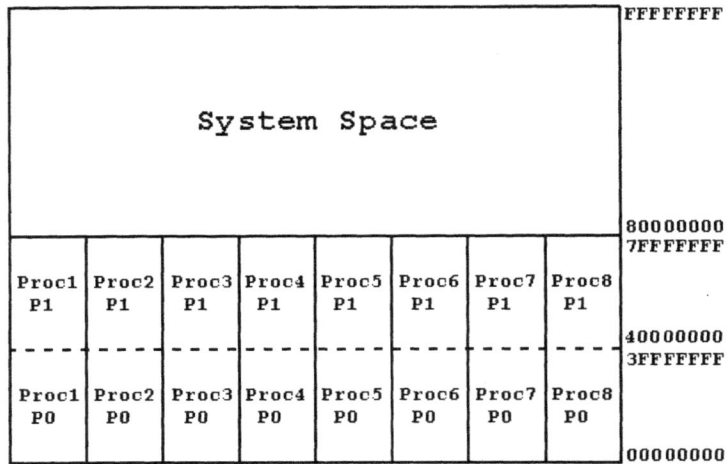

```
                                                                    FFFFFFFF


                        System  Space



                                                                    80000000
                                                                    7FFFFFFF

Proc1 | Proc2 | Proc3 | Proc4 | Proc5 | Proc6 | Proc7 | Proc8
  P1  |   P1  |   P1  |   P1  |   P1  |   P1  |   P1  |   P1
                                                                    40000000
- - - - - - - - - - - - - - - - - - - - - - - - - - - - - - -      3FFFFFFF

Proc1 | Proc2 | Proc3 | Proc4 | Proc5 | Proc6 | Proc7 | Proc8
  P0  |   P0  |   P0  |   P0  |   P0  |   P0  |   P0  |   P0
                                                                    00000000
```

Figure 17-2 Virtual Memory Regions

OpenVMS uses each of these regions for specific purposes, as follows:

- *P0 Space* Known as the program region, this is the area in which programs are mapped when they execute. Programs are executed as the result of the DCL RUN command, many other DCL commands, and foreign commands. When a program is interrupted, it is not immediately removed from this region, but when a new program starts, the existing contents of this region are destroyed. This is why the CONTINUE command can be used to continue an interrupted program only if no other program has been executed. When a program ends (as opposed to being temporarily interrupted), this region is reset to an initial state.

- *P1 Space* Known as the control region, this area contains items of a more permanent nature than the contents of the P0 space. The DCL command interpreter resides here, which is why you can interrupt a program and execute other DCL commands before resuming the program (again, with the stipulation that you have not executed another program in between). This area also contains the four per-process stacks, information used by the file- and record-management services, the DCL command table, the DCL symbol table, scratch memory for a variety of purposes, and various other information that must survive program termination.

- *System Space* In contrast to the P0 and P1 regions, which are unique to each process, system space is common to all processes. This feature allows each process to reference systemwide data from within its own context. System space addresses are not mapped into the memory management data for each process. Instead, the translation of a virtual memory address (described later) at or above 80000000 causes a reference to system space through a common set of address translation data.

System space contains the OpenVMS operating system itself, as well as systemwide code and data, including system service vectors (tables to locate OpenVMS routines), memory management databases, dynamic storage pools (described further on), the interrupt stack, and data structures describing each process.

Moving OpenVMS from 32 to 64 Bits

Early versions of OpenVMS Alpha simulated the 32-bit VAX environment through a straightforward technique known as *sign extension*. In technical terms, it copied the highest bit of a 32-bit address to each of the high 32 bits of the 64-bit address. Any VAX address at 7FFFFFFF or lower has a clear first bit, which caused the first 32 bits of the corresponding Alpha address to be clear also. Any VAX address of 80000000 or higher has the first bit set, thus setting the first 32 bits of the Alpha address.

In practical terms, it mapped the first 2GB of VAX address space to the lowest 2GB of Alpha address space, and the high 2GB of the VAX space to the highest 2GB of Alpha space. All the extra addressing space in between, nearly all of the available 64-bit space, was unused:

```
VAX address          Alpha address
00000000             0000000000000000
00000123             0000000000000123
40000000             0000000040000000
7FFFFFFF             000000007FFFFFFF
                     0000000100000000  (Unused)
                            .
                            .          (Unused)
                            .
                     FFFFFFFF7FFFFFFF  (Unused)
80000000             FFFFFFFF80000000
85004444             FFFFFFFF85004444
```

Later versions of OpenVMS Alpha began using the previously unused sections of the 64-bit address space. Since the VAX system space (80000000x and above) was starting to get crowded, the OpenVMS engineers began moving certain components to unused portions of the address space. Data for the Distributed Lock Manager were among the first to be moved, and since that time, various other components have been moved to newly defined regions of system space.

Process Scheduling

A small OpenVMS system may have only a few processes and a single CPU, whereas a large system may have multiple CPUs and thousands of processes. OpenVMS must keep track of which process is currently executing on a given CPU, decide when to remove it from execution, and select the next process to execute.

This section describes how OpenVMS manages the scheduling of processes. We start by examining the various process scheduling states and then move on to the dynamics of scheduling.

Process States

OpenVMS assigns various states to processes to indicate their eligibility for scheduling. A process is in exactly one state at a given time. Most of the possible process states are as follows:

> **Note:** Use the SHOW SYSTEM command to see a list of all processes, including their current states.

- *CUR (current)* This process is currently executing on a CPU. If the system has more than one CPU, the SHOW SYSTEM display will indicate which CPU is executing the process, as in "CUR 06." Your own process will always be shown as current when using SHOW SYSTEM.

- *COM (computable)* This process is ready to execute and will be placed into execution when a CPU becomes available, subject to priority-based selection. It is waiting for no system resources other than CPU availability.

  When a process in a wait state becomes eligible for processing (the event for which it waited has occurred), it is placed into COM state, where it awaits selection for execution.

- *LEF (local event flag wait)* The process is waiting for some event that must occur before the process can proceed. Typically, the process is waiting for the completion of a disk I/O operation or keyboard input. A "local event flag" is an indicator within a process that will be triggered when the associated event occurs. A process may wait for a single event or wait for any one of a set of events, awaiting whichever event occurs first.

- *CEF (common event flag wait)* This is like the LEF state, except that the flag(s) for which the process waits are shared by more than one process. Common event flags are most often used for interprocess synchronization or communication.

- *HIB (hibernating)* The process has voluntarily placed itself into a wait state from which it will be awakened at a prescheduled time or at the explicit request of another process. Processes that perform some task at regular intervals or that need to execute only when certain system events occur often place themselves into this state while waiting.

- *PFW (page fault wait)* The process has been stalled by the memory management subsystem. It has made a reference to some part of its address space that is not currently in physical memory (caused a page fault). When the memory management code has made the memory page ready, the process will be resumed at the operation that caused the page fault.

- *MWAIT (miscellaneous wait)* The process is waiting for one of a number of conditions. Various wait states are grouped together and identified by this category.

- *RWxxx (resource wait)* Wait states beginning with RW indicate a resource wait, and the subsequent characters describe the particular resource for which the process waits. For example, RWMPB means modified page writer busy, a type of memory management wait, and RWSCS means system communication services, a wait for the Distributed Lock Manager.

- *SUSP (suspended)* The process has been suspended, most likely by the SET PROCESS/SUSPEND command. It will remain suspended until explicitly resumed by another process.

- *COLPG (collided page wait)* Another memory management wait. The process has referenced a shared memory page for which another process was already in PFW state.

- *Outswapped* OpenVMS supports swapping, which is the removal of an entire process from memory. When memory is tight, idle, or nearly idle, processes will first be "trimmed" (have their physical memory usage reduced). Then, if sufficient memory cannot be reclaimed, a trimmed process will be moved entirely out to disk (outswapped).

  A process that is outswapped will be in a state corresponding to the one it occupied at the time it was outswapped. It may be in HIBO (Hibernating,

Outswapped) or LEFO (Local Event Flag Wait, Outswapped), for example. When the process becomes eligible for execution, it will be placed into COMO (Computable, Outswapped), and will subsequently be brought into memory (Inswapped) and placed in COM state.

Scheduling in Action

In order to execute user programs, an operating system must relinquish control of the CPU to the user program. Most modern operating systems, OpenVMS included, contain a mechanism to ensure that the operating system can regain control of the CPU from a user process.

This mechanism is implemented as an *interrupt*, an event that causes the CPU to suspend its normal operation and perform a small piece of software known as a *service routine*. Some interrupts are generated at regular intervals by timers in the computer hardware. Others are generated by hardware or software in response to various conditions.

By using a combination of hardware and software interrupts, OpenVMS gains control of a CPU at frequent intervals (several times per second) and determines whether the current process should be removed from execution in favor of another one. It is normal for a CPU to switch among various processes many times per second. This is what gives the appearance of many processes proceeding at once.

Processes waiting for CPU service are in COM state and are organized into queues according to their *priorities*. If a process at a higher priority is ready to run, the current process is placed at the end of the COM queue for its own priority, and the new process is loaded.

If an equal-priority process is waiting, OpenVMS may not switch to it immediately. Instead, the current process may be allowed to continue until it has used an adjustable time limit called QUANTUM.

Processes may also be removed from execution as a result of their own actions. A process may need to wait for the completion of an I/O operation, or it may make a reference to a memory address not currently in physical memory. When a process reaches a point at which it cannot continue, OpenVMS places it into the appropriate wait state and selects another process.

Furthermore, if a higher-priority process becomes computable, the current process can be immediately preempted in favor of the new process. This can happen as the result of an interrupt. Let's say a process initiates a disk I/O operation and then enters LEF state while waiting. Another process is executed during the wait. When the disk I/O is finished, an interrupt is generated. In response to the interrupt, the CPU executes the appropriate service routine, which makes the original process ready. The original process may have a higher priority than the current process (see "Process Priorities," next), in which case the current process is immediately preempted.

Process Priorities

As mentioned above, processes may possess different priorities. OpenVMS always schedules the highest-priority computable process for execution.

Normal process priorities are from 0 through 15, with the default interactive priority at 4. Higher numbers represent higher priorities. OpenVMS grants temporary priority boosts to normal processes under certain conditions, including the completion of an I/O operation. This allows the process to resume operation sooner and results in smoother overall system performance. These priority boosts are taken away once the process has been current for a short time.

There exists a range of *real-time* priorities, from 16 through 31, which follows different scheduling rules. Specifically, real-time processes stay current until preempted by a higher-priority process or until they give up the CPU. Real-time priorities are intended for specific purposes only; do not assign a priority in this range to a process without a specific reason. Misuse of the real-time priority range can render the system unresponsive under certain conditions.

Note: OpenVMS has internal data structures in place to support 64 priority levels, as required by certain Open Systems standards. Currently, only 32 levels are used.

At this point, the reader may wonder whether a process executing at one priority (say, 4) can permanently prevent a process at a lower priority (say, 2) from executing. Normally, the answer would be yes, but OpenVMS ensures that all processes receive a small amount of CPU service, regardless of their priority. This prevents a low-priority process from locking a systemwide resource and then becoming starved for CPU service. Otherwise, the low-priority process might never be able to release an important resource, adversely affecting other processes.

Scheduling on Multiple CPUs

Early versions of OpenVMS supported only computers with one CPU. At that time, OpenVMS had a special process called the *NULL process* that ran at the lowest possible priority and did no real work. Its only purpose was to consume CPU cycles whenever the machine was otherwise idle. This provided an easy solution to an otherwise complex scheduling problem.

These early versions also synchronized access to important resources using the *interrupt priority level* (IPL) mechanism. Each CPU has a special register indicating its current IPL. In order to access a certain resource, the CPU has to raise its IPL to the proper level, access the data, and then lower its IPL. Interrupts of lower priorities are blocked until the CPU lowered its IPL. This technique prevented accidental damage to the data by preventing overlapping accesses.

VAX/VMS Version 5 introduced support for *symmetric multiprocessing* (SMP), the ability to support multiple CPUs running at once. The introduction of additional CPUs meant that the system could execute more than one process at a time, one per CPU. However, it also meant that the traditional synchronization methods would no longer be sufficient.

With multiple CPUs, IPL is no longer adequate to synchronize access to critical data structures. Since IPL is specific to each CPU, a CPU could access a critical data structure regardless of the IPL of any other CPU. To solve this problem, *spinlocks* were added. A spinlock is a software construct maintained by OpenVMS, with a rank correlating to the IPL level it supplements. In modern versions of OpenVMS, a CPU raises its IPL as well as acquiring the proper spinlock to access a particular data structure. A given IPL may have several associated spinlocks, each protecting a specific group of data structures.

The NULL process has also been removed. Now, when there are no ready processes, the extra CPU cycles are taken up by a routine within the scheduler code. While idle, each CPU continually checks to see whether a process has become ready.

Chapter 18 — Virtual Memory Management

Virtual memory is a technique that allows processes to use (or at least, appear to use) more memory than is actually available on a computer. A process can reference any address within a 4GB virtual address range. The virtual memory management subsystem of OpenVMS is responsible for allocating system resources in such a way that a process is unaware that the memory it uses is not "real."

Several processes together, or even one process, may have memory requirements far exceeding the physical memory available on the computer. OpenVMS conceptually divides physical memory into small units called *pages* that are allocated to processes on an as-needed basis. A combination of techniques known as *paging* and *swapping* is used to ensure that memory is always available, or will become available.

Note: Other operating systems may use the terms paging and swapping interchangeably. Under OpenVMS, each has a separate meaning.

Paging assigns physical memory pages to processes, associating them with a specific page of the process virtual address space through complex *page tables*. When a process references a memory address, the memory-management hardware locates the physical memory page assigned to hold that virtual address. When memory is scarce, pages may be taken away from processes for other uses. When this occurs, OpenVMS ensures that the current contents of the pages can be reconstructed later when they are needed again.

Swapping is the technique of removing entire processes from physical memory to free nearly all pages associated with that process (the only data left in memory are necessary to locate and inswap (reload) the process when it is needed). OpenVMS uses a variety of other methods to reclaim memory before resorting to swapping[1]. When selecting a process for outswapping (removal from memory), OpenVMS locates a process that has been idle for some time and has been trimmed (had its number of physical pages reduced to a minimal level).

A Paging Example

There are many types of virtual pages. Some are private to one process; others are shared. They may be assigned to represent a block in an image file or allocated to hold new data. They may be writeable or read-only, or they may be accessible only at

---

1. Some experienced system managers intentionally tune their systems to encourage early swapping to leave more pages for those process that remain in memory.

certain privileged access modes. This example will use an ordinary process-private data page for illustration.

Let's start with the idea of a page already in physical memory that was modified by its owner process several seconds ago. A few seconds later, let's say that several other processes suddenly increase their memory requirements. The computer is now running low on free memory.

The system must do something to make more memory pages available. Our example memory page is selected by the memory management subsystem to be freed. Because the process has modified the page, its contents must be preserved before the physical page can be freed. The memory management subsystem takes several steps that result in the page being copied to a special file on disk called a *pagefile*. The page tables are updated to reflect the location of the data, and the physical page is made available for other processes.

Some time later, the process makes a reference to a memory address previously contained on that page. During the virtual-to-physical address translation, the memory management hardware discovers that the virtual page is not currently in physical memory. It signals a condition called *translation not valid*, otherwise known as a *page fault*. The process is placed into PFW (page fault wait) state while waiting for the page to be made ready. The memory-management subsystem locates a free page of memory and fills it with the contents stored in the pagefile. When this is complete, the page tables are updated with the new address information. The process is placed into COM state, and when it is selected for execution, the same instruction that caused the page fault will be retried. This time, it will not cause a page fault, and the process will continue.

Paging Details

The preceding paragraphs have described the basics of virtual memory management, paging, and swapping. As might be expected, paging and swapping can impose a significant amount of overhead on a system. This section will briefly describe some of the OpenVMS components involved in paging and some techniques employed to reduce memory-management overhead.

Before examining the specifics of paging, some terminology associated with virtual-memory techniques must be introduced. After that, paging will be examined with the focus first on a single process, then on the entire system.

Virtual-Memory Terminology

Backing Store A location on disk where the contents of a memory page are stored. This can be in a pagefile for pages whose contents have been modified. It can also be the original location of the data, such as a page in an image (program) file, for unmodified pages. The backing store is used to refill the contents of a virtual page if it has been removed from and later restored to physical memory.

Working Set This is the set of pages in the process virtual address space actually in physical memory. It includes pages dedicated to memory management and pages that describe the working set itself. It does not include pages whose contents exist only in a pagefile or other backing store.

Free Page List A list of pages available for allocation. It consists mainly of pages that have been removed from process working sets. If a process makes a reference to a page that has been removed from its working set and placed on the free page list, it can be moved immediately back into the working set of the process. Once a page has been used for another purpose, this is no longer possible.

Modified Page List A list of pages that have been removed from process working sets after being modified, but have not yet been saved to backing store. This means that they cannot be reused until the contents of the page have been copied to backing store. If the process that most recently owned a page makes a reference to it, it can be placed immediately back into the working set of that process. Periodically, OpenVMS flushes modified pages to backing store and moves the associated pages to the free page list.

Pagefile A special file on disk used to hold memory contents temporarily. When the system must free a page of physical memory that has no current backing store, its contents are copied to a block in a pagefile before the memory page is used for another purpose. OpenVMS supports the simultaneous use of multiple pagefiles.

Paging Within a Process

The OpenVMS paging scheme attempts to force processes to page against themselves. Put another way, if one particular process is memory-hungry and causes a large number of page faults, the unavoidable performance degradation should come at the expense of that process, not of other processes.

OpenVMS attempts to achieve this goal by setting a limit upon the working set size of a process. The paging behavior of a process (whether it causes few or many page faults) causes automatic adjustment of the working set size within predetermined limits (discussed later).

Note: The term *working set size* refers to the number of entries in the process working set list. Not all entries may be in use at a particular time. Therefore, the number of pages actually in use may be less than the size of the working set. The term *size* is used to avoid confusion with *limit*, which is the number to which a size can grow.

If a process generates a page fault, the system adds a page to the process working set to hold the additional page if an entry is available. If no entry is available, OpenVMS may try to expand the process working set size, as described below.

When a process generates a page fault, but cannot add a page to its working set, one of the process's own pages must be removed from its working set to make room for the new page. Certain pages that have not been modified can simply be discarded; they can be loaded again from the same source as before. Other pages may have been modified and therefore have no backing store from which they can be recreated. The system must make arrangements for modified pages to be saved in a pagefile.

If the process generates page faults at a fast rate—greater than a limit called *page fault rate high limit* (PFRATH)—the size of its working set is automatically adjusted upward, within limits. If the rate of page faults is very slow—lower than *page fault rate low limit* (PFRATL)—its working set size may be reduced, but many system managers disable this downward adjustment. In this case, pages are removed as the result of program termination or explicit requests from within programs. The system manager may adjust each of these thresholds.

Depending on system conditions, the size to which a working set can grow can be one of two limits. At the start of a program, the number of working set entries is set to a relatively small size called *working set default* (WSDEF). As the program executes, its page fault rate may exceed the threshold value. If the page fault rate stays high, the working set will grow to a limit called *working set quota* (WSQUOTA).

This limit prevents a process from unnecessarily degrading the performance of other processes by consuming too much physical memory. However, if the system has ample free memory, a process is allowed to grow even further. If a certain number of pages is available on the free page list, a process may grow beyond WSQUOTA to a final limit called *working set extent* (WSEXTENT). Just as WSQUOTA keeps one process from interfering with others, WSEXTENT keeps a process from being artificially constrained when resources are available.

Paging on the Entire System

OpenVMS manages the working set of each process as described above, but when considering the system as a whole, several nuances emerge. Each process will generate some number of unavoidable page faults, but steps can be taken to reduce their number or to lessen the overhead associated with paging.

Secondary Page Caches

When selecting a page for removal from a process working set, it would be helpful to select a page that would not be needed soon. When the data contained on that page are referenced again, yet another page fault is needed to bring it back into the working set, increasing overhead.

Unfortunately, it is not possible to predict with any real accuracy which pages should be removed from a working set to best reduce the number of future page faults. Attempts to analyze paging behavior can introduce even more overhead than they avoid.

OpenVMS attempts to solve the page-selection problem by providing an environment in which the consequences of a bad choice are held to a minimum. OpenVMS makes no attempt to select a page for removal intelligently; a heavily used page may be faulted out, only to be faulted back in shortly. A seldom-used page is equally likely to be faulted out, but won't come back as soon.

As a process executes programs, a pattern sometimes emerges. A program will often generate a flurry of page faults at its start and then concentrate mainly on a certain set of pages for a longer period of time. Eventually, so long as the required number of pages can fit in the working set, the extraneous pages will naturally get removed, leaving only the frequently accessed pages.

OpenVMS provides two special caches to reduce the performance degradation caused while the population of the working set is sorting itself out. The free page list and the modified page list serve as secondary page caches, reducing the damage done by indiscriminate page removal.

When a page is removed from the working set of a process, it is placed on the free page list (if it has backing store or is no longer needed) or on the modified page list (if no backing store exists and the page is still needed). When a page is placed on the free page list or modified page list, its contents are not immediately destroyed.

This means that when a page is removed from a working set, *it remains available in physical memory for some time.* If a page fault is generated while the contents of the target page are still valid, the page can simply be moved from the free or modified list back into the process working set. Therefore, heavily used pages removed from a process working set stand a good chance of being retained in memory until they are referenced again.

Of course, other processes continue to allocate pages from the head of the free page list for various purposes. Pages not faulted back into a working set will eventually be erased as they come to the head of the free page list.

When a page fault can be resolved from the free or modified page list, it is known as a *soft fault*, whereas faults that must be resolved from backing store are called *hard faults*. Soft faults can be serviced many times faster than hard faults. The ratio varies according to processor and disk speed, but a ratio of 100:1 is traditionally accepted.

Applications that make poor use of memory resources might rely (intentionally or not) on the secondary page caches to increase their performance. However, since all processes share these page caches, they cannot be relied on to make the application perform well, particularly on a heavily loaded system. This also implies that the poorly written application can adversely affect all other processes. The programmer remains responsible for making careful use of system resources.

Modified Page Writing

Pages on the modified page list are not written to backing store immediately, but only on certain conditions. These include the modified list exceeding a certain size and the free page list falling below a certain size.

This allows OpenVMS the opportunity to group modified pages together for writing to a pagefile. Writing modified pages in large clusters saves a significant amount of overhead.

OpenVMS also supports multiple page files on separate disks to increase the overall speed of the paging mechanism.

Dynamic Storage Pools

In addition to paged virtual memory, OpenVMS maintains two memory pools—the *nonpaged dynamic storage pool* and the *paged dynamic storage pool*. They are generally referred to as the "nonpaged pool" and "paged pool" and are located in the system virtual address range.

The nonpaged pool, as its name implies, is not paged. None if its contents are removed from physical memory. It is used to store data that must be resident in memory at all times, such as data structures describing open files and I/O operations in progress. The paged pool contains certain systemwide data that may be paged out, including a list of mounted disk volumes, for example.

Within the pools, OpenVMS maintains lists of *packets* available for allocation by a process or for use by OpenVMS itself. The packets are of varying sizes designed to satisfy a wide variety of requirements while balancing wasted space against processing overhead.

Processes usually allocate pool space indirectly as a result of OpenVMS routines. Special privileges are required to manipulate pool contents directly.

Chapter 19 — Images

OpenVMS programs are known as *executable images* or just *images*, and the process of starting program execution is called *image activation*. Under OpenVMS, image files have the filetype .EXE. The term *image* refers to the contents of the executable file—some sections of the file contain program contents exactly as they are to be laid out in memory. Hence, some sections of the executable file are exact images of their memory counterparts.

Image executions are requested directly by using the DCL RUN command or a foreign command, and most other DCL commands invoke an image to carry out the requested action.

When a user process invokes a normal image, it is mapped into the P0 region of the process. Note the use of the term *mapped* rather than *loaded*. OpenVMS does not directly load image pages into memory, but instead updates the process page tables to use pages in the image as backing store. Because of this, pages of the image are faulted in as needed. Pages in the image file that are never needed will not unnecessarily consume physical memory.

For most images, activation includes steps that allow the inclusion of a debugger, image dump facility, or traceback facility. The *debugger* is a special program that allows detailed control and examination of a running program. The *image dump facility* enables memory contents to be saved to disk in case of a severe error, allowing for examination at a later time. Lastly, the *traceback facility* displays debugging and stack information about some types of serious errors. For security reasons, support for these features is disabled for some types of images, including installed images, described later.

Some images are simple, self-contained programs and require no further preparation. However, a simple main image may be linked against (contain references to) shareable or installed images (described later), calling for additional preparation before being executed.

When the program has reached its end, has aborted due to a severe error, or has been manually aborted (not merely interrupted), *image rundown* occurs. This refers to the steps taken to return the process to the same state it was in before the image ran. This includes restoring process privileges and the working set size to their initial values and deleting P0 and portions of P1 space. After image rundown, control is returned to DCL, if present. If the process has no CLI (as is the case with some detached processes), the process is terminated.

Sharable Images

A *shareable image* is a special type of image that allows several processes to use functions stored in a single image file concurrently. For instance, most higher-level language compilers are supplied with shareable images containing their library routines. When generating main object files, the language compilers do not include code for their library routines in the main object, but instead include calls to the routines in the shareable image.

As an example, every C language program that uses the printf() function need not contain its own internal copy of the printf() code; they can all use the common routine in the C Runtime Library shareable image. When considering the number of main programs and the number of library routines used within them, considerable disk space and physical memory can be saved.

Sharable images can (if properly designed) undergo considerable change without relinking all of the main images that use them. Features can be added, and problems in library routines can be fixed by replacing a single shareable image file.

Note: OpenVMS uses a combination of compilers and linkers to produce executable files, as opposed to systems that do not use linkers. This means that modules written in a variety of languages can be combined into a single executable image. The OpenVMS *Procedure Calling Standard* ensures that modules written in different languages can work together.

OpenVMS shareable images are roughly equivalent to dynamic link libraries (DLLs) as implemented within the Microsoft Windows environment.

Installed Images

Certain images can be *installed*. This does not refer to software installation, where new programs are loaded from a distribution medium. An installed image, also called a *known file*, is a file registered via the DCL INSTALL command to have special attributes.

Installed images may be assigned elevated privileges, temporarily granting those privileges to any user who executes the image. An example is the OpenVMS MAIL facility. To send mail to another local user, a file in that user's login directory must be modified, something that other users are not normally permitted to do.

To allow this special circumstance, the MAIL program is installed with the privileges necessary to write files in someone else's directory. Any user running the MAIL program is granted those privileges only while the MAIL program is executing. When the MAIL program exits, the user's privileges are returned to normal.

Note: Because of their sensitive nature, installed images do not include support for the debugger, image dump, or traceback facilities.

Installed images may also be used to conserve system resources. They may be specified as permanently open and have their image headers resident in memory at all times. When frequently used images are installed in this manner, their startup time is significantly reduced. Many of the OpenVMS operating system images are installed this way.

Chapter 20 — The Files-11 File System

A *file system* is that part of an operating system that controls the storage and manipulation of files on media, such as disks. At first thought, that may seem like a rather straightforward task. However, to carry out this function, a file system supporting a multiuser operating system must perform a variety of difficult jobs.

A successful file system must do the following:

- Impose upon a blank medium a structure capable of representing highly organized data (The structure must usually be hierarchical, that is, to support files in directories and subdirectories)

- Be able to multiplex the use of storage units among many concurrent accessors

- Contain internal synchronization for all accesses

- Enforce security by allowing data access only to those who have legitimate authority

- Manage the sharing of individual files by multiple accessors concurrently

- Isolate faults stemming from imperfect physical media or improper access (This implies minimizing the potential for data loss due to hardware faults.)

- Provide a standard set of interface routines to upper layers of the operating system and user programs and make them apply equally to devices with dissimilar interfaces.

Finally, a file system must do all these things with minimal impact on system performance.

The file system supplied with OpenVMS is Files-11. Within the Files-11 design, there are two main specifications for the physical arrangement of data on a disk. They are ODS-2 (for On-Disk Structure level 2, used for most of the history of OpenVMS) and ODS-5 (a newer disk structure that has been gaining popularity for the past few years).

Note: The Files-11 file system is concerned with files, directories, and free space on a disk. It is not to be confused with OpenVMS Record Management Services (RMS), which is concerned with the data format within files.

Most of the information presented here applies to both structure levels, and exceptions are noted. For the general user, the most important practical difference is a more flexible set of file-naming rules introduced with ODS-5. Examples in this book conform to ODS-2 rules.

Multivolume Sets

The OpenVMS file system provides support for several types of multivolume disk sets, including volume sets, shadow sets, hardware- and software-based stripe sets, and RAID arrays.

Volume sets are multiple volumes treated as a single unit, wherein a portion of a new file may be stored at any available location on any volume. No data redundancy is provided; each cluster of file data resides exclusively on a single volume. The term *volume set* may apply to ISO 9660 volume sets, also supported by OpenVMS, as well.

Shadow sets are two- or three-disk sets in which all volumes contain exactly the same information. Each write operation is applied to all volumes, and read operations can be performed by a single volume. Read performance can be increased by assigning separate read operations to separate volumes.

Stripe sets are multivolume sets that have their logical block numbers interleaved between volumes. They can be roughly envisioned as several disks "stacked" atop one another so that a single cylinder encompasses the same track on all volumes.

RAID arrays are typically hardware-based multivolume sets that split each data byte across all volumes, such that if one disk were to fail, the data could be reconstructed from the remaining members.

A given multivolume set can be constructed so as to use two or more of the techniques discussed above. For example, two RAID sets could be combined into a volume set.

File System Terminology

Block The basic unit of disk storage. It is 512 bytes in size, the same size as a VAX memory page or the Alpha pagelet. Making the disk and memory units the same size simplifies the virtual memory management code.

Volume The basic disk storage medium under Files-11. It is treated as an array of logical blocks, which must be randomly addressable. Today, this usually means a single disk drive, or sometimes several separate drives bound by hardware in such a way as to act as a single unit. Historically, the concepts of volume and disk drive were different in that a large stationary disk drive could contain a removable disk volume.

This is less often the case today. Currently, the concept of a floppy diskette drive provides a close approximation: The device (the diskette drive) remains fixed and retains the same device name regardless of what volume (the floppy diskette) currently resides in it.

Logical Block A disk block numbered relative to the start of the disk. The file system treats a disk volume as a contiguous array of logical blocks, numbered zero through $n-1$, where n is the number of blocks on the disk. This number is not concerned with any bad-block replacement, number of actual drives, surfaces, etc. This allows most software above the disk driver to treat a disk as an abstract device with no media defects.

Physical Block A block at a certain surface/track/sector on a drive. When presented with a logical block number, the disk driver calculates the physical disk block that contains the data.

Virtual Block A block assigned to a file, relative to the beginning of that file, starting with virtual block 1. A virtual block always has an associated logical block, but a logical block has an associated virtual block only if it is assigned to a file. Keep in mind that whereas logical blocks start with 0, virtual blocks start with 1.

Bad-Block Replacement Most disk surfaces contain media defects. Disks come from the factory with internal lists of blocks that cannot reliably hold information. Each drive has some empty spare blocks to be used as replacements for bad blocks discovered later. Some time after the disk enters service, additional blocks may fail. These are added to the list of bad blocks and are assigned a replacement block. This process is sometimes handled by operating system software, but increasingly, with modern disks it is handled within the disk unit.

Cluster Factor The unit of space allocation on a volume, expressed in blocks. For example, a certain disk may have a cluster factor of three. When blocks are allocated, they are allocated in units of three blocks at a time. The system manager selects this number as a balance between a reduced number of allocation operations and unused (wasted) blocks at the ends of files. Also known as cluster size.

Disk Driver A piece of operating system software that controls the actual operation of a disk drive. The disk driver is not aware of a file system structure on disk; it moves raw blocks of data as directed by the file system.

File Header An entry in INDEXF.SYS describing a file. Most files have one header, but files with many extents (fragments) and/or files with many ACL entries may have more than one header due to space limitations in the first header.

Seek The mechanical movement of *disk heads* to a different track. Tracks are the concentric rings of data storage areas on a disk surface.

File Fragmentation The process of a file being stored to discontiguous ranges of logical blocks (parts of the file being scattered over the disk). This is an expected by-product of file system operation over time, but it extracts a performance penalty. Retrieving all parts of the file requires extra mechanical movements of the disk hardware, slowing performance.

Retrieval Pointers Pairs of numbers describing the location and size of each file extent (part of the file). They are stored in the file header.

Common File Operations

Create To establish a new file. This involves allocating and filling a file header, creating an optional directory entry for the file, and usually securing an initial allocation of disk blocks to hold the first portion of the file. When "creation" is complete, this does not imply that all of the file contents are written to the file. On the contrary, the file is usually still open for write access.

Open To establish a context for reading or modifying an existing file. A file may be opened to be read, to be read and written to, or to be appended. Files-11 does not fully support write-only files.

Read To copy data from the file into memory.

Write To modify the contents of the file. This may mean appending data onto the end of the file, or it may mean overwriting existing contents.

Extend To add additional empty blocks onto the end of the file—usually done in anticipation of appending data to the file.

Truncate To deallocate some (or all) of the file storage space without deleting the file. Truncation occurs from the end of the file, so any data left will be the first portion of the previous contents.

Delete To remove a file. The delete process deallocates the header and the directory entry (if any) and frees the disk blocks allocated to the file. This generally does not involve erasing the actual file contents, but only removing the pointers to the data. Generally, the data continue to exist until overwritten by a new file.

File Layout on Disk

A new disk must be *initialized* before being used as a Files-11 volume. Initialization establishes INDEXF.SYS and the other reserved files (see "reserved files", further on).

On a new disk, the bulk of INDEXF.SYS is located near the middle of the disk (around the middle-numbered logical blocks) by default. Some small portions of INDEXF.SYS containing backup copies of critical information are placed at other locations on disk, selected for their redundancy against certain types of hardware failures. The portion of INDEXF.SYS containing the boot block and the home block is located at the beginning of the disk, starting at logical block zero. The remaining reserved files are created, and all of the remaining logical blocks are made available for use.

As files are created, they are generally placed at the lowest available logical block numbers, although certain other factors can cause different locations to be selected. The system maintains a cache of block numbers from recently deleted files in memory, so that space for subsequent creations can be found without examining the storage bitmap. The first available spaces will also be skipped if they are not of sufficient size, and certain options are used while creating the file.

The actions of creating, extending, and deleting files eventually result in files being broken into pieces (properly known as *extents*, but commonly called *fragments*), each of which may be stored at a different location on disk. File fragmentation is also caused by the process of extending a file when it is not known how large the file will eventually be. This prevents the proper amount of space from being allocated in the first place. If too little is allocated and the next block of free space is taken by another file, the first file must continue at another location. If too much space is allocated, there will be a range of free space between two existing files. An example of this process is presented further on.

Fragmentation degrades performance for two reasons: processing overhead and disk seeks. The processing overhead involves handling lists of pointers to various parts of a file and accounts for a small amount of the lost performance. The bulk of the damage comes from the extra seeks caused when the disk heads must physically move to a different part of the disk, given that the mechanical motion is extremely slow compared with processing speed.

Special programs called *defragmenters* collect the various pieces of fragmented files together to make them contiguous. Defragmenters for OpenVMS are available from Hewlett-Packard and third-party vendors.

File System Operation

Since Files-11 is used on systems with many concurrent users, it must be able to satisfy a variety of requests from a variety of sources. At any given time, some users may be creating files, others may be deleting files, and yet others may be extending existing files. These are operations that must be serialized, because they move disk blocks between the allocated and free states. Ordinary operations, such as reading files and writing to them (defined here as filling blocks which have already been allocated) may not need any serialization, so long as each open file has a maximum of one potential writer at once.

Note: The activities listed here are concerned with data at the block level only. OpenVMS RMS, described later, has already performed any necessary record-level processing.

Processes request file system services through a construct known as an I/O *channel*. Each process has a fixed number of channels. A given channel holds context information, such as which device and/or file is accessed on it. When a process initiates an I/O operation, the process uses a system service called queue I/O request ($QIO) to which it supplies the channel on which to act, as well as a number of arguments describing the action to be carried out.

Note: I/O channels are used with all types of devices, not just disks.

A particular part of the file system known as the *extended $QIO processor* (XQP) performs tasks that cannot be performed by the $QIO system service or by the device driver. Such tasks include intervening when there is not enough virtual-to-logical block mapping information in memory and operations that do not involve a data transfer, such as associating a file with an I/O channel. The XQP essentially replaces the older-style ancillary control process (ACP) approach. An ACP is a dedicated detached process that handles these operations for a certain class of device, and they are still used in certain circumstances. The XQP was developed, in part, because ACPs can become performance bottlenecks and the XQP code can be mapped into each process's P1 space, distributing the load.

To maintain the states of devices and files and the accesses to them, the file system maintains various *control blocks* linked together in lists. For example, a channel on which a file is accessed will have an associated *window control block* (WCB), which maintains mapping information (copied from retrieval pointers) for the file being accessed. This WCB will itself be associated with a *file control block* (FCB), which contains information about the file, including information about other accessors to that file.

As files are created, extended, deleted, read, and written, these control blocks are kept updated to reflect the current state of the file system. Attempts to perform unauthorized or inconsistent operations, such as writing to a read-only file or reading a file to which you are not allowed access, are rejected.

OpenVMS supports *asynchronous I/O*, wherein a process requests an I/O operation and then may perform other work while the I/O operation is in progress. When the I/O is complete, the process is notified, usually via an event flag (see "Process Scheduling" in Chapter 17, "The Process").

File Fragmentation

System performance can suffer when files are fragmented. Why then, is it allowed to happen? It happens because it is a side effect of allowing multiple accesses to a disk, whether concurrent or not. Consider the two following scenarios, both of which cause file fragmentation.

In scenario 1, two users are creating files at the same time. If two users request the creation of files at the same time, the file system must synchronize these events to happen one at a time. In this case, let's assume user 1's request is honored first. Some disk blocks are allocated to the file (the initial allocation) in anticipation of the user's writing data to it. However, the file system must not indefinitely stall user 2's request. When the creation[1] of the first file is finished, the file system will create file 2 and allocate some blocks for it. As both users write data to their respective files, their initial allocations will eventually be filled.

At this point, file 1 must be extended, but the initial allocation of file 2 occupies the next logical blocks on the volume. The next part of file 1 must be placed at some other location. Thus, file 1 becomes fragmented.

---

1. The term creation refers only to allocating a header, a directory entry, and the initial blocks of a file; no data have yet been placed into the file.

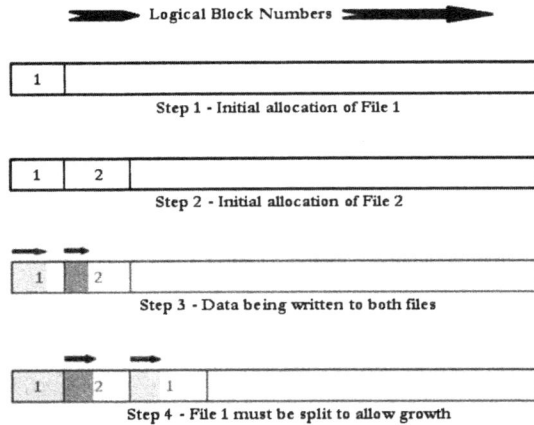

Figure 20-1 File Fragmentation

In scenario 2, a single user is writing multiple files. It is easy to envision how a single user creating two or more files at once can create fragmented files in exactly the same way as two users creating one file each.

In addition, the file system must work around portions of files already existing on the disk and eventually use free space that becomes available as files are deleted. At any given time, there may not be a single range of free blocks large enough to hold the data to be written, or, frequently, a file may be opened without the system knowing how much data will be written to it. In this fashion, files on the disk will become fragmented.

Reserved Files

All of the data describing the layout of files on a disk is contained on the disk itself. When a disk is first accessed (after a reboot or the mounting of a new disk), there must be some way to locate enough information to get started. In order to accomplish this, Files-11 places certain key information in known locations.

A certain number of *reserved files* exist on disk, some portions at specific locations, which allows Files-11 to learn the state of all information on a disk. During system operation, the contents of these files are kept updated with the latest file system information[1].

---

1. For performance reasons, certain information may be allowed to be temporarily out-of-date. None of the data are unrecoverable; should the system fail while some file system data are obsolete, all of this information is automatically checked and, if necessary, reconstructed the next time the disk is mounted.

The main reserved files holding disk structure information are named in the following paragraphs.

INDEXF.SYS This is the central file containing the names, attributes, and physical locations of files on disk. In addition, it contains much of the information needed to begin accessing a disk on system startup. Its contents are described the next section.

BITMAP.SYS This file contains a map representing free space on the volume. Each bit in the file represents one cluster (not block) of disk storage, indicating at a glance whether or not it is free. While it is possible to determine the same information from INDEXF.SYS, it would be an unreasonably slow process.

000000.DIR This file is the top-level directory for the volume and represents the starting point for directory operations. Please note that INDEXF.SYS contains complete information about all files on the volume and that directories are merely a means to represent a hierarchical relationship among files. From a technical perspective, directories are not strictly necessary for using a Files-11 disk volume.

INDEXF.SYS Contents

The INDEXF.SYS file is the central location for information about the files on a volume. Part of INDEXF.SYS is stored at a known location on disk so that a system just starting up can find certain key information, which is then used to locate the remainder of the file system data. Within this file are the following elements:

- *The Boot Block* This block is used only on disks that contain a copy of the OpenVMS operating system. It is stored at the first logical block on the volume and contains information needed to locate OpenVMS during system startup.

- *The Home Block* This block is stored at the second logical block and contains such things as the volume name, creation date, cluster factor, and other volumewide information.

- *Backup Blocks* INDEXF.SYS contains backup copies of important blocks such as the home block and the header describing INDEXF.SYS. These backup copies provide the ability to access the volume should the primary copies be lost due to media defects.

- *Index File Bitmap* A bitmap (not to be confused with BITMAP.SYS) containing information about which file headers within INDEXF.SYS are unused. This is used to quickly locate a free header when a file is created.

- *File Headers* Most of INDEXF.SYS contains file headers, which are blocks describing each file on the volume. Among the header contents for a file are the file identification (FID), record attributes, file characteristics, protection codes, file owner, file name, creation date, modification date, and retrieval pointers.

Most files are represented by a single header. However, since each extent (fragment) of a file needs one retrieval pointer in the header and headers are of a fixed size, severely fragmented files may require additional headers.

OpenVMS Record Management Services

Whereas the basic units used by the file system are *files* and *blocks*, Record Management Services (RMS) is concerned with the internal structure of files. Even though programs are allowed to access virtual blocks directly, most programs handle data as collections of *records*. RMS provides record-oriented services and handles the file system interface on behalf of a program.

RMS provides support for a variety of different file and record formats, many more variations than are found on most operating systems. File formats are typically sequential, indexed, and relative. Records may be of fixed or varying length and possess a variety of carriage-control attributes. A program may use RMS to create a file with certain file and record characteristics and then simply supply records to RMS. RMS handles the organization of records into blocks and makes the appropriate file system calls to store the file on disk. Likewise, when opening an existing file, RMS can interpret the file and record characteristics automatically and supply the data to the program in the form of records.

Most language compilers use RMS to implement their built-in I/O routines, but a programmer may choose to use RMS or the file system (via $QIO) directly. This can provide for more flexibility and, if used properly, superior performance to built-in I/O routines. The programmer should bear in mind, however, that doing so decreases the portability of the program to other operating systems.

Chapter 21 — Clustering and Galaxy Systems

VMS Clusters

Clustering is a technique whereby two or more computer systems are coupled together more tightly than in a simple network. VMScluster systems can share disks and other resources and provide clusterwide access to them.

It is possible to configure a VMScluster in such a way that it does not matter which cluster member a user logs into; each system acts identically to all the others, and all the same files, printers, and queues are available.

VMScluster members may also use the same system disk (boot device), sharing one on-disk copy of the OpenVMS operating system. Certain features of the file system make it possible for each system to have some private and some shared files. This permits the sharing of a system disk while providing for some system-specific files.

The OpenVMS queuing mechanism (batch, printer, and server queues) is clusterwide; a user on each system can submit a job to any queue available in the cluster.

The network manager can also specify a single DECnet nodename to refer to the entire cluster. This name is called an *alias node identifier* or *cluster alias*. Users accessing cluster systems can use this alias as if it were an actual nodename to achieve the same kind of abstraction via DECnet.

In order to understand the implications of this type of resource sharing, imagine two users updating a record in a file at the same time. Both users could simultaneously attempt to read the same record in the same file, modify the data, and then update the record on disk. If there were no mechanism in place to coordinate such accesses, whichever update occurred first would be overwritten by the update that occurred second. In order to avoid this problem, one user's read-modify-write sequence must execute uninterrupted. The second user's accesses must be stalled until the first user is finished.

Most operating systems can perform this type of synchronization among different processes on the same system, but cluster systems can provide this service to all processes anywhere in the cluster.

The key to this type of resource sharing is the Distributed Lock Manager. The Lock Manager is made up of a clusterwide database of *resource locks* and the software to manage it.

When a process needs to access a resource, the Lock Manager provides the process with a resource lock for that resource, associating it with the process intending to use the resource and the type of access requested. The Lock Manager ensures that all cluster members are updated with the same lock information.

A resource lock has one of six modes, indicating the type of access requested. They are as follows:

1. *EX*—Exclusive. No other process will be allowed any access.

2. *PW*—Protected write. This process will be allowed to read and write the resource. Other processes may only read it.

3. *PR*—Protected read. This process intends to read the resource. No other process may write it.

4. *CW*—Concurrent write. This process can read and write the resource. Other processes are under no restrictions.

5. *CR*—Concurrent read. This process intends to read the resource. Other processes are under no restrictions.

6. *NL*—Null. The process does not intend to access the resource at this time, but is expressing a potential future interest in the resource. Converting an existing lock from one mode to another is faster than acquiring a new lock, so processes with intermittent interest in a resource usually lower an existing lock to NL mode, rather than releasing the lock between accesses.

Should another process anywhere in the cluster request access to the same resource, the Lock Manager grants the request only if the intended access is compatible with existing locks. Otherwise, the requesting process must wait until the other locks are released or converted to a compatible mode.

The compatibility among the lock modes is shown in Figure 21-1. One axis represents a lock already held (you may select either axis), and the other axis represents the mode of a lock being requested. The table indicates whether the requested lock is compatible with the existing lock and, therefore, whether it will be immediately granted.

	EX	PW	PR	CW	CR	NL
NL	YES	YES	YES	YES	YES	YES
CR	NO	YES	YES	YES	YES	YES
CW	NO	NO	NO	YES	YES	YES
PR	NO	NO	YES	NO	YES	YES
PW	NO	NO	NO	NO	YES	YES
EX	NO	NO	NO	NO	NO	YES

Lock Mode Compatibility

Figure 21-1 Lock Mode Compatibility

Adherence to the rules of the OpenVMS Lock Manager is voluntary. A process could access a resource without acquiring a lock, thereby causing synchronization problems.

Therefore, most OpenVMS language compilers include inherent support for the Lock Manager in their I/O routines, relieving the programmer from manually acquiring locks for each resource. BLISS and Assembly Language (Macro) do not include this support, so programmers using those languages must manually call Lock Manager system services.

Clusters and Storage Controllers

VMSclusters permit devices, such as disks and tapes to be connected directly to a given cluster node and served by the Mass Storage Control Protocol (MSCP) server to other cluster nodes.

A cluster may also contain one or more dedicated *storage controllers*—separate computers to which disks and tapes are attached. OpenVMS systems access those disks and tapes through the storage controller.

Certain devices may be *dual-ported*, which means they have two separate interfaces through which they may be accessed. These devices may be simultaneously attached to two separate storage controllers, providing failover capability in the event of a component failure.

OpenVMS processes need not be aware of the physical configuration of storage controllers and devices; OpenVMS provides transparent access to the devices without processes having to be concerned with the data path used.

Galaxy Systems

The Galaxy software architecture allows multiple instances of OpenVMS to run simultaneously on a single computer. CPUs, blocks of physical memory, and I/O ports can be assigned to different instances of OpenVMS, and these resources can be reassigned from one instance to another.

For example, if a given computer has 6 CPUs and 6GB of physical memory, a system manager may decide to allocate 2 CPUs and 2GB of physical memory to each of three instances of OpenVMS running concurrently. He may further decide to form a VMScluster comprised of the three instances.

A given CPU may be reassigned to another instance while the Galaxy system is running without interrupting any applications running on any instance.

These features offer several benefits. For example, different versions of OpenVMS may run on the same computer at the same time. Thus, entire systems can undergo operating system upgrades without shutting down more than one instance at a time, minimizing application interruptions. The ability to reassign hardware resources enables the system manager to respond to changes in workloads among instances; a CPU can be reassigned from a nearly idle instance to one temporarily requiring more CPU power.

Chapter 22 — DECnet Details

This section presents some background information on DECnet that is not necessary to use DECnet effectively, but provides a better understanding of the underlying technology.

DECnet Routing

Some DECnet nodes are *routers*, while others are *end nodes*. Routers maintain a database of the network layout and can forward network traffic to and from end nodes. Routers may have physical connections to two or more separate local area networks (LANs) and have the responsibility to forward information between nodes on separate LANs. Routers can also perform any function that an end node can.

DECnet routers maintain tables allowing them to forward traffic between any two nodes properly, even if there are several routers between the nodes or there are several possible paths.

LANs

A networking scheme like DECnet or TCP/IP is a conceptual abstraction used on collections of concrete networks—for example, LANs. A LAN consists of one or more nodes connected by a physical network medium, such as an Ethernet cable (including any hubs). All nodes on a LAN may communicate directly with one another because they share the same physical medium. A DECnet or TCP/IP network may consist of many separate LANs, with DECnet or TCP/IP assuming responsibility for connecting them and directing traffic via routers. Different networking schemes including DECnet, TCP/IP, and many others may coexist on the same physical networks at the same time.

DECnet end nodes can communicate directly with other DECnet nodes on the same LAN, but must rely on a router to communicate with machines on other LANs.

Routing is based on *cost*, an arbitrary value assigned by the network manager to each step in a possible path (hops). Between two nodes, the path with the least total cost is preferred. When network problems occur, or when certain routers are unavailable, a new path is chosen at the next lowest cost.

DECnet Versions

On a given OpenVMS system, you may encounter DECnet Phase IV or DECnet Phase V, otherwise known as DECnet OSI or DECnet-Plus. The general user does not need to be concerned with which version his system is using, although the technical details differ from one to the other.

DECnet Phase IV

DECnet Phase IV is commonly considered the traditional DECnet and is still used on many OpenVMS systems, several years after the introduction of DECnet OSI.

DECnet Phase IV is based on the Phase IV Digital Network Architecture (DNA) and is still offered as an alternative to Phase V because a strong, vocal portion of the customer base prefers Phase IV. A system manager might choose Phase IV for his years of familiarity with it or because its routing functions impose a lighter load on the resources of older, slower systems.

Phase IV routing is performed by the proprietary DECnet Routing Protocol (DRP).

DECnet Phase V (DECnet OSI)

DECnet Phase V, or DECnet OSI, is based on the *OSI (Open Systems Interconnect) reference model*, and is intended to supercede DECnet Phase IV. DECnet OSI provides backward compatibility with the proprietary protocols at the upper layers of DECnet Phase IV and introduces support for many standard OSI features.

DECnet OSI routing is performed by standard OSI routing protocols.

DECnet Protocols

DECnet Phase IV supports several proprietary protocols, including those shown below (this is not a complete list):

- *DAP* Data access protocol—provides remote file access.

- *LAT* Local area transport—provides multiplexed terminal traffic (can carry combined traffic to and from multiple terminals, such as with terminals attached to a terminal server).

- *CTERM* Command terminal—a terminal emulation protocol.

- *LAVC* Local area VAXcluster (VMScluster)—carries VMScluster traffic among cluster members.

- *SCP* Session control protocol—manages logical network links.

- *NSP* Network service protocol—provides reliable virtual connections on top of the routing protocol.

- *MOP* Maintenance operations protocol—provides utility functions, such as downline-loading of operating system software and network testing.

- *RP* Routing protocol—provides routing information to DECnet nodes.

DECnet OSI supports, in addition to many of the proprietary Phase IV protocols, all standard OSI application-layer, presentation-layer, and session-layer implementations.

Both DECnet Phase IV and DECnet OSI support popular media-access implementations, such as Ethernet (IEEE 802.3), Token Ring (IEEE 802.5), and FDDI. Data-link-layer support includes IEEE 802.2 LLC (logical link control), LAPB (link access procedure, balanced), Frame Relay, and HDLC (high-level data-link control).

Appendix A—Decimal, Octal, and Hexadecimal Notations

There are many instances in which numbers are best expressed in a radix other than decimal. For example, memory addresses are usually expressed in hexadecimal format, and User Identification Code (UIC) fields are expressed in octal format.

Hexadecimal format is convenient for memory contents and addresses because two hexadecimal digits can express any value contained in an 8-bit byte with no wasted space. Thus, eight hexadecimal digits can express any 32-bit (4-byte) value, the natural data size used by the VAX, and 16 hexadecimal digits can represent the 64-bit (16-byte) size used by Alpha and Itanium systems.

A hexadecimal digit is represented by the numbers 0 through 9 and the letters A through F in the following fashion:

Binary Value	Decimal	Hexadecimal
0000	0	0
0001	1	1
0010	2	2
0011	3	3
0100	4	4
0101	5	5
0110	6	6
0111	7	7
1000	8	8
1001	9	9
1010	10	A
1011	11	B
1100	12	C
1101	13	D
1110	14	E
1111	15	F

The relationship between bits and hexadecimal digits is shown in the following table:

Binary								Hexadecimal	Decimal
0000	0000	0000	0000	0000	0000	0000	0000	0 0 0 0 0 0 0 0	0
0000	0000	0000	0000	0011	0000	0011	1001	0 0 0 0 3 0 3 9	12345
0000	0000	0000	0000	1000	0000	0000	0000	0 0 0 0 8 0 0 0	32768
1000	0000	0000	0000	0000	0000	0000	0000	8 0 0 0 0 0 0 0	2147483648
1111	1111	1111	1111	1111	1111	1111	1111	F F F F F F F F	4294967295

A hexadecimal digit represents four bits, and an octal digit represents three bits. Octal digits are represented by the numbers 0 through 7, as follows:

Binary			Octal	Decimal
000	000	000	000	0
000	000	001	001	1
000	000	010	002	2
000	000	011	003	3
000	000	100	004	4
000	000	101	005	5
000	000	110	006	6
000	000	111	007	7
000	001	000	010	8
000	001	001	011	9

Appendix B—Additional Resources

The OpenVMS Documentation Set

The OpenVMS documentation kit is available online at

```
http://www.openvms.compaq.com:8000/
```

Because of the recent merger of Compaq and Hewlett-Packard, the above link may change.

The OpenVMS FAQ online

The OpenVMS frequently asked questions (FAQs) list is currently archived at these locations, among others:

```
http://www.openvms.compaq.com/
ftp://rtfm.mit.edu/pub/usenet/comp.os.vms/
ftp://www.faqs.org/
```

The recent merger of Compaq and Hewlett-Packard may result in a change to the first link above.

Encompass

Users of OpenVMS should consider joining Encompass. Encompass is the Enterprise Computing Association, a users group with an interest in Hewlett-Packard/Compaq products. Its membership is partially composed of former DECUS members, who were merged with a Compaq users group after Digital Equipment Corporation was taken over by Compaq. DECUS was the Digital Equipment Computer Users Society, a users' group including many particularly devoted and knowledgeable members who contributed a great deal to VAX, Alpha, and OpenVMS culture and tradition. Over the years, members contributed large amounts of useful OpenVMS freeware, collections of which are still growing today.

Members of Encompass are eligible for the OpenVMS hobbyist program. Please see

```
http://www.encompassus.org
```

The OpenVMS Hobbyist Program

The hobbyist program makes available software licenses and media for the OpenVMS operating system and approximately 100 OpenVMS software products. A few third-party commercial software vendors also make their products available to hobbyist licensees at no cost. Please see

```
http://www.montagar.com/hobbyist/index.html
```

Digital Press

In addition to this book, Digital Press publishes a number of books related to OpenVMS, other operating systems, and computing in general. Please see

```
http://www.digitalpressbooks.com
```

Newsgroups

The primary USENET newsgroup concerned with OpenVMS is comp.os.vms. This newsgroup operates in parallel with the INFO-VAX mailing list, so you may choose either method to obtain the same information.

If your ISP's news server does not carry comp.os.vms, ask your ISP to add it. Many ISPs respond quickly and happily to such requests. Alternatively, you may join the INFO-VAX mailing list.

To subscribe to the INFO-VAX mailing list, send an e-mail message to

```
Info-VAX-Request@Mvb.Saic.Com
```

including SUBSCRIBE INFO-VAX in the message body. A message whose body contains UNSUBSCRIBE INFO-VAX will remove you from the list.

Remember, it's considered proper etiquette to read a new newsgroup or mailing list for a couple of weeks before posting any messages to it. This allows you to become familiar with the style and etiquette of a particular group before posting. The OpenVMS FAQ contains particular recommendations about posting to comp.os.vms.

Another hierarchy of newsgroups, vmsnet.*, is devoted to various aspects of VAX, Alpha, and OpenVMS, but does not carry as much traffic as does comp.os.vms.

Appendix C—Default File Types

If you omit a file type in a file specification, OpenVMS may assume a certain file type, depending on what command you issued. For example, the SET COMMAND utility assumes a file type of .CLD.

The command

```
$ SET COMMAND UTILITIES
```

is interpreted as

```
$ SET COMMAND UTILITIES.CLD
```

Common default file types are listed here:

```
.ADA   ADA language source file
.B32   BLISS language source file
.BAS   BASIC language source file
.C     C language source file
.CLD   Command Definition Utility (CDU) command description file
.COB   COBOL language source file
.COM   Command procedure
.CXX   C++ language source file
.DAT   Data file
.DIF   Output from DIFFERENCES command
.DIR   Directory file
.DIS   OpenVMS MAIL distribution list
.EDT   EDT editor initialization file
.EXE   Executable image (program)
.FOR   FORTRAN language source file
.HLB   Help library
.HLP   Source files for creating .HLB files
.INI   Initialization file
.JOU   EDT journal file
.LIS   Language compiler listing file
       Default input file type for PRINT and TYPE
.LOG   Batch process log file
.M64   MACRO-64 language (Alpha Assembler) source file
.MAI   OpenVMS MAIL data file
```

```
.MAP   Memory map file produced by the Linker
.MAR   MACRO-32 (VAX Assembler or Alpha cross-assembler) source file
.MLB   Macro Library (used with MACRO assembler)
.MSG   Source file for program message text
.OBJ   Object file (produced by language compilers, input to Linker)
.OLB   Object Library file
.OPT   Linker options file
.PAS   PASCAL language source file
.PLI   PL/1 language source file
.PS    PostScript file
.STB   Symbol Table (produced by the Linker)
.SYS   OpenVMS system image file
.TJL   Journal file for the ACL editor
.TLB   Text library
.TMP   Temporary file
.TPU   EVE editor command file
.TPU$JOURNAL EVE editor journal file
.TXT   Text file
.UPD   File containing traces of changes to MACRO source file
```

Glossary

ASCII (American Standard Code for Information Interchange) A popular character set using one of 256 byte values to represent printable and non-printable characters. For example, a value of 65 represents an uppercase "A," and a value of 122 represents a lowercase "z." The ASCII character set includes upper- and lower-case English letters, the digits 0 through 9, common punctuation symbols, and a variety of non-printable control characters.

BACKUP SAVESET A file produced by the OpenVMS BACKUP utility containing the data and metadata for one or more files. Used to archive backup copies of files, directory trees, or entire disk devices to be used in the event of data loss or hardware failure.

BOOT or **BOOTSTRAP** The process of loading and starting an operating system. If the system has just been powered on, this is referred to as a "cold boot." If the system had previously been running an operating system, it is a "warm boot" or "reboot." In OpenVMS terminology, "reboot" is not synonymous with "restart." "Restart" refers to resuming an interrupted operating system already in memory.

BROADCAST MESSAGE A message sent to one or more terminals. It may be sent by OpenVMS or by an appropriately privileged user.

CHARACTER One element in an array (string) of text or other information. In the context of OpenVMS, the term usually refers to a member of the ASCII character set. A character is a single letter, digit, punctuation mark, or control character. *See also ASCII.*

CLI (Command Line Interpreter or Interface) That part of computer software that accepts user commands, either typed at a keyboard or read from a file, and causes them to be carried out. The default CLI under OpenVMS is the Digital command language (DCL).

COMPILED PROGRAM A program produced by a language compiler from one or more language source files. OpenVMS compilers produce object files, which are then linked, creating executable programs.

CONSOLE SUBSYSTEM Software that, among other things, assists with loading or bootstrapping an operating system, diagnostic functions, and updating CPU microcode. It may run on a dedicated processor, or on the main CPU of the system. It usually has control of the hardware when an operating system is not running. *See also SRM.*

CONSOLE TERMINAL A special terminal that receives system messages and security alarms, whose device name is OPA0:. For security reasons it is often located in a physically secure location.

CPU (Central Processing Unit) A component in a computer that executes operating system and program instructions. A given computer system may have more than one CPU.

DCL (Digital Command Language) The default command line interpreter of OpenVMS.

ENVIRONMENT VARIABLE A setting stored in the nonvolatile memory of the computer, used to customize the actions of the console subsystem. Used to store such settings as the default boot device and what action to take when the computer is powered on.

EXTENT One portion of a file stored on disk—also known as a fragment. A given file may be stored as one or more discontiguous extents.

FILE FRAGMENTATION The occurrence of files being broken apart and stored at discontiguous locations on a disk. This is a normal by-product of file system activity. Utility programs exist to gather file fragments back together periodically to aid performance.

FILE HEADER A 512-byte block in the reserved file INDEXF.SYS used to describe another file on the disk. Nearly all file attributes (name, owner, protection, size, etc.) are stored in the header.

HIBERNATE The act of a process voluntarily entering a wait state until explicitly awakened by another process or by a scheduled wake-up request—also the name of the associated process-scheduling state.

LEXICAL FUNCTIONS A set of function provided by the Digital command language providing a variety of services, including returning information about files and converting time formats.

MIPS (Millions of Instructions Per Second) One measure of CPU performance. Used alone, it is not necessarily a reliable way to compare CPUs of different architectures.

ODS-2 (On-Disk Structure Version 2) The primary on-disk file system layout used by OpenVMS.

ODS-5 (On-Disk Structure Version 5) A newer file system layout providing for better compatibility with other file systems, such as those used with UNIX or Windows.

PAGEFILE A special file on disk used by the virtual memory management subsystem. It is used to store memory contents when memory space is needed for other purposes. Its contents are used to recreate the contents of memory pages when they are needed again.

PAGE TABLE A database in memory containing virtual-to-physical memory mapping information. Used by the computer hardware to resolve process-generated memory addresses into their actual locations in physical memory. The contents of a page table change over time to reflect paging, swapping, and virtual memory creation and deletion. Its contents are kept current by the operating system.

PDF (ADOBE® Portable Document Format) A file format capable of storing text and graphics images as if they were arranged on a newspaper or magazine page.

PERL A scripting or "shell" language common on UNIX systems and other operating systems. It is the UNIX system's counterpart to the OpenVMS DCL (Digital command language) scripting capability. PERL is available for OpenVMS.

PRIMARY CPU A CPU capable of carrying out any operating system function or one that controls the actions of other CPUs. For example, a certain hardware architecture or operating system may allow any CPU to carry out general instructions, but restrict I/O operations to the primary CPU. The primary CPU also begins the bootstrap process and causes any other CPUs to be started at the appropriate time.

PROCESSOR A component in a computer system that carries out programmed instructions. Computer systems have numerous special-purpose processors in addition to one or more central processing units. When the term *processor* is used alone, the term usually refers to a central processing unit. *See also CPU.*

RETRIEVAL POINTER A piece of data in a file header indicating the size and location of a file, or a portion thereof.

RMS (OpenVMS Record Management Services) A part of OpenVMS that provides record-oriented I/O functions to programs.

SRM The Console Subsystem used with OpenVMS. *See also* "Console Subsystem."

TELNET A TCP/IP utility program providing remote login capability among computers on a network.

THREAD A separate schedulable path of execution within a process. All threads in a process share the same process context, but may execute simultaneously on different CPUs.

X WINDOW SYSTEM A suite of graphics software forming the basis for the DECwindows and Common Desktop Environment (CDE) graphical user interfaces.

XQP (extended $QIO processor) A portion of the OpenVMS file system providing services that cannot be performed by the disk driver, including accessing a file on an I/O channel and providing virtual-to-logical block mapping.

Index

F

FCB (file control block), 266
File Manager application (New Desktop), 203–4
File Manager control (New Desktop), 197
File menu (DECwindows FileView application), 221
File protection, 93–97
    access categories, 94–95
    ACL-based, 93, 96–97
    classes of users, 94–95
    deleting subdirectories and, 90–91
    overview, 93
    privileges overriding, 97
    UIC-based, 93, 94
Files, 63–75
    common file operations, 264
    copying, 72, 73
    copying to the desktop, 210–11
    creating, 72
    DECnet foreign file specifications, 180–81
    defined, 63
    deleting, 72–73
    deleting previous versions, 74
    disk structure levels, 65–68
    displaying contents, 72
    displaying list of, 68–69
    fragmentation, 264, 265, 267–68
    highwater marking, 144
    indexed, 65
    layout on disk, 265
    logical names for, 101–2
    overview, 63–64
    printing, 78–79
    reading and writing from command procedures, 124–26
    relative, 65
    remote file access using DECnet, 179–80
    renaming, 73
    reserved, 91–92, 268–69
    saving e-mail messages to, 162
    sending as e-mail messages, 161
    sequential, 64
    sizes, 69, 70
    specification defaults, 70
    UIC protection categories, 30–31
    version limits, 74–75
    wildcards for specifying, 69, 70–71
    See also Files-11 system
Files-11 system, 261–70
    common file operations, 264
    criteria for successful file systems, 261
    directory structure, 91–93
    file fragmentation, 264, 265, 267–68
    file layout on disk, 265
    file system operation, 266–67
    INDEXF.SYS file, 92, 265, 269–70
    multivolume sets, 262
    Record Management Services (RMS) vs., 261, 270
    reserved files, 268–69
    terminology, 262–64
File systems, 261
FileView application (DECwindows), 219–23
    Commands menu, 221–22
    directory navigation, 220–21
    File menu, 221
    Options menu, 222–23
    overview, 219–20
    Utilities menu, 222
    Views menu, 221
Finding batch and print queues, 81–82
Folders for e-mail messages, 158–59, 163–64
Foreign commands, 76–77
Formatting text in EDT, 173–74
Forwarding e-mail messages, 161
Fragmentation of files, 264, 265, 267–68
Free page list, 251
Freezing the terminal display, 150
Front panel (New Desktop)
    applications, 203–9
    controls, 196–99
    overview, 194–95
    subpanels, 199–203
    Window menu, 195
    workspace switch, 195–96
FTP vs. SCP, 236

entering, 44–46
overview, 42, 44–45
parameters vs., 45–46

L

Labels in command procedures, 129–30
Lexical functions (DCL), 57–58
Local DCL symbols, 50–51, 122–23. *See also* DCL symbols
Lock control (workspace switch), 196
Log files, verification for batch jobs and, 80
Logging in
    changing expired password during, 142
    to DECnet node, 183–84
    from directly connected terminals, 34
    first time, 33
    GUI-based workstation access, 36
    login failures, 37
    login sequence, 36–39
    modem access, 35
    to OpenVMS GUI, 192–93, 215
    personal OpenVMS systems, 228
    Telnet access, 34
    terminal server access, 35–36
    user account for, 33
    welcome message, 37, 38
    See also LOGIN.COM file;
        SYLOGIN.COM file
Logging out
    from New Desktop, 194
    from OpenVMS, 40, 138
    from remote DECnet node, 184
    workspace switch Exit control for, 196
Logical names, 100–103
Logical operators, 59–61
LOGIN.COM file
    conditional execution of, 105–6
    creating DCL symbols using, 52
    execution during login, 39
    overview, 103–5
    preventing from running, 106
    printer definition in, 78
    verification setting and batch jobs, 80
LOGOUT command, 40, 138

LOGOUT/FULL command, 40, 138

M

Mailer application (New Desktop), 204
Mailer control (New Desktop), 197–98
MAIL facility, 155, 157–58. *See also* E-mail
MAIL.MAI file, 158–59
Mapped images, 257
Maximizing windows, 189–90
Member number in UICs, 30
Memory layout of processes, 241–43
Menu bars (OpenVMS GUI), 186, 192
Messages
    broadcast, 106–7
    command procedure error-handling,
        125–26
    multiple, from one command, 49–50
    overview, 48–49
    PHONE facility for, 111–13
    severity levels, 49
    "User authorization failure," 37
    See also E-mail
MicroVAX, 2
MicroVMS, 2
MIME utility, 165–66
Minimizing windows, 188–89
Modem connection and login, 35
Modified page list, 251
Mouse functions in OpenVMS GUI, 187–88
Moving
    e-mail messages between folders, 164
    text in EDT, 173
    window behind others (DECwindows),
        217
    windows between workspaces (New
        Desktop), 209–10
Moving around
    directories in DECwindows, 220–21
    directories in OpenVMS, 86–88
    in EDT, 171–72
    e-mail folders, 163
Multiple CPUs, scheduling processes on,
    247–48
Multiuser systems

logical, 59–61
Options menu
    DECwindows, 223–24
    DECwindows FileView application, 222–23
    OpenVMS GUI, 193
.OR operator, 59, 60, 61
OWNER UICs, 31

P

P0 space (program region), 241, 242
P1 space (control region), 241, 242
Paged dynamic storage pool, 254–55
Pagefile, 251
Paging
    details, 250
    entire system, 252–53
    example, 249–50
    modified page writing, 254
    page faults, 250, 252–54
    page tables, 249
    secondary page caches, 253–54
    terminology, 251
    within a process, 251–52
PALcode procedures, 15
Parameters (DCL)
    entering, 43–44, 45–46
    keywords vs., 45–46
    overview, 42–43
Passwords
    changing, 141–42
    expired, changing during login, 142
    in login sequence, 36, 37, 38
    protection by OpenVMS, 139–41
    security issues, 139
    system password, 36
    for user accounts, 27
Paths (DCL), 76–77
PCSI (POLYCENTER Software Installation Utility), 234
PDP series computers, 1–2
Percent sign (%)
    beginning DCL messages, 49
    as wildcard character, 71

PERL scripting language, 109–10
Personal Application control (New Desktop), 197
Personal OpenVMS systems, 225–36
    console subsystem, 225–33
    installing software, 234–35
    Internet connections, 235–36
    logging in, 228
    software licenses, 233–34
    system shutdown, 225, 229–33
    system startup, 225, 226–29
PHONE facility, 111–13
    answering calls, 113
    canceling calls, 112
    placing calls, 112–13
    rejecting calls, 113
    starting, 111–12
    terminating calls, 113
Physical terminals, 145–48. *See also* Terminals
PIPE command, 108–9
Pipelining commands, 108–9
Placing PHONE calls, 112–13
POLYCENTER Software Installation Utility (PCSI), 234
POP3, 156–57
Positional qualifiers, 43–44
PRINT command, 78–79
Printing
    files, 78–79
    using New Desktop Default Printer, 198
Print queues
    finding, 81–82
    overview, 22, 23
    printing files, 78–79
Priorities of processes, 110, 246, 247
Privileged architecture library (PALcode), 15
Privileges
    basic, 29
    defined, 29
    list of, 29–30
    overriding file protection, 97
    process, adjusting, 110–11

for SYSTEM account, 33
Processes, 239–48
    control region (P1 space), 241, 242
    defined, 18, 239–41
    examining system processes, 20–21, 244
    login processes, 39
    memory layout, 241–43
    moving OpenVMS from 32 to 64 bits, 243
    NULL process, 247, 248
    paging within, 251–52
    priorities, 110, 246, 247
    privileges, adjusting, 110–11
    program region (P0 space), 241, 242
    scheduling, 244–48
    spawning subprocesses, 107–8
    states, 244–46
    system space, 241, 242–43
    types of, 18–21
    user account limits, 28
Program region (P0 space), 241, 242
Programs
    custom commands for, 77
    DCL paths and, 76–77
    foreign commands for, 76
    images, 257–59
    installing on personal OpenVMS
        systems, 234–35
    passing embedded data into, 127
    passing keyboard data into, 127–28
    RUN command for, 75–76
    running, 75–77
    software licenses, 233–34
    See also Applications (New Desktop)
Proxies (DECnet), 180
PURGE command, 74, 144

Q

Qualifiers (DCL), 42–44, 46
QUANTUM time limit, 246
Queues, 77–84
    batch, 22, 24, 79–82
    batch mode caveats, 80–81
    commands for interacting with, 22
    defined, 22, 77
    deleting entries, 83

entry numbers, 83–84
examining entries, 82–83
finding batch and print queues, 81–82
generic, 22, 23
modifying entries, 83
modifying procedures already queued,
    80–81
overview, 22
print, 22, 23, 78–79, 81–82
printing files, 78–79
server, 22, 24
submitting batch jobs, 79–80
Quotas
    disk, 38
    resource, 28
Quotation marks (“”)
    in DCL commands, 43
    for exclamation marks used literally, 48

R

READALL privilege, 97
READ command, 124–26, 133, 159
Recall buffer, 149–50
RECALL command, 149–50
Receiving e-mail messages, 159
Record Management Services (RMS), 261,
    270
Reduced instruction set computer (RISC),
    14–15
Rejecting PHONE calls, 113
Relative files, 65
Relative notation for directories, 87–88
Remote file access using DECnet, 179–80
Removing. *See* Deleting
RENAME command, 73
Renaming files, 73
Replying to e-mail messages, 161
Reserved files, 91–92, 268–69
Resizing windows, 190
Resource locks, 271–73
Restoring windows, 189
RISC (reduced instruction set computer),
    14–15
RMS (Record Management Services), 261,

freezing the display, 150
hardcopy terminals and EDT, 168
network vs. physical, 145
processes associated with, 18–19
recall buffer, 149
RECALL command for, 149–50
SET TERMINAL command for, 148–49
settings, 145–48
terminal servers, 35–36
Terminating PHONE calls, 113
Text editors
for e-mail messages, 160
overview, 167
See also EDT
Threads, 21
Three-arrow prompt, 226
Times, specifying, 99–100
TMPMBX privilege, 29
Traceback facility, 257
Trash Can control (New Desktop), 199, 209
Tree structure of directories, 86–87
TYPE command, 72, 182

U

UAF records, 27–28
UICs (User Identification Codes)
classes of users, 94–95
file protection categories, 30–31
identifiers for, 32
non-uniqueness of, 31
overview, 30–31
UIC-based file protection, 93, 94
UNIX, Alpha compatibility with, 15
User account records, 27–28
User accounts, 27–32
captive, 143
classes of users, 94–95
disk quotas, 28
identifiers, 31–32
obtaining, 33
passwords for, 27
privileges, 29–30
resource quotas and limits, 28
SYSTEM account, 33

User Identification Code (UIC), 30–31
username for, 27
"User authorization failure" message, 37
User Authorization File, 28
User Identification Codes. *See* UICs (User
Identification Codes)
Username
in login sequence, 36, 37, 38
overview, 27
Utilities menu (DECwindows FileView
application), 222

V

Variables, DCL symbols as, 54
VAX architecture
continued support for, 1, 4–5
design goals, 1
history, 1–4
OpenVMS support by, 13–14
overview, 13–14
Verbs (DCL)
abbreviating, 46
entering, 43–44
overview, 42
redefining using DCL symbols, 53–54
Verification, batch jobs and, 80
Version limits for files, 74–75
Viewing. *See* Displaying
Views menu (DECwindows FileView
application), 221
Virtual memory management, 249–56
dynamic storage pools, 254–55
modified page writing, 254
overview, 249
page faults, 250, 252–54
page tables, 249
paging details, 250
paging example, 249–50
paging on the entire system, 252–53
paging within a process, 251–52
secondary page caches, 253–54
swapping, 249
terminology, 251
VMSclusters. *See* Clustering

VMS$COMMON.DIR file, 92

W

Warning messages. *See* Messages
WCB (window control block), 266
Wildcard characters
    DIRECTORY command with, 69
    for directory specifications, 88–89
    for file specifications, 69, 70–71
Window Manager (DECwindows), 215–17
Window menu
    New Desktop front panel, 195
    OpenVMS GUI, 190–92
Windows 2000, Alpha compatibility and, 15
Windows NT, Alpha compatibility with, 15
Windows (OpenVMS GUI)
    keeping action windows open, 214
    making active, 188
    maximizing, 189–90
    minimizing, 188–89
    moving between workspaces, 209–10
    overview, 186
    resizing, 190, 217
    restoring, 189
    See also DECwindows interface
Windows PCs, VAX emulator for, 6
Working sets, 28, 251
Workspace switch (New Desktop), 195–96
WORLD UICs, 31
WRITE command, 124–26
WRITE SYS$OUTPUT command, 56–58

X

XQP (extended $QIO processor), 266

www.ingramcontent.com/pod-product-compliance
Lightning Source LLC
Chambersburg PA
CBHW080926220326
41598CB00034B/5693

* 9 7 8 1 5 5 5 5 8 2 7 9 1 *